Software Engineering Quality Practices

Software Engineering Quality Practices

Ronald Kirk Kandt

 Auerbach Publications
Taylor & Francis Group
Boca Raton   New York

Published in 2006 by
Auerbach Publications
Taylor & Francis Group
6000 Broken Sound Parkway NW, Suite 300
Boca Raton, FL 33487-2742

© 2006 by Taylor & Francis Group, LLC
Auerbach is an imprint of Taylor & Francis Group

No claim to original U.S. Government works
Printed in the United States of America on acid-free paper
10 9 8 7 6 5 4 3 2 1

International Standard Book Number-10: 0-8493-4633-9 (Hardcover)
International Standard Book Number-13: 978-0-8493-4633-0 (Hardcover)
Library of Congress Card Number 2005053554

Library of Congress Cataloging-in-Publication Data

Kandt, Ronald Kirk.
  Software engineering quality practices / Ronald Kirk Kandt.
      p. cm. -- (Applied software engineering series)
  Includes bibliographical references and index.
  ISBN 0-8493-4633-9 (alk. paper)
  1. Software engineering. 2. Computer software--Quality control. I. Title. II. Series.

QA76.758.K35 2005
005.1--dc22   2005053554

Taylor & Francis Group
is the Academic Division of T&F Informa plc.

Visit the Taylor & Francis Web site at
http://www.taylorandfrancis.com

and the Auerbach Publications Web site at
http://www.auerbach-publications.com

Contents

List of Illustrations

List of Practices

List of Tables

Preface

I have developed software for more than 30 years. My experience in developing software is probably little different, although broader, than that of most people. I went to college and majored in computer science, where I learned a lot about data structures, analysis of algorithms, automata theory, formal languages, programming languages, compiler construction, operating systems, and artificial intelligence. I even had two classes in software engineering, although I really had not learned how to develop quality software. Sure, I had learned to define requirements before designing software, to design software before implementing it in a classical waterfall development model, and a few other things, but that is only a small amount of the knowledge that a software engineer needs to know to develop good software. Although this knowledge has been extremely valuable, it did not enable me to develop quality software that must evolve over time.

While at college, I wrote numerous programs. These included a one-pass linking loader, a Smalltalk-72 interpreter, and a source-to-source transformation system. My college experience ended when I developed a software system to capture design knowledge for later reuse. Development of this system required that I build a knowledge representation language, a hypertext system, and a graphical presentation system. By the time I finished college I had written well over 100,000 lines of code in various languages, although predominately in assembly language, Algol, and Lisp.

Immediately after leaving college, I worked for numerous research organizations. On my first assignment, I helped develop a real-time operating system. After this, I helped build numerous knowledge-based systems to support image understanding applications and an advance programming environment. My research career culminated with the development of numerous planning and scheduling systems to support the definition of space transportation architectures and the allocation of spacecraft resources.

By this time, about 15 years had gone by and I largely developed software like most people still do today. During this time, I had developed numerous heuristics for developing software but my method of developing software was still ad hoc. Even so, most people considered me a good programmer. I became a good programmer largely because I was a compulsive programmer who made a lifetime's worth of mistakes in a relatively short time period. To overcome these mistakes, I devised various techniques to minimize the consequences of bad decisions and my own cognitive limitations.

However, I still had much to learn about developing good software. In 1995, I contracted with a software engineering organization that had been certified as being CMM® (Carnegie Mellon University, Pittsburgh, Pennsylvania) Level 3. Consequently, its personnel used a defined development process. Part of this process required that all system builds include an accounting of the extent to which the software had been tested. Consequently, every source file delivered as part of a system build had to run through software that computed statement coverage. My response to this requirement was that it was not applicable to me because I had written an extensive test suite to test my code. This argument carried no weight, so the code coverage tool was applied to the source code that I wrote. Surprisingly, about 10 percent of the functions had not achieved 100 percent coverage. Afterward, I was a firm believer in the application of statement coverage tools, as well as other tools that provide measures of software quality.

In 1998, I went to work as the chief architect for a large financial institution to develop a financial planning system. During this tenure, I wrote a program to solve an optimization problem. At one stage in the processing of the program, there were three possible outcomes: (1) no solution existed; (2) a solution existed and the algorithm could proceed without transforming the initial solution; and (3) a solution existed, but the initial solution had to be reformulated before continuing to solve the problem. Because I was now a firm believer in testing and measuring the test adequacy of a test suite, I asked the program manager to purchase a software coverage tool. This request was denied.

Hence, I had to devise a testing strategy that would thoroughly test the program, although I did not have the ability to measure it. So how many test cases were needed to adequately test the software? I decided that creating 25,000 randomly generated test cases would be more than sufficient to thoroughly test the code. The test suite was successfully executed and the project team assumed that the module functioned correctly. A couple of years later, there were no reported defects in the optimization module.

A couple of years after that, I translated the code from C++ to Java and ran the test suite against it. All 25,000 test cases were successfully executed. I then built a graphical user interface for the optimization module and began testing it. About 20 percent of the test cases entered from the user interface failed. Upon investigation, I determined that I had introduced a minor defect during translation. While isolating the defect, I discovered that the extensive test suite did not thoroughly test the three decision outcomes of the stage of the program described previously. One path was executed twice, another path was executed 24,998 times, and the final path was never executed. That is, the extensive test suite was not effective or efficient.

Purpose and Scope of the Book

The purpose of this book is to describe how to develop quality software in an effective, efficient, and professional manner. It is intended to convey practical advice as briefly as possible and avoid the dogmatism that surrounds the software profession. This book ignores advanced engineering topics, such as formal methods of verification, mathematical models of reliability, and advanced approaches to software reuse based on, for example, domain-specific languages. Instead, it concentrates on understanding what the real requirements of a system are, what constitutes an appropriate solution, and how one ensures that the realized solution fulfills the desired qualities of the relevant stakeholders. It also discusses how an organization attracts and keeps people who are capable of building these high-quality systems. The target audience of this book is the practicing software engineer and the managers who supervise them.

Acknowledgments

I have learned much from several of my professors. Martin Kay challenged me in my first computer science class, which motivated me to change my major from mathematics to computer science. Arvind taught me operating systems and taught me a great lesson — that understanding a problem is half its solution. Kim Gostelow taught me everything I know about automata theory and formal languages. The work of Arvind and Gostelow in the mid-1970s on data-flow computer architectures also had a profound impact on much of my thinking. Thomas Standish provided many thought-provoking lectures in data structures and compiler design. He also got me interested in automatic programming, as did James Neighbors, whose ideas on domain analysis and domain-specific programming languages have significantly influenced my own. Peter Freeman taught me much of what I know about software engineering. Somehow, all these people taught me how to think without me really knowing it. I am especially grateful to have learned so much from them.

I have also had the support of many fine individuals in the workplace. When I worked at Hughes Research Laboratories, Bruce Bullock and David Tseng provided a great atmosphere for performing research in knowledge-based systems. At the Information Sciences Institute of the University of Southern California, I had the pleasure of working with Bob Balzer and Neil Goldman on challenging problems in advanced programming environments. When I consulted at Rockwell International Science Center, Bill Pardee provided many thought-provoking discussions. At the Jet Propulsion Laboratory of the California Institute of Technology, Milton Lavin gave me tremendous support while I worked on a software process improvement project.

In addition, Bruce Bullock, Gerard Holzmann, Milton Lavin, Elmain Martinez, Dwayne Nebeker, James Neighbors, and Bill Pardee reviewed early drafts of this book, or chapters thereof. Several of their comments improved the quality of this book. I greatly appreciate their efforts.

Finally, some of the work described in this book was performed at the Jet Propulsion Laboratory, California Institute of Technology, under a contract with the National Aeronautics and Space Administration.

Ronald Kirk Kandt
Simi Valley, California

Chapter 1

Introduction

This chapter demonstrates that industry has found it difficult to efficiently develop quality software since at least the 1960s. It further identifies the qualities and key drivers that underlie software products and their production. Finally, it identifies the four common approaches to improve product quality and suggests that an integrated approach based on the key drivers of software quality is necessary to meet the quality needs of the consumers of software products.

In the early 1970s, software engineering teams seldom produced applications on time or within budget. When completed, applications often did not meet system requirements or the expectations of their customers. Both industry and government had observed that these problems occurred with alarming frequency. Command and control systems, for example, had as much as 95 percent of the code rewritten to meet operational needs [1]. The World Wide Military Command and Control System proved very unreliable, sometimes falsely warning of Russian nuclear attacks. The Federal Aviation Administration's Air Traffic Control Center software, which was originally projected to cost $1.8 million and take 17 months to implement, still was not finished after five years and expenditures exceeding $19 million [1]; several years later, its direct software costs grew to more than $100 million [2]. Similarly, the OS/360 operating system constructed by IBM exceeded its estimated development costs and initial delivery was several years late [3]; each new release also contained roughly 1000 new software errors [4].

In the mid-1990s, there was still a *software crisis* [5]. Today, *Software Engineering Notes* publishes tens or hundreds of catastrophic software failures in every issue, which demonstrates how widespread the problem remains. At Jet Propulsion Laboratory, the situation is no better. In 1999, it suffered two catastrophic mission failures partially because of inadequate software processes [6]. In sum, the experiences of the Federal Aviation Administration, IBM, and Jet Propulsion Laboratory are not unique; instead, these problems are common and only illustrative of the experiences of most organizations.

This is a frightening thought considering that Floyd, in his 1979 Turing Award acceptance speech [7], said that describing this situation as a software depression would be more appropriate. Twenty-five years after this statement, the *software depression* still exists, and it is worsening. Consider that from the early 1960s through the late 1980s, the size of NASA software systems increased 20 to 25 percent annually, although productivity increased only 4 to 6 percent per year [8]. During the 1990s, NASA personnel have observed the same growth rates. What this means is that without any change in these trends, future software will be developed with either greater risk, greater cost, or both greater risk and greater cost. Consequently, there is a critical need to develop a practical methodology for effectively and efficiently developing quality software. The benefit of such a software development methodology is significant because defect avoidance, detection, and correction activities alone consume about 50 percent of the labor to create software [9] and as much as 75 percent of total software life-cycle costs [10]. Hence, the software industry must significantly improve productivity to meet demand while producing quality systems. This can be achieved by introducing improvements that have a one-time or continual affect. Figure 1.1 illustrates the current trends and the effect of improvements.

1.1 Qualities

When developing software, we are concerned with both product and process qualities. *Product quality* reflects the essential character, features, and properties of artifacts and is a reflection of how well they support stakeholder needs. A *stakeholder* is any group, individual, or organization that is affected by, or can affect, a product, project, or organization. *Process quality*, on the other hand, reflects on how a product is produced. Because the relative importance of each of these qualities affects overall product quality, one should measure each quality [11]. Furthermore, when developing software, the benefits of these general qualities, as well as those specific to a product, affect users in three, possibly unanticipated, ways [12, 13].

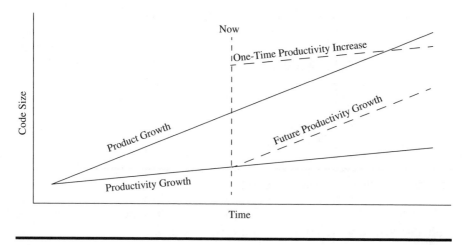

FIGURE 1.1 Current trends in product and productivity growth and desired changes.

1. *Conventional quality* results in stakeholder satisfaction when it is present in a product and in dissatisfaction in its absence.
2. *Essential quality* reflects the attributes of an artifact necessary to achieve a minimum level of customer satisfaction. The presence of an essential quality has little impact on the overall perception of the quality of a product but its absence will have a significant detrimental impact on customer satisfaction.
3. *Attractive quality* represents a product characteristic that is not expected to be present in a product; when it is present, the product's customers are delighted.

Hence, to classify a product or process quality as providing essential, conventional, or attractive quality, one must consider what happens both when one does not provide it and when one does. For example, the absence of either essential or conventional quality will displease a stakeholder. Alternatively, the presence of conventional or attractive quality will please a stakeholder. However, improving an already acceptable essential quality provides less stakeholder value than improving an acceptable conventional or attractive quality [12]. Figure 1.2 illustrates the characteristics of the three forms of quality.

1.1.1 Characteristic Qualities of Products

Software product quality is generally associated with the absence of defects in a software artifact. However, quality is also related to many other properties, characteristics, and attributes that people value. The ones that

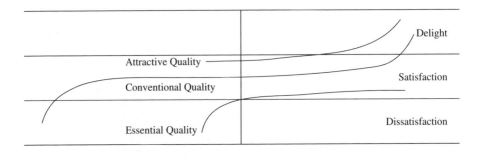

FIGURE 1.2   The three types of quality.

most affect software success are availability, efficiency, maintainability, portability, reliability, reusability, and usability.

Quality 1.1.   Availability. Availability is the readiness of a software system for immediate use at any time. Hence, a system can be highly reliable yet still be rarely available. For example, a software system may require significant *downtime* for system maintenance or upgrade.

Quality 1.2.   Efficiency. Efficiency is the capability of a system to productively perform its function without wasting system resources. For example, efficient products run faster and consume less primary and secondary memory.

Quality 1.3.   Maintainability. Maintainability is the extent to which software artifacts facilitate change [14]. The following qualities enable maintainable systems.

Quality 1.3.1. *Extensibility.* Extensibility is the extent to which software can be expanded or enhanced [11]. In an idealized world, user needs, adopted technology, development team composition, and funding commitment would rarely change. However, in the real world, user needs change, technology changes, personnel change, and funding changes. Consequently, to develop quality systems on time and within budget that satisfy and delight customers requires that software engineers preplan products for evolution. Therefore, extensibility should be planned into the development of every nontrivial software system.

Quality 1.3.2. *Modularity.* Modularity is the extent to which one plans a software system in terms of a collection of standardized units for use together. Modular systems decompose into smaller components, each solving a fragment of a larger problem. Modularity reduces defects, reduces work in later maintenance efforts [15], and increases the possibility of reusing modules, assuming they have well-defined interfaces and loose coupling with other modules.

Quality 1.3.3. *Simplicity.* Simplicity is the extent to which a software system contains only essential complexity. Thus, software systems should only include those features that it needs to achieve its purpose. Adding non-essential features simply creates greater risk because nonessential features often do not fit well with the overall design and increase its complexity and reduce its elegance [15]. That is, software systems should have *conceptual integrity*, which reflects one set of integrated ideas that work well with one another. In addition, because the enormous complexity associated with developing most modern software systems quickly stresses the intellectual limitations of people, the best solutions are generally simpler ones [16] that cost less to develop and have fewer defects [17].

Quality 1.3.4. *Testability.* Testability is the extent to which software facilitates the verification of its operation.

Quality 1.3.5. *Understandability.* Understandability is the extent to which people can comprehend the behavior of a software system [11], which generally results in the development of more reliable software systems. The understandability of software systems can be increased, for example, by using improved design and documentation methodologies.

Quality 1.4. Portability. Portability is the extent to which code can operate in different computer configurations and environments [14]. It is also a measure of the effort to modify a program to run in a new environment.

Quality 1.5. Reliability. Reliability is the probability that a program will function without failure over a specified time [14]. In addition, reliable products perform their intended tasks in a manner consistent with user expectations and yield the same results when given the same inputs. Unfortunately, reliability is not free. In general, it costs 50 percent more to develop high-dependability software products than to develop low-dependability software products. However, such an investment is generally cost-effective if a project involves significant operations and maintenance activities [18]. Achieving reliability depends on three other qualities: accuracy, completeness, and robustness.

Quality 1.5.1. *Accuracy.* Accuracy is the extent to which the preciseness of program output satisfies its intended use.

Quality 1.5.2. *Completeness.* Completeness is the extent to which all parts of a software system are fully developed.

Quality 1.5.3. *Robustness.* Robustness is the extent to which a software system can continue to operate despite anomalies and perform as intended [11].

Quality 1.6. Reusability. Reusability is a measure of the ease with which a software artifact can be used by a software project other than the one for which it was originally intended.

Quality 1.7. Usability. Usability is the extent to which code satisfies its purpose without wasting the time of its users [14]. It is also a measure of the effort required to learn, use, and prepare input for a program and interpret its output. One way to develop usable software systems is to use concepts, terms, and behaviors familiar to users [11].

1.1.2 Characteristic Process Qualities

Process qualities are related to how people develop products. There are three key product qualities: effectiveness, efficiency, and predictability.

Quality 1.8. Effectiveness. Effectiveness is the extent to which one can produce a product that is ready for service. Thus, effective products meet the needs of their users and provide a quality of service that pleases them. This should be a minimum standard; going one step beyond this is to provide products that delight customers by doing something unexpected but of great value [12].

Quality 1.9. Efficiency. Efficiency is the extent to which a software system is developed using a minimum expenditure of energy, resources, time, and money. The cost to develop and maintain products should be achieved as efficiently as possible to reduce waste. There are two primary ways to achieve such efficiency. The first way is to build only what is needed. Thus, products should provide only necessary or high-value features to their users because the addition of features that do not meet this criteria tends to lower product quality. The second way is to minimize product development cost by efficiently using human resources, whose benefits generally increase at a greater than linear rate. To efficiently use software development personnel, an organization must assign personnel having the appropriate skills to tasks and provide a work environment that enhances their productivity.

Quality 1.10. Predictability. Predictability is the extent to which one can declare something in advance based on observation, experience, or reason. In software development, one needs to reliably predict the required resources, delivery date, and cost of a software development effort. To do so requires the establishment of a measurement program, as well as a way to define stable requirements. To define stable requirements, an organization must manage the definition of requirements, assign work tasks based on the requirements and related requirement groupings, evaluate the effects of adding and changing requirements, and control the realization of such requirements.

1.2 Quality Drivers

In 1981, Boehm documented his extensive research into the drivers of software cost [19]. In 1996, Clark pursued a similar line of research into the drivers of software quality [20]. In 2003, Neufelder identified numerous drivers of software reliability, an important quality of many mission-critical systems, in a presentation given at Jet Propulsion Laboratory and described in [21]. Table 1.1 identifies what these researchers concluded to be the top drivers affecting software quality. It should be noted that the first two drivers for each category were much more important than the others.

Thus, from these three studies it is clear that the most critical factors affecting software cost and quality are product complexity and human capabilities. Vital human capabilities include knowledge of the problem domain, modern programming practices, and software tools. Other important factors include various timing and space constraints, product reliability needs, and the stability of the adopted technologies and the personnel who use them. Furthermore, Nikora's results, which indicate that software complexity, size, and volatility are the primary drivers affecting software quality, are consistent with these three studies [22]. Similarly, Jones queried numerous practitioners about what they consider to be significant software risks [23]. A root cause analysis of their answers indicates that projects largely fail because of requirements volatility, excessive schedule pressure, project management malpractice, inaccurate cost estimating, and inadequate configuration management.

TABLE 1.1 Software Quality Drivers

	Boehm's Rankings	*Clark's Rankings*	*Neufelder's Rankings*
1	Personnel/team capability	Product complexity	Domain knowledge
2	Product complexity	Analyst capability	Non-programming managers
3	Required reliability	Programmer capability	Use of unit testing tools
4	Timing constraint	Constraint on execution time	Use of supported operating systems
5	Application experience	Personnel continuity	Testing of user documentation
6	Storage constraint	Required reliability	Use of automated tools
7	Modern programming practices	Documentation	Testing during each phase
8	Software tools	Multi-site development	Reviewed requirements
9	Virtual machine volatility	Application experience	Use of automated FRACAS
10	Virtual machine experience	Platform volatility	Use of simulation

Furthermore, several studies have identified the most common types of software defects, including explanations for their occurrence [24–26]. During the requirements definition phase, requirements are often incompletely, inconsistently, or vaguely stated, and many needed requirements (e.g., maintainability, reliability, and usability requirements) are often left undefined whereas many unneeded requirements are defined. Some of the causes of such problems include using the wrong people to define requirements who often misunderstand their responsibilities, lack adequate experience or knowledge, suffer from unclear reasoning and biases, incorrectly understand the assumptions or facts underlying requirements, and select solutions before they understand the user's needs or requirements. Likewise, stakeholders often do not completely understand their needs or computer capabilities and limitations, often have conflicting views, and seldom participate in requirements engineering.

A consequence of these problems is the definition of unstable requirements, which is one of the most common sources of cost and schedule overruns and project cancellations [23, 27, 28]. Hence, volatile requirements generally have a significant impact on product development and either must be eliminated before development occurs or managed as they arise during development. However, because some domains can only be understood over time and organizational goals often change because of broader organizational change, organizations must learn to embrace change as a necessary part of survival because the tractability and invisibility of software exposes it to continual requirements churn [3, 29, 30]. Furthermore, because individual skills, team experience, and proper domain knowledge are important factors in requirements definition, organizations should attempt to develop teams of highly skilled software engineers and managers with high levels of domain knowledge to obtain more predictable performance [31, 32].

As mentioned, complexity is one of the largest drivers affecting software quality. Complexity is often incidentally introduced into software, which sometimes increases its size. Both size and complexity work against the development of quality software. Therefore, software should be developed adhering to good design practices that reduce complexity and size. Fortunately, simple metrics can be used to measure design quality. Note, however, that this approach simply attempts to deal with human cognitive limitations by placing bounds on software design tasks, which are unlike most engineering problems that are constrained by physical properties and laws.

Defects that arise during coding have been extensively studied [9, 22, 33–35]. These analyses have identified several common types of coding defects. Table 1.2 shows the most common ones, which are grouped by major categories.

Finally, Jones showed that defects had the following characteristics: 20 percent of defects were introduced while defining requirements, 25 percent during design, 35 percent when coding, 12 percent while writing documentation, and 8 percent when repairing defects [36]. He also showed that the number of defects remaining in delivered software were introduced during requirements definition 31 percent of the time, in design 25 percent of the time, in coding 12 percent of the time, in documentation 16 percent of the time, and during repairs 16 percent of the time. It is interesting to note that the highest defect removal rate, in percentage terms, occurs during coding, followed by design, and then by requirements definition. This is probably not coincidental; it is probably a result that verification of earlier stages of software development typically occur later in the software development life cycle. That is, requirements are usually

TABLE 1.2   Common Types of Coding Defects

Control flow defect types	Data reference defect types
• Multi-way branch assumption • Infinite loop • Non-terminating function • Unreachable code • Incorrect loop termination	• Unused variable • Uninitialized variable • Multiply initialized variable • Illegal array reference • Illegal memory reference • Use of incorrect variable
Data declaration defect types	Other common defect types
• Undeclared variable type declaration • Incorrectly declared variable type declaration • Under-constrained variable type declaration • Implicitly initialized variable • Improperly initialized variable • Incorrect variable storage class specification • Incorrect variable length specification	• Inconsistent data type comparison • Mixed data type comparison • Different length variable comparison • Use of incorrect comparison operator • Use of incorrect logical expression • Use of exact floating-point comparison operator • Incorrect specification of the number of function arguments • Incorrect order of function arguments
Computation defect types	• Incorrectly declared type of a function argument • Inappropriate modification of actual input argument • Incorrect handling of input, output, or other exception • Illegal function input or output • Unused enumeration items
• Use of non-arithmetic data type in arithmetic operation • Use of different numerical types in arithmetic operation • Data truncation during variable assignment • Occurrence of underflow or overflow exception • Illegal division by zero • Inaccurate numerical computation • Invalid range of numerical variable • Incorrect operator precedence assumption	

created, followed by the creation of designs and then code. After this, the code is usually checked, followed by the verification of the design, and finally by the verification of the requirements. Thus, a logical outcome of this is that software engineers should verify requirements and designs immediately after they are completed, and adopt an iterative software development life cycle to get quicker feedback on the quality of software.

1.3 Common Approaches to Developing Quality Software

Several approaches have been proposed to develop quality software. Probably the most commonly proposed software development approaches recommend automating software development, introducing software modeling methodologies, adopting mature software development processes, and reusing existing software.

1.3.1 Software Automation

The automation of processes and procedures has two primary benefits. First, it guarantees that an organization consistently applies them, which means that it is more likely to produce quality products. Second, automation improves the productivity of the people that must execute the processes and procedures because such automation reduces the tasks that they must perform, which permits them to perform more work.

In the early days of software automation, people were dedicated to developing systems programs, such as compilers and linking loaders. Later, the field dedicated itself to the development of automated methods for program generation, verification, and testing. These efforts, unlike the ones before them, largely failed because they required application generators to represent and manipulate higher forms of knowledge. However, many of these efforts led to the development of fourth generation languages, which were successful in several application domains.

1.3.2 Software Modeling Methodologies

Numerous *software modeling methodologies* have been introduced over the years. By the early 1990s, various structured methodologies (e.g., [37]) were widely used that emphasized the use of data flow, entity-relationship, and state-transition diagrams. These structured methodologies helped minimize the design of complex systems by limiting what software engineers consider at any given moment. When using a structured methodology, a software engineer gradually introduces complexity into a system by decomposing it into several meaningful layers of abstraction. During the abstraction process, a software engineer refines the representation of a prior abstraction by repeatedly adding more detail until a final solution results. Using abstraction, software engineers clearly define the relationships between system components, which results in the efficient development of quality programs [38].

Following the structured design movement, several information-engineering methodologies (e.g., [39]) were introduced. Their primary representation schemes are entity-relationship, data flow, and entity-type hierarchy diagrams, which identify the relationship between entity types. These methodologies also included traceability matrices that identify the relationship between business functions and the entities they manipulate.

Now, object-oriented analysis and design methodologies represent the leading edge of technology (e.g., [40]). Such methodologies tend to emphasize the use of class, sequence (control flow), and state-transition diagrams. They, however, differ from prior paradigms by encapsulating data and function together into highly reusable concepts using message-based communication [41]. Unfortunately, as with every new computer technology, many have been marketed as a *silver bullet* [42], although no one paradigm has proven better than another. Maybe that is because the modeling techniques of each paradigm are largely similar. Each advocates the use of abstraction as a means of composition and address coupling and cohesion issues, although in different ways. Intuitively, modeling is beneficial and its use widespread, although there is no objective evidence that supports this belief.

1.3.3 Software Process Improvement

Software process improvement attempts to improve the quality of software by improving the processes used to develop it. The belief that underlies this approach is that if an organization controls and improves its processes, improved product quality will follow. Several organizations have reported impressive results with this approach, although many of its detractors have criticized the results as being inaccurate. Some of the critics have said that poor measurements were performed and that other factors contributing to improvement were ignored. In fact, the Software Engineering Institute, which created the most popular models used within the United States, has even said that the best organizations of its lowest model ranking often outperform the worst organizations having the highest ranking. For example, Barbacci said [43]:

> "Process maturity does not translate automatically into product quality. Software quality requires mature technology to predict and control quality attributes. If the technology is lacking, even a mature organization will have difficulty producing products with predictable performance, dependability, or other attributes."

In sum, there is no conclusive evidence that shows the benefit of any software process improvement model, although intuitively software process improvement models do make sense.

1.3.4 Software Reuse

Software reuse is the application of a previously developed work product to a new software development effort. Software reusability is important for several reasons: less personnel are required to develop software systems because there are fewer components to develop; reused components are more reliable because other applications and users have repeatedly tested them; properly designed reusable components can be integrated into a software system for little or no cost; and software reuse lessens the maintenance and evolutionary costs that occur after product delivery because the reused components are generally better documented and understood.

Software reuse can be traced to 1968 when McIlroy advocated the use of mass-produced components [44]. This concept has been successfully applied in two well-understood problem domains: mathematics and graphical user interfaces. As a result, numerous mathematical libraries and application programs exist to solve a variety of mathematical problems. Similarly, a variety of windowing systems and toolkits have evolved, which are largely based on a common set of ideas.

The best software development organizations generally achieve reusability levels of about 75 percent when they concentrate on developing one or more product lines [41]. However, few organizations achieve this level of software reuse for several reasons: educational institutions never teach practitioners how to reuse software; many practitioners prefer the challenge of developing a component instead of reusing one; few practitioners are capable of identifying patterns of reuse and developing general schemes for providing reusable solutions; few organizations understand the benefits of developing reusable software artifacts; and few organizations have the process maturity to establish a successful reuse program. Consequently, to avoid failure, an organization should provide adequate tools and training to its practitioners; create a separate group of people having special skills and knowledge to develop reusable components; only insert documented and robust components into a reusable library that provide functionality that have historically proven to be repeatedly needed; and establish a software process improvement program.

1.4 An Integrated Approach for Developing Quality Software

This chapter indicates that few organizations are capable of cost-effectively developing quality software. The key *technical* issues that affect the development of quality software include extreme requirements, such as reliability and performance needs; limited resources, such as processor speed and memory capacity; product complexity; and product size. The key *human* issues that influence the development of quality software include software engineers and managers who have sufficient knowledge of the problem domain and modern programming practices, software engineers who are skilled in software tool use, and software managers who properly manage projects. The key *process* areas that have the largest effect on quality include configuration management, cost estimation, project management, requirements engineering, and verification. Cost estimation, however, is still more of an art than an engineering discipline. The key *environmental* factors impacting software quality include the stability and support of computing systems, operating systems, adopted technologies, and personnel. Thus, an organization should concentrate on improving these key aspects of software development. More specifically, a software engineering organization should consider performing the following tasks:

1. Develop an employment program that hires and retains a highly skilled, learning workforce. This is because people are the most important element in the development and maintenance of computer software. Numerous studies have shown that the very best programmers are generally 15 to 30 times better than the worst ones [45–50]. No tool, technique, or methodology yet developed yields an order of magnitude improvement as does hiring the very best software professionals. Thus, no one can dispute that staffing an organization with the very best people is the best way to increase human productivity and improve product quality. Therefore, an organization must develop a rigorous procedure for selecting the very best software talent and further developing that talent. This means that the organization must:
   - Define rigorous requirements for identifying qualified candidates for employment
   - Define a progression of several job categories with associated roles and responsibilities
   - Define the minimum skills, education, and certification requirements for each job category
   - Define methods for objectively assessing job skills
   - Develop objective criteria for evaluating performance
   - Define objective measures and procedures for advancing and retiring staff members, as well as defining remedial procedures for personnel who do not meet expectations
   - Establish a rigorous training program and mandate its attendance for software engineers and managers

2. Develop a configuration management procedure that:
   - Ensures that every software delivery can be exactly recreated at any time in the future
   - Identifies rules for when and how artifacts can change
3. Develop a requirements engineering procedure that:
   - Defines availability, efficiency, extensibility, portability, reliability, reusability, robustness, testability, and usability requirements
   - Inspects requirements to eliminate unneeded features and corrects those that are incompletely, inconsistently, or vaguely stated
   - Involves users in the definition of requirements
4. Develop a design procedure that:
   - Measures the coupling of each system component
   - Refactors designs to maintain acceptable levels of coupling
   - Inspects designs to identify that modules fulfill a single responsibility
   - Thoroughly documents system architectures and module interfaces
5. Develop a project management procedure that specifies:
   - How a project manager should plan for change
   - How a project manager should manage requirement change
   - How a project manager should identify qualified people to define requirements who understand their responsibilities, have domain experience and knowledge, and follow a sound reasoning process
   - How a project manager should assign mentors to inexperienced people
   - How a project manager should monitor work and react to deviations from expectations by replanning work, if necessary
6. Establish a measurement program focusing on the key software risks and desired qualities.
7. Adopt an iterative software development life cycle to get quicker feedback on the quality of software [3].
8. Adopt or develop an integrated tool suite that supports the activities identified in Tasks 2 through 7. This tool suite should include test tools to perform unit testing and tools to automate bookkeeping and workflow activities to reduce human workload [51].
9. Develop a procedure for reliably defining development costs, dependent on schedule time.
10. Define a small number of reference architectures that define common computing environments for the types of applications that an organization builds. Typically, the technologies to consider include computers, mass storage devices, operating systems, databases, programming languages, and windowing systems.

11. Define a small number of solution frameworks for different lines of businesses, different problem domains, or different aspects of either one. Such frameworks should only be developed for aspects of an organization's business that it must repetitively do.

This book specifies procedures based on known best practices that address Tasks 1 through 7. Further, these procedures heed the advice given by Booch, Jacobson, and Rumbaugh [52]:

> *"To develop software rapidly, efficiently, and effectively, with a minimum of software scrap and rework, you have to have the right people, the right tools, and the right focus. To do all this consistently and predictably, with an appreciation for the lifetime costs of the system, you must have a sound development process that can adapt to the changing needs of your business and technology."*

1.5 Summary

People have always had difficulty creating quality software for large systems. This is true today although numerous efforts have been taken to improve our ability to produce quality software predictably and cost effectively. However, despite these efforts, the growth of software is accelerating about four times faster than human productivity. The result of this fact is that systems delivered today are less reliable and cost more to develop than previously. The majority of these systems are so bad that they are not even delivered to customers.

Many qualities influence the process of developing software and can be found in it. Some product qualities, for example, are efficiency, maintainability, and reliability. Important process qualities are effectiveness, efficiency, and predictability. However, these qualities may be of varying importance for different systems. In addition, they may affect customer perceptions of value in different ways. For example, some system features may be expected, but if the system does not provide them, the customer may be dissatisfied with the system regardless of its other features; yet, if the features are available in the product, they may have little effect on customer satisfaction.

There are several drivers that influence the quality of software. The ones having the greatest impact are personnel and team capabilities, product complexity, required product reliability, extreme resource constraints, and the adoption of testing tools. Of these drivers, an organization can directly influence only two: (1) the selection of personnel and (2) the use of testing tools. The other drivers can only be managed by the introduction of good decision processes that control complexity in light of reliability needs and resource limitations.

There are several approaches to developing quality software. Of these, software automation, modeling methodologies, process improvement, and reuse are the most common. Unfortunately, little effort has been made to identify a way to hire and retain people best able to develop quality software, although the overwhelming evidence indicates that quality people are the most vital asset that a software development organization has. Hence, this book proposes an integrated solution based on people, tools, and techniques. To this end, it identifies practices and procedures for hiring and retaining the best people and identifies effective practices and efficient procedures for them to use.

References

1. Engelman, C., Towards an Analysis of the LISP Programming Language, Mitre Corporation, Report 2648-IV, 1973.
2. Hirsch, P., What's Wrong with the Air Traffic Control System?, *Datamation*, August 1972.
3. Brooks, F.P., Jr., *The Mythical Man-Month: Essays on Software Engineering Anniversary Edition*, Addison-Wesley, 1995.
4. Boehm, B.W., Software and its Impact: A Quantitative Assessment, *Datamation*, May 1973.
5. Gibbs, W.W., Software's Chronic Crisis, *Scientific American*, 86, September 1994.
6. Casini, J. et al., Report on the Loss of the Mars Climate Orbiter Mission, Jet Propulsion Laboratory, Internal Document D-18441, 1999.
7. Floyd, R.W., The Paradigms of Programming, *Commun. of the ACM*, 22, 455, 1979.
8. Shaw, M., Toward Higher-Level Abstractions for Software Systems, *Data and Knowledge Engineering*, 5, 119, 1990.
9. Beizer, B., *Software Testing Techniques*, Van Nostrand Reinhold, 1990.
10. Myers, G.J., *Software Reliability: Principles and Practices*, Wiley, 1976.
11. Freeman, P., *Software Perspectives: The System is the Message*, Addison-Wesley, 1987.
12. Pardee, W.J., *To Satisfy and Delight Your Customer: How to Manage for Customer Value*, Dorset House, 1996.
13. Smart, K.L., Assessing Quality Documents, *ACM J. of Computer Documentation*, 26, 130, 2002.
14. Weigers, K.E., *Creating a Software Engineering Culture*, Dorset House, 1996.
15. Metzger, P. and Boddie, J., *Managing a Programming Project: Processes and People*, Prentice Hall, 1996.

16. Dijkstra, E., The Humble Programmer, *Commun. of the ACM*, 15, 859, 1972.
17. McConnell, S., Less is More, *Software Development*, October 1997.
18. Boehm, B. and Basili, V.R., Software Defect Reduction Top 10 List, *IEEE Computer*, 2, January 2001.
19. Boehm, B.W., *Software Engineering Economics*, Prentice Hall, 1981.
20. Clark, B.K., The Effects of Software Process Maturity on Software Development Effort, Ph.D. dissertation, Computer Science Department, University of Southern California, 1987.
21. Neufelder, A.M., System Software Reliability Training Program, Reliability Analysis Center, 2003.
22. Nikora, A.P., *Software System Defect Content Prediction from Development Process and Product Characteristics*, Ph.D. dissertation, University of Southern California, 1998.
23. Jones, C., *Assessment and Control of Software Risks*, Prentice Hall, 1994.
24. Hooks, I.F. and Farry, K.A., *Customer-Centered Products: Creating Successful Products through Smart Requirements Management*, AMACOM, 2001.
25. Kotonya, G. and Sommerville, I., *Requirements Engineering: Processes and Techniques*, Wiley, 1998.
26. Lauesen, S. and Vitner, O., Preventing Requirement Defects: An Experiment in Process Improvement, *Requirements Engineering*, 6, 37, 2001.
27. Lederer, A.L. and Prasad, J., Nine Management Guidelines for Better Cost Estimating, *Commun. of the ACM*, 35:2, 51, 1992.
28. Vosburgh, B.C. et al., Productivity Factors and Programming Environments, in *Proc. of the Int. Conf. on Software Engineering*, 1984, 143.
29. Christel, M.G. and Kang, K.C., Issues in Requirements Elicitation, Software Engineering Institute, Carnegie Mellon University, Technical Report CMU/SEI-92-TR-012, 1992.
30. Chudge, J. and Fulton, D., Trust and Co-operation in System Development: Applying Responsibility Modelling to the Problem of Changing Requirements, *Software Engineering J.*, 193, May 1996.
31. Boehm, B. and Egyed, A., Software Requirements Negotiation: Some Lessons Learned, in *Proc. of the Int. Conf. on Software Engineering*, 1998, 503.
32. Hofmann, H.F. and Lehner, F., Requirements Engineering as a Success Factor in Software Projects, *IEEE Software*, 18(4), 58, 2001.
33. Kelly, J.C., Sherif, J.S., and Hops, J., An Analysis of Defect Densities Found during Software Inspections, *J. of Systems and Software*, 17, 111, 1992.
34. Lutz, R.R. and Mikulski, I.C., Requirements Discovery during the Testing of Safety-Critical Software, Jet Propulsion Laboratory, unpublished report, 2002.
35. Myers, G.J., *The Art of Software Testing*, Wiley, 1979.
36. Jones, C., *Software Assessments, Benchmarks, and Best Practices*, Addison-Wesley, 2000.
37. DeMarco, T., *Structured Analysis and System Specification*, Yourdon Press/Prentice Hall, 1978.

38. Freeman, P. and Wasserman, A.I., *Software Design Techniques*, IEEE Computer Society, 1980.
39. Martin, J., *Information Engineering*, Volumes 1-3, Prentice Hall, 1990.
40. Rumbaugh, J. et al., *Object-Oriented Modeling and Design*, Prentice Hall, 1991.
41. Yourdon, E., *The Decline and Fall of the American Programmer*, Yourdon Press/Prentice Hall, 1993.
42. Brooks, F.P., Jr., No Silver Bullet: Essence and Accidents of Software Engineering, *IEEE Computer*, 20(4), 10, 1987.
43. Barbacci, M.R., Klein, M.H., and Weinstock, C.B., Principles for Evaluating the Quality Attributes of a Software Architecture, Software Engineering Institute, Carnegie Mellon University, Technical Report CMU/SEI-96-TR-036, 1996.
44. McIlroy, M.D., Mass Produced Software Components, in *Proc. of the NATO Conf. on Software Engineering*, 1968.
45. Humphrey, W.S., *Managing Technical People: Innovation, Teamwork, and the Software Process*, Addison-Wesley, 1997.
46. Putnam, L.H. and Myers, W., *Measures for Excellence: Reliable Software on Time, within Budget*, Yourdon Press, 1992.
47. Sackman, H., Erikson, W.J., and Grant, E.E., Exploratory Experimental Studies Comparing Online and Offline Programming Performance, *Commun. of the ACM*, 11, 3, 1968.
48. Sackman, H., *Man-Computer Problem-Solving: Experimental Evaluation of Time-Sharing and Batch Processing*, Auerbach, 1970.
49. Weinberg, G.M., *Understanding the Professional Programmer*, Dorset House, 1988.
50. Weinberg, G.M., *Quality Software Management: Systems Thinking*, Dorset House, 1992.
51. Hunt, A. and Thomas, D., *The Pragmatic Programmer*, Addison-Wesley, 2000.
52. Booch, G., Rumbaugh, J., and Jacobson, I., *The Unified Modeling Language User Guide*, Addison-Wesley, 1999.

Chapter 2

Organizational Change Management

Chapter 1 indicated that industry has had difficulty producing quality software for decades, discussed prior approaches to improving software quality, and proposed an integrated approach based on key software quality drivers. This chapter, on the other hand, identifies numerous practices an organization should perform to enhance its ability to improve software development processes and, as a result, software systems. Many of these practices address the cultural issues of a proposed organizational change, which often is the primary deterrent to introducing sustainable change.

The *software crisis* or *depression* is more than 40 years old. Problems that existed in developing software in the early days of computing still exist today. These problems include the delivery of low-quality products, actual development costs that exceed expected development costs, and actual development time that exceeds expected development time. To overcome these problems, the software industry has adopted several software process standards, requirements, and guidelines. However, overcoming these problems is an extremely challenging undertaking that is seldom undertaken properly because organizations largely ignore or incorrectly handle the human issues surrounding organizational change [1–5]. It has even been said that an organization may take ten or more years to build a foundation and *culture* — a set of shared beliefs, goals, and values — that will sustain continuous process improvement [6]. Consequently, 55 to 90 percent of all change efforts fail [7].

This chapter discusses those practices that this author has found to significantly ease the introduction and sustainment of a software process improvement program that fosters a quality-oriented culture. This information represents the knowledge this author has gained through both success and failure at several organizations, and is consistent with what others have said [1, 5, 8–12]. It is based on four imperatives that involve the understanding, commitment, and involvement by the members of an organization:

1. An organizational vision must be clearly defined and communicated to the entire workforce so that each individual can understand the organizational goals, how he or she helps satisfy those goals, and how he or she best performs work in a manner consistent with satisfying those goals.
2. Each level of the entire organization, and nearly every member of it, must commit to the achievement of the goals identified in the organizational vision.
3. Involvement by practitioners in defining how to achieve the organizational goals is essential for success [13]. Note that the review of policies, procedures, and processes is insufficient for sustaining successful change. Successful change can only occur by involving practitioners in the definition of these policies, procedures, and practices.
4. The defined policies, procedures, and processes must be clearly communicated to those affected by them. This means that these people should understand what is expected of them in the future, how it differs from the current situation, how they are expected to change, and how the organization will help them change.

2.1 Practices for Management Personnel to Follow

Management plays a critical role in organizational change management. Without its leadership, successful change seldom occurs. Following are numerous practices that management personnel should follow to change an organization.

Practice 2.1. Inculcate an organizational vision. A vision statement identifies what an organization should be, do, and create. Hence, a vision statement should identify the financial, human, and product values of an organization; reflect the organization's uniqueness; and set standards for

TABLE 2.1   Standard Topics of a Vision Statement

Applicable laws	Ethical conduct
Change	Methods of communication
Commitments	Product safety
Continuous product improvement	Protection of the environment
Employee development and recognition	Satisfaction of internal and external customers

productivity and quality that guide how work is done [14, 15]. These standards typically discuss the items contained in Table 2.1.

Every vision statement should define a core strategy based on achieving operational excellence, product leadership, or customer intimacy. Furthermore, lower-level organizational units should refine the vision statement of an organization and create links between each job description and this vision statement. This traceability permits each individual to understand his or her contribution to the organization and the relevance of proposed organizational changes. Without logically consistent, cascading vision statements, people will tend to resist change because they will not understand the relevance of a proposed change to the organization or how it affects them.

The top-most software development organization should create a vision statement that identifies software process improvement as a goal of the organization and articulate a compelling need for it. A *compelling need* for software process improvement is a forceful, convincing, and necessary argument that identifies its usefulness or merit. Compelling needs are driven by various events and situations. Common ones include:

■ The survival of an organization and the jobs of its employees [1, 16]
■ A reaction to a near-term crisis, such as a competitive threat posed by a new competitor or the loss of an important customer
■ Support of long-term business needs and goals identified in higher-level vision statements [8, 11, 17–19]

Compelling needs encourage people to embrace change and increase the odds of a successful software process improvement effort [20, 21]. There are three common ways to identify a compelling need. An organization can:

1. Compare itself against its competitors and other best-of-breed organizations
2. Identify and measure its core business needs and processes [22]
3. Identify business threats and opportunities [20]

Software process improvement efforts commonly use the first two methods and could benefit from using the third approach. Regardless, an organization should use only the most compelling threats and opportunities to convey an understanding of the reasons for change to its employees. Furthermore, an organization should communicate the compelling need of a change to its people in the terms most important to them [15]. Thus, a communication strategy should relate a software process improvement effort to the roles that people perform in satisfying the organizational vision.

Practice 2.2. Commit to a software process improvement program. Floyd indicates the value of such a practice when he gave the following advice, well before anyone used the words "software," "process," and "improvement" in the same sentence [23]:

> *"Spend part of your working day examining and refining your own methods. Even though programmers are always struggling to meet some future or past deadline, methodological abstraction is a wise long-term investment."*

The importance of management commitment to a software process improvement program cannot be understated. Boehm, for example, said [24] that "significant software productivity improvements are not achievable without the full commitment of higher management." Similarly, Weigers stated [25] that "the single biggest threat to a software process improvement program is lack of management commitment." Hence, a commitment to change should flow down from the highest level to the lowest level of management [18, 24, 26–28].

A change sponsor should have the authority to legitimize a change, provide adequate resources to it [29], and ensure that it becomes an organizational goal. In addition, change sponsors must be willing to publicly and continually support the change, demonstrate behavior consistent with it, reward desired behaviors, and discourage undesirable ones [14]. Management cannot downplay their informed commitment because most change failures involve a lack of it. Indications of a lack of commitment include:

- Organizations do not follow processes in times of crisis.
- Organizations postpone or reduce work to accommodate schedule slips.
- Organizations do not specify quality goals.
- Organizations do not provide training to enhance critical skills.

Sometimes an organization will have to significantly change its structure to correct inadequate management commitment. Executive management may need to realign the entire organization so that software personnel have the absolute responsibility, accountability, and authority over software personnel and development processes. For example, one company's president required process improvement across the entire company and made all software personnel report to the corporate vice president for systems and software engineering, which was a newly created position [30]. Another mature software development company also made the software organization manager the focal point of the software process improvement effort and asked every member of the organization to accomplish software process improvement as part of their normal job [28].

Practice 2.3. Create a software engineering steering group. To foster change, an organization should create an active software engineering steering group composed of executives and senior line management [11]. Line managers contribute resources to a software engineering process group and provide input to it as interested customers. Because line managers ultimately are responsible for implementing change, key line managers should help sell changes. The executives of a software engineering steering group, on the other hand, champion the software process improvement effort, identify improvement targets, assign resources, monitor change processes, remove progress barriers, and exchange ideas about what works and what does not. A chief executive officer generally leads a software engineering steering group. If not, another senior-level *fixer* must head the software process improvement effort and have the authority and resources to negotiate among those affected by a change [11].

There are three basic approaches for improving software processes. The autocratic approach advocates using top leadership to define a change, which an organization enforces using compliance mechanisms. This approach assumes that there is no need to address human and organizational issues although mandates are rarely successful and often delay the acceptance of a change [31]. Another approach uses top leadership to determine what needs to change, who then selects a group of people to develop and apply key strategies to align the organization and gain commitment from people. While more effective than the autocratic approach, this approach often falls short of achieving the desired results because it relies on the wisdom and skills of a small number of strategic-thinking and influential people. A third approach, the enlightened approach, uses stakeholders affected by the change to identify the new behavior and develop transition strategies [4, 15]. This approach requires more people and time to define solutions, but results in a larger group *owning* them [3, 10, 19, 32, 33]. It also capitalizes on the wisdom of senior leadership as well as other people throughout the organization, which results in a greater probability of success than other approaches. Consequently, effective software process improvement efforts should follow an enlightened change approach.

Practice 2.4. Create a software engineering process group. The software engineering process group focuses on software process improvement by working with managers and engineers from software development organizations to track, evaluate, and install new software development methods and technology [34]. The software engineering process group:

- Obtains support from all levels of management
- Facilitates process assessments
- Helps line managers define and set expectations for software processes
- Maintains collaborative working relationships with practitioners
- Arranges for software process improvement training
- Monitors and reports on the progress of specific software process improvement efforts
- Creates and maintains process definitions and a process database
- Consults with projects on software development processes. In this capacity, it:
  - Tailors process priorities, definitions, standards, and related material, such as document templates
  - Suggests process improvement methods
  - Analyzes process measurements
  - Infuses technology improvements
  - Facilitates communication among groups with similar interests or issues

Where the software engineering process group fits into an organization is vitally important to its success. Therefore, it should be located in the part of the organizational structure that enables it to influence the definition of the software development processes of all projects. For a line organization, the software engineering process group should be organized as shown in Figure 2.1. This figure indicates that the software engineering process group is distributed among each project and aligned with the organization to which the projects report. The way this works is that the software engineering process group assigned to each project is responsible for tailoring the institutional software development process to support its specific needs. Once a project begins following the tailored software development process, the project's software engineering process group

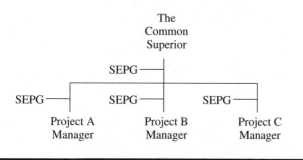

FIGURE 2.1   The software engineering process group of a line-structured organization.

inputs measurements and learned lessons back to the higher-level software engineering process group so that it can capture that information in the institutional software process repository and potentially modify the institutional software development process to improve the organization's effectiveness and efficiency.

For a matrix organization, the process is basically the same. Figure 2.2 shows the organization of a software engineering process group for an institution using a matrix organizational structure [34]. The reason that software engineering process groups are not assigned to the resource managers is that it would not guarantee that a project would follow a common, coordinated software development process. That is, it is more likely that incompatibilities may result in the software development processes of a project if the software engineering process groups are assigned to resource managers instead of project managers.

The reader may be wondering which organizational structure is more desirable. The leaders of the NASA Software Engineering Laboratory reported that when it switched from a line to a matrix structure, two things occurred [35]. First, the loss of *line authority over project development* led to its loss of contact with developers and a loss of continuity among development teams, which resulted in loss of direction for the NASA Software Engineering Laboratory and to differing and inconsistent development processes for each project. Second, the reorganization caused the departure of committed senior management, which eventually led to the collapse of the NASA Software Engineering Laboratory. That is, in the line organization, one only needs the commitment of one person — the project manager; whereas in a matrix structure, the commitment of each resource manager is needed, which is usually more difficult to obtain.

A software engineering process group should be chartered to continually improve software engineering processes, and should be given the authority to enforce them [33, 36]. Because its personnel are vitally

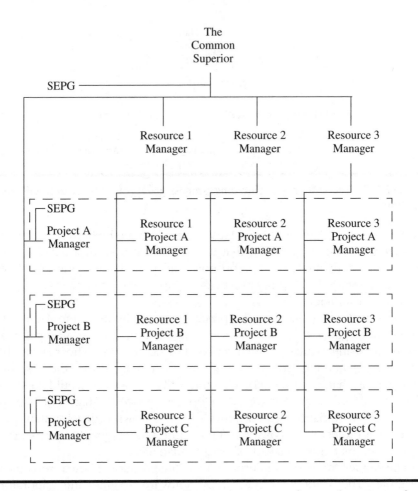

FIGURE 2.2 The software engineering process group of a matrix-structured organization.

important to successful change, they should be highly respected people [10, 19, 29, 37], having expertise in software engineering, process definition, organizational change, and information technology [10, 17, 26, 34, 38]. They also should be highly motivated and should generally have spent most of their lives building systems, which reassures practitioners that their advice is both meaningful, practical, and relevant. The work experiences of these people should also have involved a variety of employers, work environments, positions, software development processes, phases of the software development life cycle, and problem domains [34]. If these people do not have these characteristics, expertise, and respect, a change effort will fail because the software process engineering group will lack the necessary credibility for it to succeed [5, 11].

Consequently, an organization should consider receiving nominations from the practitioners regarding the composition of a software engineering process group [39]. Finally, Fowler and Rifkin state [34]: "The quality and appropriateness of the choice of process group leader will clearly indicate the degree of management commitment to software engineering process improvement." Therefore, executives should be very careful in choosing the leaders of software engineering process groups.

A software engineering process group should comprise about four percent of the initial workforce and about two percent of the sustaining workforce [40]. The NASA Goddard Space Flight Center actually imposed a ten percent overhead cost on projects to support the NASA Software Engineering Laboratory for collecting and processing data, although these costs initially were only five percent and were later reduced to less than two percent [35]. However, when including data analysis, total costs were around ten percent [35]. In the opinion of the founders of the NASA Software Engineering Laboratory, it would not have succeeded without this resource commitment [35].

A software engineering process group should consist of both full-time people, to maintain continuity, and practitioners, who understand the processes that an organization actually performs [5, 32]. A good policy is to maintain a staff whose composition is one third software process experts, who are permanent members of the team; one third software development experts, who are elected by the practitioners and serve three-year terms [34]; and one third practitioners, who serve one-year internships and whose purpose is to indoctrinate them in practical software engineering and process improvement ideas.

The practitioners should actively participate about half time in the software engineering process group while they work on real projects. The rationale for this approach is that successful technology transfer occurs when personnel have software process knowledge and personally transfer that knowledge to their home organizations. Another way of looking at this is that a software engineering process group is centralized, yet supported by local improvement staffs [33, 41]. This approach is consistent with the organizational structure identified in Figures 2.1 and 2.2. This approach is also consistent with how the NASA Software Engineering Laboratory deployed new technology to projects [35]. It actively sought *customers*, learned what their needs were, and then tailored the institutional software development process to best fit their needs. That is, NASA Software Engineering Laboratory personnel became active participants in, or informal members of, project development teams.

When selecting the personnel of the software engineering process group, an organization should choose only those individuals who have demonstrated a commitment to process improvement. This is because many organizations have software process improvement teams that act immaturely [5, 19] although they are advocating changes to improve organizational maturity. Typical problems of such groups include lack of defined processes, realistic and specified requirements, project plans, defined milestones, and schedules. That is, software engineering process groups should be run like a software development project.

Practice 2.5. Align the human resources organization. The human resources function of an organization could have the most significant impact on a software process improvement program because people are the most important resource that an organization has. Unfortunately, this fact has largely gone unnoticed within the software process improvement field. Consequently, the following activities are seldom discussed, although they could significantly enhance the ability of an organization to improve its software development processes. In fact, ignoring these issues will almost certainly lead to failure. The scope of these issues concentrate on personnel selection, improvement, and retention and the appropriate assignment of personnel to project tasks.

Hire a resilient workforce compatible with the characteristics of the desired organizational culture.

Resilient people are positive, focused, flexible, organized, and proactive. Resilient people absorb disruptive change while displaying minimal dysfunctional behavior [42]. These people help develop an adaptive culture, whose characteristics are its focus on innovation, willingness to assume risk, ability to eliminate and correct problems, focus on long-term goals, and willingness and enthusiasm to change. To select these kind of people, the human resources department should develop hiring criteria that evaluate character, self-discipline, motivation, education, training, and skills [43]. The benefits of such selective criteria are improved performance and lowered personnel turnover.

Generate thorough job descriptions.

Job descriptions typically identify the required education, knowledge, and skills of a person that will assume a position, as well as the duties and responsibilities that the person will perform. However, job descriptions seldom specify the rationale for creating the position, or the linkages between or among positions and across functions. Without such information, the person performing the job will be unaware of the organizational agenda and may not operate in a manner consistent with the goals of the entire enterprise [14, 43]. Therefore, the goals and objectives of every job description must be traced to a vision statement [44]. This is because personnel who are not traceable to a vision statement provide no value to the institution and should be eliminated from it or given a new role — one of value to it. Hence, every employee at the institution should have a job description that identifies the rationale for the position, the work relationships of the position [45], and how the position helps achieve the institutional goals and objectives. If process improvement is an objective of the organization, then every job description should identify process improvement expectations and measurements [20].

Furthermore, to be an effective team player, a person should know the objectives of the team. Consequently, a job description should identify the direct suppliers to and customers of the team, the resources that the team consumes and manages, and the objectives of the team, which are aligned with the corporate objectives. Each objective should have quantifiable team and individual performance criteria. In sum, when a job description includes all this information, it will be clear what the job contributes to an organization, which will increase employee satisfaction and help the organization operate cost-effectively.

Establish a defined career path for software professionals. This should be based on certifications, education, experience, skills, and training. Note that a skill involves the effective and efficient application of knowledge to solve problems, although most people view a skill as the ability to use a tool or technique without consideration to how effectively or efficiently a person can apply that knowledge [22, 44]. Furthermore, the criteria for promotions must be quantitative and objective instead of qualitative and subjective, which is contrary to a basic tenet of process improvement — measuring effectiveness and efficiency — and adversely affects employee morale.

Provide a problem-solving-based training program focused on quality. This is because employee competence should be a part of any strategic plan. This is especially important since Boehm has observed [24] that "the demand for new software is rising much more rapidly than the supply of capable software people." Thus, organizations should be interested in improving core, enduring skills [14]. Hence, a training program should focus on three things:

1. Analytical thinking, because it helps people to better identify and solve problems and creates an adaptive workforce that can achieve changing business needs and adopt new technology [8, 20, 43, 44]
2. Quality, because it clearly defines concepts of acceptable work [21]
3. The latest tools and techniques that support the development of quality products [3, 10, 22, 44, 46]

If an organization does not provide such training, old practices will render new organizational changes meaningless and a business's operating units will not function more efficiently or effectively.

Align the reward system with the objectives of a software process improvement program. This alignment should clearly communicate to the workforce through job descriptions the behaviors that will be rewarded as statements of accountability [5, 19, 22, 43]. Freeman, for example, said [47]:

> *"The most important quality policy with respect to quality is one which effectively promotes paying attention to it, for example, by tying bonuses and promotions, at least in part, to measures of product quality. The second most important quality policy is one which establishes objective, measurable standards for quality."*

He further illustrates the dysfunctional behavior that will arise if the reward system is not aligned with the objectives of a software process improvement program in his following comments [47].

> *"It is only common sense that people will pay attention to something if properly motivated. In most organizational settings, if quality is preached, but rewards are unconnected to quality, little real attention will be paid to it. For example, several years ago an organization became concerned with quality and set up a new organization and set of procedures for checking the quality of all software developed. The development work products were carefully checked by an independent group at several stages (preliminary design, detailed design, etc.); however, the approval to proceed to the next stage of development was independent of the quality checks, at least partly because the manager's bonus was tied to schedule, not quality. Several times, a system was found to be below desired quality standards, but rather than delay development until it passed the standards, work proceeded while a half-hearted attempt to fix the problems was undertaken in parallel!"*

Aligning the reward system to reinforce desired behaviors is especially important when trying to invoke change [5, 19, 43]. Thus, the reward system must clearly communicate the required behavioral changes that will be rewarded in the future. In conclusion, every reward system must do three things:

1. Align the desired behaviors with a vision statement to show orga-nizational value [14].
2. Assess individuals based on both individual and team performance [48].
3. Use objective, fair, and open criteria for merit increases and pro-motions that substantially differentiate pay between top, middle, and low performers [44, 48, 49].

2.2 Practices for Software Engineering Process Groups to Follow

Software engineering process groups have the primary responsibility for making successful software change happen. They create tactical plans that fulfill the strategic business goals of the organization. Consequently, soft-ware engineering process groups manage the day-to-day activities focusing on improving organizational software processes. Following are several practices that software engineering process groups should perform to promote successful change.

Practice 2.6. *Assess the maturity of the organizational development pro-cesses.* An assessment is a self-audit that provides information to help an organization establish a baseline and define its priorities. An assessment should describe how an organization functions, identify improvement opportunities, and provide recommendations regarding a course of action. Completing a thorough assessment of an organization will help the soft-ware engineering process group anticipate how a change will affect the organization and how it should respond to the change. The results of an assessment will shape the general approach for the change by determining initiatives and strategies that will move the organization to the desired state. Assessments should be done periodically to determine progress and refine the software process improvement approach.

Because a software engineering process group should assess the ability of an organization to adopt a change, it should study [50]:

■ The method an organization has used to handle past change because it affects the success of future changes
■ The activities of past software process improvement efforts that worked well and contributed to success, as well as those that did not

- The frequency of change that the organization has undergone during the past three years and the dominant effect these changes had on members of the organization
- Employees' view of the most recent organizational change, in addition to the prevailing attitude toward change
- Whether employees have understood new policies in the past and if these policies met their needs
- Employees who will perceive a software process improvement effort as a threat (or an enhancement) to job security, social status, or power because these people most likely will resist (or support) change

Practice 2.7. Identify changes and their scope. A software process improvement effort should address the most promising improvement activities for each business unit [15, 25, 51]. For most business units, improvements in their project management, requirements engineering, and validation and verification activities generally yield the greatest benefit. Regardless, a software engineering process group should perform four tasks to identify improvement activities:

1. It should focus a software process improvement effort on new or important projects that can most benefit from change [2, 21].
2. It should identify what the customer values most and determine the processes, policies, and strategies it can change to add customer value [21].
3. It should identify strategic and core competency processes that it can improve [9, 27, 28, 30].
4. It should analyze global inefficiencies caused by redundancies performed within activities of the overall business process.

Because an organization needs a gradual approach to change [5, 11, 15, 17, 24, 25, 46], it should change no more than three processes at any given time [1] and introduce changes in three- to six-month time frames. The reason for this is to prevent personnel from becoming confused about the goals and objectives of the effort or exceeding their emotional limit to change. By limiting the amount of concurrent change, an organization will improve its ability to change because of the clarity presented by a small number of goals and objectives.

In addition, a software engineering process group should develop and document a vision for each process it expects to change [18, 20]. Each vision statement should describe the new capabilities of the process and identify realistic performance and quality improvement expectations [3]. Further, each vision statement should identify how an organization will support the changed processes, respond to customer needs, and respond to competition. A new vision should include measurable objectives for each new process that illustrate dramatic improvement, and fact-based analysis must drive the vision. By creating a vision for each process undergoing change, a software engineering process group provides employees with a sense of how they will perform work in the future, which will lower resistance to change by allaying fears that arise when people are uncertain about their futures.

Markus, for example, observed [39] that "a thorough analysis of the existing situation should be conducted to identify factors that will facilitate or hinder the change. Examples of such factors can be inappropriate reporting relationships among individuals or groups, incentive schemes that do not reward the desired behavior or punish undesired behavior, and unclear allocation of responsibility for certain tasks." He goes on to say [39] that "people will resist ... when the costs outweigh the benefits (received wisdom)." Acknowledging this fact, Leffingwell and Widrig [52] indicate that an organization should consider "automating some of the manual, record-keeping, and change management aspects of the process that would free scarce resources to focus on higher value-added activities."

Practice 2.8. Demonstrate a quantitative financial benefit for each change. The importance of demonstrating a beneficial and realistic financial return on investment has been noted by several researchers [10, 15, 53]. The best way to demonstrate a financial benefit is to address the needs of the organization by improving important products; improving processes is relevant only if they have measurable positive impact on product improvement [35]. The NASA Software Engineering Laboratory, for example, was not interested in improving a key process area or achieving higher levels of a process maturity model if such improvement had no demonstrated improvement on product quality [35].

Unfortunately, most software process improvement efforts attempt to demonstrate the value of the effort in measured terms of lowered number of defects, increased productivity, and shortened schedules. The problem with this approach is that these measures are difficult for managers, especially high-level executives, to translate into financial value. March indicates that Juran knew this too when he states the following [21]:

> *"Although Juran's analytical methods could identify areas needing improvement ... they were in the language of the shop floor ... for this reason, he advocated a cost-of-quality (COQ) accounting system [that] provided management with a dollar cost for defective products."*

Thus, a cost-of-quality accounting system permits executives to compare the value of a software process improvement effort with another competing program. In addition, such a system provides a means for determining whether the rate of return is greater than some minimal level that the organization expects to obtain from every investment. This is what most software professionals forget — a software process improvement effort is an investment! Therefore, if an organization has determined that it wants a return of eight percent on every investment, then a software process improvement program must convincingly demonstrate that it will achieve at least that much. If not, it will not be able to acquire or sustain a commitment from executive management, unless it is forced to do so by its customers.

The most sophisticated, and most appropriate, model for computing return on investment is the discounted-cash-flow model because it considers the time value of money. That is, it discounts future cash flows to their present values. To use this model, one first assumes some minimum desired rate of return, set by an organization to cover risk and the cost of money, and then calculates the rate of return, as specified by the model. If the sum of the discounted values of future cash flows is greater than the payout, then the project is viable; otherwise, the project costs more than it returns. For every viable project, the excess of the present value over the payout indicates its merit, which an organization can use to compare one proposal with another. This, of course, assumes that there is a limitation of funds and that all beneficial proposals compete with one another.

To perform this computation, the personnel of a software process improvement effort must translate defect and productivity improvements into financial terms. Initially, they must prepare defect and productivity rates and costs based on available data from other organizations. It is best to use data from within the same industry or from those who work on similar problems. Then, the team should revise these rates and costs based on cultural and personnel issues. Be aware that an organization's executives will expect justification for the proposed expected defect and productivity rates and costs.

Readers may be asking themselves whether this advice is also applicable to nonprofit organizations. It is because there is no reason to expect that any funding source will not involve competitive selection. Assuming this, a software process improvement program must demonstrate that it has greater value than another project or any other form of investment. Of course, this argument assumes that the people who select projects to fund desire to spend their money wisely, which is otherwise known as the *prudent man* assumption.

Practice 2.9. Obtain the commitment of practitioners. Software organizations that deploy new methodologies often encounter significant resistance [54]. Therefore, software development organizations need to understand the key factors that influence the adoption of a process change. There are four significant factors [55]:

1. A belief that a change will enhance one's job performance
2. The voluntariness of a change
3. The consistency of a change with one's existing values, needs, and past experiences
4. The importance of a change by those one respects

Furthermore, because the usefulness and compatibility of a new methodology with existing work processes has significant influence [33, 43], bottom-up change has been accepted by software engineering process groups as a standard way of doing business [56]. This is because most practitioners are interested in improving how they work, given a supportive environment.

Of all the pressures that an organization can use to impose change, the measurement and reward structure is probably the most important [55]. Therefore, the more strongly practitioners feel that a technology will not help them achieve higher performance levels or become more productive as defined by existing measurement and reward systems, the more important it is for an organization to change the measurement and reward systems to reinforce the desired change [55]. This is especially true during a change in technology because the benefits of such a change are generally not apparent for a long time, whereas the costs incurred by the practitioners are immediate and obvious.

Another effective method for obtaining the commitment of practitioners is to constantly engage them. Communication is one of the most effective tools an organization can use to obtain acceptance of a change [15, 18, 19]. Hence, it should occur frequently [44, 57] and be performed in one-on-one or in small group situations [11]. Consider, for example, that the Chief Executive Officer of one firm spent six months communicating and justifying his vision to small focus groups when he wanted it to produce personal computers [1]. When communicating with the workforce, the organization should perform the following actions to build trust and foster positive change [14]:

■ Explain the shortcomings of a change followed by its benefits [46] because presenting a balanced view of the change will help build trust with those affected by it.
■ Listen to the workforce and encourage feedback.

- Inform employees how the software process improvement effort will affect them, honestly, simply, and straightforwardly [15].
- Communicate the result of a change to the affected personnel [48].
- Tailor messages to target audiences [20, 27, 58]. Note that practitioners are generally motivated to change when they see visible success of software process improvement initiatives, are given adequate resources, and observe successful initiatives that peers initiate [59]. Thus, communications with practitioners should focus on these issues.

Practice 2.10. Measure personnel productivity and product quality. Freeman indicates that quality can only be achieved by measuring product quality when he says the following [47]:

> *"The best policies regarding quality are those that motivate people to pay attention to quality. For example, one can implement an objective measure of the thoroughness of testing in terms of the percentage of paths through the software that have been tested; this is one aspect of testing quality. Likewise, the quality of a software design at the architectural (structural) level can be measured in terms of the number and strength of connections between its component parts."*

In addition to measuring product quality, an organization should use metrics to measure its progress in transitioning to a desired state because it permits it to compare the rate of actual change against its planned change [5, 30, 36, 56, 60]. This results in three key benefits:

1. It demonstrates value to management and engages them on a continual basis, which encourages their continual support.
2. It provides feedback to the software engineering project group, which allows them to alter existing plans so that it can be more effective.
3. It encourages practitioners to participate in software process improvement.

These metrics should measure the effectiveness and efficiency of each process and the acceptance of new or changed processes [14, 20]. These measurements should form a hierarchy, such that the higher-level measurements relate directly to organizational goals and the lowest level goals relate to detailed individual measurements, such as total labor hours per developed line of code. Thus, the movement of lower-level indicators will predict movement of the higher-level indicators.

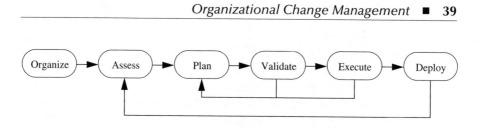

FIGURE 2.3 **The organizational change management procedure.**

2.3 A Procedure for Making Change Happen

The change procedure involves a sequence of several activities. First, an organization organizes the change effort. Second, the software engineering process group assesses the organization. Third, it plans the change effort. Fourth, it validates the change effort because the situation may have changed enough to make the plan invalid. If the situation did change, then planning is resumed. Fifth, the software engineering process group executes the plan. Afterward, the software engineering process group standardizes the aspects of the plan that worked well by documenting what worked, what did not work, and the reasons for success or failure. Then, the software engineering process group either deploys the plan or revises it. That is, during the execution phase, the software engineering process group applies the plan to a small organizational unit; but during the deployment phase, it applies the plan to the entire organization. Figure 2.3 graphically illustrates this procedure.

> **Step 1.** Organize the change effort. To foster change, an organization may need to create several focus groups to develop and share ideas. Two essential groups for improving software processes are the software engineering steering group and the software engineering process group [11]. Personnel in these two groups fulfill several useful functions, as described below:
> - The line managers of the software engineering steering group contribute resources to a software engineering process group and provide input to it as interested customers. Because line managers ultimately are responsible for implementing change, key line managers should be on work teams to help sell the software process improvement initiative.
> - The executives of a software engineering steering group sponsor and champion the software process improvement effort. They also define policies and goals, identify improvement targets, assign resources, select key personnel for the software engineering steering and process groups, monitor progress, and

remove progress barriers. A chief executive officer generally leads the software engineering steering group. If not, another senior level *fixer* must lead it and have the authority and resources to negotiate among those affected by a software process improvement program [11].

■ Members of the software engineering process group identify new work processes and develop process measurements, targets, and implementation plans. Each implementation plan must specify a budget and the needed resources to be successful. While performing these tasks, the software engineering process group makes presentations to the software engineering steering group, which approves work and recommits to the software process improvement effort.

   To support this work, these groups must create a vision statement that relates a change effort to the strategic business plan of the organization. This statement must clearly specify what the organization will look like, feel like, and be like once it has successfully adopted the change. If the software engineering process group determines that something about the current organization is not adequate to meet the change goals, it must determine what the organization needs to do to sustain the desired effect.

Step 2. Assess the organization. An *assessment* is a self-audit that provides information to help an organization establish a baseline and define its priorities. An assessment should describe how an organization functions, identify improvement opportunities, and provide recommendations regarding a course of action. Completing a thorough assessment of an organization will help the software engineering process group anticipate how a change will affect the organization and how it should respond to the change. The results of an assessment will shape the general approach of a change effort by determining the initiatives and strategies that will move the organization to the desired state.

A software engineering process group must identify what information it needs and how it will obtain it. To this end, it must identify:

■ Who will provide and gather the assessment data
■ Who will be involved in documenting and reviewing the gathered information
■ How it will document the acquired information
■ How it will document the assessment findings and their implications
■ Who is the intended audience of an assessment report

A software engineering process group must also assess the ability of an organization to adopt a change. Consequently, it must identify:

- The frequency of change that the organization has undergone during the past three years and the dominant effect these changes had on members of the organization [50]
- Employees' view of the most recent organizational change, in addition to the prevailing attitude toward change
- What aspects of prior change efforts contributed to success and failure
- Employees who will perceive a change effort as a threat to job security, social status, or power because these people most likely will resist change
- The magnitude of change needed to achieve the desired state
- Whether a change requires a substantial change in workforce attitudes and motivation and in budget and resource availability
- Whether a substantial change in work methods, rules, and procedures is required
- Whether a change in key personnel is required
- Existing or forthcoming political dynamics that might influence the change

Step 3. Plan the change. In this phase, the software engineering steering group works with the software engineering process group in preparing the organization for change. Because there is seldom a consensus for change, achieving change is extremely challenging. Typically, 20 to 30 percent of employees will quickly adopt change, 20 to 30 percent will never accept change, and the remainder will go with the flow [61]. Thus, a software engineering process group does not have to spend a lot of time with those who resist change; it only needs to help and protect those who want to change.

Therefore, a software engineering process group must always anticipate the response of employees to change. If the organization is not prepared for the response, the change effort may fail. Because the transition period is a time of reorientation and uncertainty, the software engineering process group must do whatever it can to reduce individual stress caused by the change. Because people often feel that they have lost control of their environment during a change effort [5], the software engineering process group must identify what the changes will be beforehand, as well as identify how these changes will personally affect its employees. Sometimes, people do not want to make the effort to adopt new ways. Consequently, the software engineering process group must reduce the effort required for them to do so [5]. That is, people do not fear change; instead, they fear having to give up those things they value.

Productivity loss is initially associated with a change effort because the transition period requires individuals to learn and adopt new behaviors. Therefore, a software engineering process group should communicate the rationale for a change, its expected outcome, and what will and will not change to enhance success. In addition, it must give people enough time to assimilate the change before introducing new changes or placing other demands on them. Throughout this process, the software engineering process group must set short-term goals, focus on priorities, and support change by providing training and maintaining open communication paths between it and those affected by the change. To do this, it must perform several tasks and document them in a plan.

■ A plan must identify the change sponsors, software engineering steering group, software engineering process group, change advocates, and all other stakeholders. It must identify the role of each individual and group, including their responsibilities, accountabilities, and authorities. It must also identify the concerns and interests of each individual and group. Step 1 of the change process should have accumulated most, if not all, of this information.

■ A plan should specifically identify whether any important stakeholder poses a potential barrier to change. In addition, the plan should identify potential cultural and structural barriers. The software engineering process group should assess each potential barrier and propose a solution strategy for each one. Some of this information is sensitive; thus, the software engineering process group must tailor this portion of the plan for different audiences.

■ A plan must identify the current situation, including what is wrong and right about it. This description must include a description of the existing software development processes and tools. Further, it should include a description of all support processes, such as those that human resources and training groups typically perform. The plan must also identify the desired situation in a similar manner. An outcome of Step 2 of the change process provides most, if not all, of the information describing the current state, whereas an outcome of Step 1 provides the high-level, qualitative goals of the desired state. From these goals, the software engineering process group must develop lower-level, quantitative goals and develop very specific objectives that achieve them.

- A plan must contrast and compare the functional differences between the current and desired states. More specifically, it must identify those processes and tools that the organization will adopt and those that will be changed or no longer used. In addition, the plan must identify how individuals, business units, and the organization must change to support the defined objectives. This change also necessitates linking new requirements to methods of satisfying them. For example, if a new requirement mandated that all programmers achieve a specific certification then the organization should provide relevant training.
- A plan must identify the scope of a change. To this end, it must first identify those business units that can have a positive return on investment when adopting the change. Then, it must identify cultural and political barriers that would make it difficult for some of these business units to adopt a change, at least initially, and eliminate them from consideration. Next, a plan should identify the remaining business units for deploying the change. After this, it should rank these business units according to their probability of successfully adopting a change, which it will use to determine the sequence of candidates for executing the plan.

Step 4. Validate the plan. After developing a sound transition plan, the software engineering process group should review it to make sure that it will meet organizational needs. Remember that the change should address a business imperative and contribute to the goals of the organization. This is the time to confirm that the drivers still call for the desired state and that the plan will help the organization achieve it. If a driver has changed or the software engineering process group needs to adjust the plan, it should reassess the situation and alter the plan. Validating the plan not only serves the software engineering process group, but also serves as an excellent communication tool for involving the software engineering steering group. By confirming that the plan is sound, a software engineering process group will once again increase commitment and support for a software process improvement effort.

Step 5. Execute the change. Deploy the change to a single group. If the pilot effort is successful, then deploy the change to the entire organization. If the change was not beneficial, then replan the change effort.

Step 6. Deploy the change. Once a software engineering process group has successfully piloted a transition plan, it should deploy the plan to the entire organization. This activity is the largest in scope of the entire implementation because everyone affected by the change will be significantly involved. Remember that while change is stressful for even the healthiest organization, the best change leaders are those who expend the least amount of organizational energy in exchange for positive results. This is the idea of economic choices, or effectiveness and efficiency. Remember that the goal is to change as little as possible and to affect as much as possible. The critical elements for successful deployment are an organizational support infrastructure, a good product, and effective promotion [46]. Furthermore, to increase deployment effectiveness, a process asset library requires a role-based hypertext system backed up by a database system [46].

During deployment, be aware of the reactions of the members of the organization. By constantly monitoring behavior in the transition period, a change team can see new roadblocks and determine how to combat them. Skilled change leaders arrange for quick, visible, positive outcomes. They then use feedback about the level of stress or concern brought on by the change as a barometer for determining how to adjust the pace or approach of the transition strategies.

2.4 Summary

Proponents of software process improvement claim improved product quality, reduced time to market, better productivity, increased organizational flexibility, and greater customer satisfaction. The NASA Software Engineering Laboratory is a good example of the benefits that can be derived from a successful software process improvement effort. During 1987 to 1991, it was able to decrease software defect rates by 75 percent, reduce costs by 55 percent, and improve software reuse by 300 percent [35]. During 1991 to 1995, it further reduced defect rates by 37 percent, reduced costs by 42 percent, and improved reuse by 8 percent [35]. Overall, reuse rates actually grew to 80 percent on flight dynamics systems [35]. However, about two thirds of software process improvement efforts fail [62]. Some organizations have even found it difficult to establish simple metrics programs [63].

Addressing these issues, this chapter has proposed several practices to improve the success of software process improvement efforts. The basic premise is that to effect change, software organizations must address both social and technological aspects. For an organization to succeed with software process improvement, it must successfully achieve four critical objectives. Failing to successfully perform any of these objectives will cause the software process improvement effort to fail. The first critical objective is to construct the vision of the new organization and the individual changed processes. Unfortunately, this is seldom addressed by software process improvement plans nor discussed by software process improvement professionals. This is somewhat strange considering that modern software development processes usually specify the development of a concept of operations, which essentially outlines the vision of a proposed software system. So why is it that software process improvement professionals think that they can create a new system — a software process — without doing what they themselves advocate to software practitioners? Thus, a software process improvement program must develop an operational concept and support it with several operational scenarios. In addition to explaining what the future will look like, operational scenarios may also help identify who will resist change [11].

The second critical objective is to obtain commitment at all organizational levels [62]. Obviously, the most desired form of commitment is to have employees identify and be involved with a software process improvement effort because other forms of commitment are only sustained through reward or organizational control systems. However, these methods are useful for sustaining commitment when commitment is adversely affected by current attitudes, circumstances, and organizational factors [62].

Obtaining executive-level commitment for a software process improvement effort is the most important of all levels to achieve. Without high-level commitment, the commitment of others most likely will not be forthcoming. To obtain executive-level commitment, a software process improvement team must successfully demonstrate how the software process improvement effort supports the organizational strategy and business needs. For example, if the addressed business need is to reduce software development costs by ten percent, then the software process improvement effort must demonstrate how it will reduce those costs.

The third critical objective is to involve practitioners in the development of the software process improvement initiative [24]. Such involvement should include 10 to 25 percent of the workforce, depending on the size of the organization. Without such involvement, an organization will not be able to gain acceptance of a software process improvement effort because practitioners will resist what they did not help to create. In addition, when seeking user involvement, intentions must be genuine. Markus states [39] that "where powerful authorities have decided that a specific change, unpopular with users, will take place ... users are likely to resent strongly a tactic that is meant to make them feel as though they have some say in the matter, when they obviously do not."

The fourth critical objective is to clearly communicate the software process improvement effort — the vision, its benefits, its differences, and so on — to the entire workforce. The software engineering process group will have to do this for executives, middle-level managers, and practitioners. For each of these groups, the software engineering process group should develop a different message. For high-level executives, the message should concentrate on the alignment of the software process improvement effort with the business goals and needs of the organization and the financial return on investment. For practitioners, the message should emphasize the difference between how they do work today and how they will do it in the future. The software engineering process group should emphasize the personal benefits of the change, as well as tedious operations that practitioners currently have to perform manually that will be automated in the future. Finally, the software engineering process group should motivate middle-level managers by emphasizing the benefits in terms of improved product quality, reduced schedules, and greater predictability of schedules. That is, the software engineering process group should emphasize that managing projects will be easier in the new state than in the prior one.

In conclusion, this chapter has provided a procedure for introducing change and identified numerous practices for changing an organization. Organizations should use this procedure and these practices to improve their software process improvement efforts. To promote success, an organization must address four critical objectives — creating a vision of the future organization, achieving executive commitment, involving practitioners in change definition, and communicating that vision to the entire organization. In addition, a select group of people, having the necessary skills and personal characteristics, should lead and participate in software process improvement efforts.

References

1. Carr, D.K. and Johansson, H.J., *Best Practices in Reengineering: What Works and What Doesn't in the Reengineering Process*, McGraw-Hill, 1995.
2. Diaz, M. and Slago, J., How Software Process Improvement Helped Motorola, *IEEE Software*, 14(5), 75, 1997.
3. Laporte, C.Y. and Trudel, S., Addressing the People Issues of Process Improvement Activities at Oerlikon Aerospace, *Software Process: Improvement and Practice*, 4(4), 187, 1998.
4. Lawrence, P.R., How to Deal with Resistance to Change, in *Management of Change*, Harvard Business Review, 1991, 77.
5. Moitra, D., Managing Change for Software Process Improvement Initiatives: A Practical Experience-Based Approach, *Software Process: Improvement and Practice*, 4, 199, December 1998.

6. Paulk, M.C. et al., *The Capability Maturity Model: Guidelines for Improving the Software Process*, Addison-Wesley, 1994.
7. Kabat, D.J., Information Technologies to Manage the Next Dynamic, in *The Change Management Handbook: A Road Map to Corporate Transformation*, Berger, L.A. and Sikora, M.J. (Eds.), Irwin, 1994.
8. Beer, M., Eigenstat, R.A., and Spector, B., Why Change Programs Don't Produce Change, *Harvard Business Review*, 68, 158, November–December 1990.
9. Burrill, C.W., Ten Ways to Kill a Quality Program, *IEEE Engineering Management Review*, 24, 105, 1996.
10. Hall, T., Rainer, A., and Baddoo, N., Implementing Software Process Improvement: An Empirical Study, *Software Process: Improvement and Practice*, 7, 3, March 2002.
11. Keen, P.G.W., Information Systems and Organizational Change, *Commun. of the ACM*, 24, 24, 1981.
12. Price Waterhouse Change Integration Team, *Better Change: Best Practices for Transforming Your Organization*, Irwin Professional Publishing, 1995.
13. Gabriel, R.P., *Patterns of Software: Tales from the Software Community*, Oxford University Press, 1996.
14. Fitz-enz, J., *The 8 Practices of Exceptional Companies: How Great Organizations Make the Most of Their Human Assets*, AMACOM, 1997.
15. Juran, J.M. and Gryna, F.M., *Quality Planning and Analysis: From Product Development through Use*, McGraw-Hill, 1993.
16. Pitterman, B., Telcordia Technologies: The Journey to High Maturity, *IEEE Software*, 17(4), 89, 2000.
17. Debou, C. and Kuntzmann-Combelles, A., Linking Software Process Improvement to Business Strategies: Experiences from Industry, *Software Process: Improvement and Practice*, 5, 55, March 2000.
18. Kotter, J.P., Leading Change: Why Transformation Efforts Fail, *Harvard Business Review*, 73, 59, 1995.
19. Stelzer, D. and Mellis, W., Success Factors of Organizational Change in Software Process Improvement, *Software Process: Improvement and Practice*, 4, 227, 1998.
20. Eckes, G., *Making Six Sigma Last*, Wiley, 2001.
21. March, A., A Note on Quality: The Views of Deming, Juran, and Crosby, *IEEE Engineering Management Review*, 24, 6, Spring 1996.
22. Ferguson, P. et al., Software Process Improvement Works!, Software Engineering Institute, Carnegie Mellon University, Technical Report CMU/SEI-99-TR-27, 1999.
23. Floyd, R.W., The Paradigms of Programming, *Commun. of the ACM*, 22, 455, 1979.
24. Boehm, B.W., *Software Engineering Economics*, Prentice Hall, 1981.
25. Weigers, K.E., *Software Requirements*, Microsoft Press, 2003.
26. Butler, K. and Lipke, W., Software Process Achievement at Tinker Air Force Base, Oklahoma, Software Engineering Institute, Carnegie Mellon University, Technical Report CMU/SEI-2000-TR-14, 2000.
27. Grady, R.B., *Successful Software Process Improvement*, Prentice Hall, 1997.

28. Haley, T. et al., Raytheon Electronic Systems Experience in Software Process Improvement, Software Engineering Institute, Carnegie Mellon University, Technical Report CMU/SEI-95-TR-17, 1995.

29. Herbsleb, J.D. and Goldenson, D.R., A Systematic Survey of CMM Experience and Results, in *Proc. of the Int. Conf. on Software Engineering*, 1996, 323.

30. Willis, R.R. et al., Hughes Aircraft's Widespread Deployment of a Continuously Improving Software Process, Software Engineering Institute, Carnegie Mellon University, Technical Report CMU/SEI-98-TR-6, 1998.

31. Zelkowitz, M.V., Software Engineering Technology Infusion within NASA, *IEEE Trans. on Engineering Management*, 43, 250, 1996.

32. Dion, R., Process Improvement and the Corporate Balance Sheet, *IEEE Software*, 10(4), 28, 1993.

33. Rainer, A. and Hall, T., An Analysis of Some Core Studies of Software Process Improvement, *Software Process: Improvement and Practice*, 6, 169, 2001.

34. Fowler, P. and Rifkin, S., Software Engineering Process Group Guide, Software Engineering Institute, Carnegie Mellon University, Technical Report CMU/SEI-90-TR-24, 1990.

35. Basili, V.R. et al., Lessons Learned from 25 Years of Process Improvement: The Rise and Fall of the NASA Software Engineering Laboratory, in *Proc. of the Int. Conf. on Software Engineering*, 2002, 69.

36. Crosby, P.B., *Quality is Free*, McGraw-Hill, 1979.

37. Wilson, D.N., Hall, T., and Baddoo, N., A Framework for Evaluation and Prediction of Software Process Improvement Success, *J. of Systems and Software*, 59, 135, 2001.

38. Humphrey, W.S., Snyder, T.R., and Willis, R.R., Software Process Improvement at Hughes Aircraft, *IEEE Software*, 8(4), 11, 1991.

39. Markus, M.L., Power, Politics, and MIS Implementation, *Commun. of the ACM*, 26, 430, 1983.

40. McGarry, F., A Presentation on Software Process Improvement, Jet Propulsion Laboratory, 2002.

41. Curtis, B., The Global Pursuit of Process Maturity, *IEEE Software*, 76, July/August 2000.

42. Conner, D.R., The Next Generation of Fire Walkers, in *The Handbook of Change Management: A Road Map to Corporate Transformation*, Berger, L.A. and Sikora, M J. (Eds.), Irwin, 1994, 257.

43. Labovitz, G. and Rosansky, V., *The Power of Alignment*, Wiley, 1997.

44. Humphrey, W.S., *Managing Technical People: Innovation, Teamwork, and the Software Process*, Addison-Wesley, 1997.

45. Rothman, J., *Hiring the Best Knowledge Workers, Techies, and Nerds: The Secrets and Science of Hiring Technical People*, Dorset House, 2004.

46. Kaltio, T. and Kinnula, A., Deploying the Defined SW Process, *Software Process: Improvement and Practice*, 5(1), 65, 2000.

47. Freeman, P., *Software Perspectives: The System is the Message*, Addison-Wesley, 1987.

48. Weinberg, G.M., *Understanding the Professional Programmer*, Dorset House, 1988.
49. Herman, R.E., *Keeping Good People: Strategies for Solving the Dilemma of the Decade*, Oakhill Press, 1997.
50. Kitson, D.H. and Masters, S.M., An Analysis of SEI Software Assessment Results, in *Proc. of the Int. Conf. on Software Engineering*, 1993.
51. Weigers, K.E., *Creating a Software Engineering Culture*, Dorset House, 1996.
52. Leffingwell, D. and Widrig, D., *Managing Software Requirements: A Use Case Approach*, Addison-Wesley, 2003.
53. Brodman, J.G. and Johnson, D.L., Return on Investment (ROI) from Software Process Improvement as Measured by US Industry, *Software Process: Improvement and Practice*, 1, 35, August 1995.
54. Kozar, K., Adopting Systems Development Methods: An Exploratory Study, *J. of Management Information Systems*, 5(4), 73, 1989.
55. Riemenschneider, C.K., Hardgrave, B.C., and Davis, F.D., Explaining Software Developer Acceptance of Methodologies: A Comparison of Five Theoretical Models, *IEEE Trans. on Software Engineering*, 28, 1135, 2002.
56. McGarry, F. et al., Software Process Improvement in the NASA Software Engineering Laboratory, Software Engineering Institute, Carnegie Mellon University, Technical Report CMU/SEI-94-TR-22, 1994.
57. Wohlwend, H. and Rosenbaum, S., Schlumberger's Software Improvement Program, *IEEE Trans. on Software Engineering*, 20, 833, 1994.
58. Berger, L.A., Change Management, in *The Handbook of Change Management: A Road Map to Corporate Transformation*, Berger, L.A. and Sikora, M.J. (Eds.), Irwin, 1994, 3.
59. Baddoo, N. and Hall, T., Motivators of Software Process Improvement: An Analysis of Practitioners' Views, *J. of Systems and Software*, 62, 85, 2002.
60. Hammer, M., *Beyond Reengineering*, HarperCollins, 1996.
61. Carr, D.K., Hard, K.J., and Trahant, W.J., *Managing the Change Process: A Field Book for Change Agents, Consultants, Team Leaders, and Reengineering Managers*, McGraw-Hill, 1996.
62. Abrahamsson, P., Commitment Development in Software Process Improvement: Critical Misconceptions, in *Proc. of the Int. Conf. on Software Engineering*, 2001, 71.
63. Herbsleb, J.D. and Grinter, R.E., Conceptual Simplicity Meets Organizational Complexity: Case Study of a Corporate Metrics Program, in *Proc. of the Int. Conf. on Software Engineering*, 1998, 271.

Chapter 3

Personnel Management

Chapter 1 indicated that people are the primary determinant of software quality and productivity. This chapter identifies numerous practices for finding, nurturing, and retaining the best people. It also defines a step-by-step procedure that incorporates these practices so that they can be easily followed.

An organization's most important asset and primary determinant of success is talented people [1–4]. Weigers, for example, has said [5]: "your team members will always be your greatest asset. ... hiring and nurturing outstanding software engineers will give you a competitive edge no process definition can best." Several studies of software projects support this hypothesis by showing that talented people solve the key problems and produce the best products [3, 6–12]. In these studies, the best programmers were generally 15 to 30 times better than the worst ones in terms of both productivity and quality factors [3, 11, 13–16]. Some of these studies claimed that the differences are even greater. For example, Gibbs said [17]:

> "You can walk into a typical company and find two guys sharing an office, getting the same salary and having essentially the same credentials and yet find a factor of 100 difference in the number of instructions per day that they produce."

At least one study has shown even larger differences. The variability of productivity of software personnel among more than 400 military software systems ranged from ten source lines of code per month to several thousand [13]. Even more surprisingly, other experiments demonstrated that some people simply cannot do the work. DeMarco and Lister conducted an experiment in which 166 programmers were tasked to complete the same assignment [8]. They found that the programmers exhibited differences in productivity of about five to one on the same small project. However, the most interesting result of the study was that 13 of the 166 programmers did not finish the project at all. In another study with similar findings, Curtis presented a group of 60 professional programmers with what he characterized as a simple debugging task [6]. Despite its simplicity, six of the professional programmers were not able to complete the task. Hence, about 10 percent of software engineers either required huge amounts of time to complete their work or others would have to complete it for them, which translates into an actual loss of net output per unit of cost.

Furthermore, the performance of these programmers had no significant correlation with years of programming experience or scores on standard programming aptitude tests. This indicates that general programming skill dominates training and on-the-job experience, which later studies confirmed [12, 18]. In sum, the most important ingredient of a successful project is to have talented people work on it [1, 19, 20]. Brooks, for example, said that good design practices can be taught; however, great designs come from great designers [21] who produce structures that are faster, smaller, simpler, cleaner, and produced with less effort [22]. Larman supports this view when he said [23]: "More important than following an official process or method is that a developer acquire skill in how to create a good design, and that organizations foster this kind of skill development. This comes from mastering a set of principles and heuristics related to identifying and abstracting suitable objects and to assigning responsibilities to them." Unfortunately, McConnell believes that 95 percent of software engineers lack fundamental design knowledge, enabling them to produce good designs [9]. I personally believe this is a good approximation of the truth, and even extends to the other aspects of the software development process — requirements definition, coding, and testing. One cause of this situation is that most practitioners do not maintain their technical skills and knowledge. According to Humphrey [3], only 19 percent regularly read technical journals and only 8 percent attend professional conferences.

The characteristics that one should expect from superior software engineers are shown in Table 3.1 [2, 3]. To put the importance of these characteristics in perspective, consider that the typical software engineer needs one to two years to become comfortable with a methodology [20].

TABLE 3.1   Characteristics of Superior Software Engineers

Committed	Driven
Communicative	Flexible
Competent	Honest
Confident	Industrious
Creative	Intelligent
Dedicated	Knowledgeable
Disciplined	Motivated

This implies that if an organization uses average talent, it cannot evolve at the rate of technological change. Thus, to keep abreast of technology, an organization must hire people who have superior comprehension capabilities [24], which allows them to use newly developed technologies.

3.1 Practices for Staffing an Organization

Few organizations know how to effectively hire talented people. This section identifies a small number of key practices that help identify these people.

Practice 3.1. Define minimal standards of knowledge for software personnel. Human performance of software personnel depends on a broad base of relevant knowledge [7, 19]. Therefore, an organization should define minimal levels of knowledge that enable people to effectively and efficiently perform a variety of tasks. Brooks says, for example, that programming knowledge, domain knowledge, and comprehension strategies are essential to understand software [25]. I generally agree with this assessment and believe that people should have a breadth of knowledge in the following topics, which provides a foundation for intuitive judgement, permitting people to grasp new issues and concepts much quicker than those who do not have this knowledge [3].

Computer science knowledge. People should have a basic understanding of algorithms, data structures, programming languages, and computer architecture. In addition, people should have used a variety of programming languages and systems and become proficient in at least one higher-level language. Furthermore, people should have deep knowledge of at least two of the following areas: algorithms, data structures, computer networks, database systems, human–computer communication, operating systems, and programming languages. Currently, the primary function of colleges and universities is to teach students this material. Unfortunately, only about 15 percent of the educational institutions in America are accredited by the Computer Science Accreditation Board, which indicates that an educational institution does a good job of teaching this material, and few outside America are accredited by it [26].

Software engineering knowledge. People should have practical knowledge about how to develop quality software and manage the risks of developing it. This practical knowledge should include an understanding of software process models and the software life cycle. People should know how to write good requirements, design suitable software systems, and produce reliable implementations. Most of this knowledge is learned on the job, if learned at all. However, recently, a few institutions have started to offer degrees specializing in software engineering.

Domain knowledge. To develop quality software for an application domain requires that people working in that domain have a good understanding of it. It is impractical for this kind of knowledge to be taught at an educational institution, so it is generally learned on the job. Hence, work assignments should be designed, in part, to enhance this learning [27]. In addition, an organization should provide other mechanisms for capturing this knowledge and transferring it to others.

Note that these requirements differ substantially from what most organizations define in a job description. For example, most organizations emphasize specific skills, such as knowledge of a specific database system or programming language. Unfortunately, requiring this kind of specific knowledge without requiring an understanding of the more general knowledge will lead to a workforce that has difficulty perceiving the real problems facing an organization or creating innovative solutions for them. Instead, an organization should stress hiring people with fundamentals that enable them to learn specific tools quickly [28].

Furthermore, an organization should quantify people's knowledge using the following seven stages of expertise [29]:

1. Innocent: an individual is unaware of the subject.
2. Aware: an individual has read an article about the subject.
3. Apprentice: an individual has attended a seminar on the subject or read a book about it.
4. Practitioner: an individual is ready to use knowledge of the subject.
5. Journeyman: an individual who uses subject knowledge naturally and automatically.

6. Master: an individual who has internalized subject knowledge and knows when to break the rules.
7. Expert: an individual who writes articles or books and gives lectures on the subject.

Practice 3.2. Use a defined process to evaluate a candidate's knowledge. This will reduce turnover and minimize overhead costs [30]. The formal process should include the following sequence of activities.

Step 1. Interview each candidate. When interviewing a candidate, have every person who might work with the candidate evaluate him [2, 27, 28], possibly as a group to increase efficiency and effectiveness [31], and inform every person who will interview a candidate the reason for hiring another person [28].

During each interview, attempt to identify the problem-solving skills of the candidate by asking situational questions [31] and analyzing the candidate's behavior. A good way to do this is to ask the candidate how he would go about solving a simple problem [28]. In addition, such a problem will help the interviewer evaluate the candidate's knowledge. A problem that I like to pose is one where I ask the candidate to develop an online phone book. I define a few brief requirements that do not uniquely define the product. Then I evaluate the decisions that the candidate makes to develop a product that satisfies my ambiguously stated needs. Throughout this process, the candidate will either verbalize his assumptions or ask me direct questions. When direct questions are asked, I answer them. When assumptions are identified, I sometimes contradict them to see how the candidate proceeds. In sum, there is no single correct answer to this open-ended problem, but it provides a great way to evaluate what the candidate knows about computer science and software engineering, as well as evaluating his decision processes.

You should also ask several more questions during the interview process [28, 31, 32]. To better understand the general work habits of a candidate, consider asking the following questions:

■ How many assignments do you like to work on at one time?
■ When you have lots of assignments to complete and only a very limited time to do them, what do you do?
■ Do you prefer work that is highly structured, somewhat structured, or unstructured?
■ Do you prefer working alone, with small groups, or in large groups?

- What's most important to you when you work with people?
- How do you work best with people?
- When working on a project, what do you do to make it a success?
- Have you encountered someone in the past who you thought was inefficient or ineffective? If yes, what did you do about the situation?
- How do you deal with problem employees?

To better understand the goals, beliefs, and values of the candidate, consider asking the following questions:

- What are your goals? And, how do you plan to achieve them?
- What matters most to you in your work? What part of it do you find most satisfying? What activities do you least like to perform?
- What most discourages you or frustrates you on your job? How do you handle this frustration?
- What skills, knowledge, and abilities do you need to develop or improve?
- Do you prefer to follow a defined process? If so, name one that you like, or provide an example of how you like to perform work.

To better understand how the candidate views himself and assesses the work he does, consider asking the following questions:

- What are your strongest skills and how were they developed?
- Of all the projects you have worked on, which one do you take the greatest pride in? Why? Similarly, which one do you take the least pride in? Why?
- What have been the most difficult problems that you encountered on a job? What did you do about them?
- What is the biggest mistake you made on a job? What did you learn from it?

To better understand how the candidate will satisfy the current needs of the organization, consider asking the following questions:

- Who determines the work you do? What role do you play in the process?
- What books or articles have you recently read? Summarize one of those articles or books.
- How have you managed or dealt with change in your organization?
- What is your experience with *a specific technology*? How did you learn how to use *that specific technology*? How does *that*

specific technology work? How does *that specific technology* compare to *another one?*
- What qualifies you for this job?
- What is most satisfying to you about this position? Why? What is least satisfying to you about this position? Why?

Following are additional questions to learn more about the candidate's ability to perform a specific job function. If you want to know more about the candidate's ability to design, implement, test, and document software, ask the following questions:
- How do you design software? What design techniques do you now use, and why? What difficulties have you encountered designing software in the past? What have you learned from these experiences?
- How do you decide what to test in a project? How do you test software? How do you track the tests that succeed and fail?
- How do you know when you have detected a defect? How do you report problems?
- How do you determine what to document? How do you document those things you have chosen to document?

If you want to know more about the candidate's ability to manage people and projects, ask the following questions:
- Have you managed a project before? How are you managing your current project?
- What is similar about this project to ones you have managed in the past? What is dissimilar about this project from those you have previously managed?
- How do you recognize when a project is going well? When a project is going well, what do you do? How do you determine when a project is not going well? When things are not going well, what do you do?
- How do you make sure that you and your people achieve the objectives for which you are responsible?
- How do you make sure you and those who report to you do quality work?
- How do you ensure that you and those who report to you satisfy deadlines?
- How do you manage difficult people?
- How do you manage relationships with those superior, at the same level, and inferior to yourself?
- How do you provide feedback to your employees?
- How do you evaluate their performance?

Step 2. Examine a portfolio of work provided by a candidate [2]. Determine its quality with respect to the quality that the organization desires and report on it. In addition, focus on the candidate's ability to convey information within the portfolio to the interviewer.

Step 3. Make candidates give a 30- to 60-minute presentation on a technical subject. Follow the presentation with a question-and-answer period. The goal of the presentation is to provide the candidate with a forum to demonstrate his technical knowledge, communication skills, and personality traits. That is, it is important to evaluate how a candidate responds to questions or criticisms, as well as to evaluate his or her speaking ability. Hence, consider asking yourself the following questions at the conclusion of a presentation:

- Was the candidate well organized? Did the candidate follow an outline? Or, did the candidate read the presentation from view graph slides?
- Did the candidate clearly explain ideas?
- Did the candidate use clear and correct pronunciation?
- Did the candidate maintain eye contact with the audience?
- Was the candidate enthusiastic about the material?
- How did the candidate respond to questions?

Step 4. Discuss the candidate's perseverance and motivation by talking to past mentors, superiors, and associates. However, motivation is largely affected by five characteristics under management control: skill variety, task identity, task significance, job autonomy, and job feedback [9]. In fact, about 60 percent of motivation is derived from properly matching a job with a person [9].

Step 5. Assess each candidate's fitness for the advertised position and the organization's desired cultural values. Consider asking the following questions to evaluate the candidate:

- Is the candidate passive, assertive, or aggressive? Is the candidate outgoing, warm, shy, or withdrawn?
- Did the candidate discuss problems and raise questions? Did the candidate explain things clearly?
- Does the candidate focus on opportunities and solutions? Does the candidate emphasize getting things done? Is the candidate tenacious or persevering?
- Is the candidate innovative? Does the candidate enjoy doing research or solving applied problems?

- Is the candidate driven to satisfy goals? Can the candidate see problems from a global, or broad, perspective? Does the candidate make objective decisions?
- Does the candidate possess specific job knowledge? Can the candidate use that knowledge to solve problems? Does the candidate think logically and systematically and perform work in a logical and systematic matter? Can the candidate focus on detailed issues?
- Did the candidate demonstrate or provide evidence of reliability, responsibility, and initiative?
- How good a fit is this person to the job opening?
- Did the candidate say or do anything that would make the interviewer reluctant to hire that candidate?
- Why is the candidate a good person to hire?

Practice 3.3. Hire summer interns and contractors on a short-term basis. This gives the organization the opportunity to judge an individual's performance before hiring him. If the performance satisfies organizational needs, then consider making the temporary worker a permanent employee. In sum, no combination of interviews, tests, and resume evaluations works as well as including the person in the organization on a trial basis.

Practice 3.4. Hire personnel who have actually delivered software systems. Shipping software is difficult because it requires a combination of skills and experience that are difficult for a person to otherwise attain. Both technical and political skills are involved in delivering a software system, and delivering small software systems is very different from delivering large ones. If the team does not have people — particularly senior leaders — who have shipped a variety of software in at least half of the key positions (e.g., development manager, test manager, program manager, and product manager), it is likely to have a very difficult time delivering a new one.

Problem 3.5. Define graduated career opportunities to support growth in workforce competencies. Graduated career opportunities identify a hierarchy of positions with associated responsibilities that require increasing levels of capability in one or more workforce competencies [27]. The purposes of a graduated career hierarchy are to:

- Motivate individuals to develop the competencies required to satisfy the organization's needs.
- Reward individuals for growth in workforce competencies.
- Enable individuals to assume positions of greater responsibility or influence.
- Ensure that careers are aligned with business strategy and direction.

An example of a graduated career hierarchy is shown in Figure 3.1. It is expected that an individual will hold each title for four to six years and will fulfill the responsibilities associated with the job title. In addition, it is expected that minimum educational and certification requirements (i.e., entry criteria) are associated with each job title. For example, one

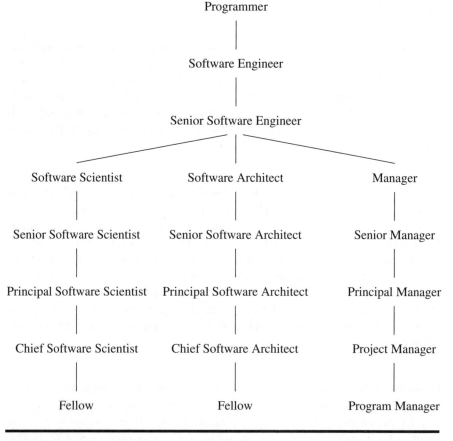

FIGURE 3.1   Recommended career hierarchy.

would expect that a Bachelor's degree in computer science or software engineering is required to enter the workforce. Similarly, one would expect that a Master's degree is required of a manager, software architect, or software scientist. For a higher-level scientist, a Ph.D. should be required. For the other two paths, senior-level people should have two Master's degrees — one emphasizing technology and the other a business function. In sum, developing thorough job descriptions is the first step of a good recruitment program [31]. The following information should be associated with each job title:

- The rationale for the position, relationship with work performed by others, and expected organizational impact
- The required education, experience (type and amount), knowledge, skills, and process abilities
- Expected past performance and accomplishments
- A task statement that identifies what and how significant duties and responsibilities are performed when work is done effectively and efficiently

Practice 3.6. Define an orientation program for new personnel. Once a person is hired, an organization should plan to integrate the new employee into the workforce through an orientation program. An orientation program should establish a comprehensive understanding of the organization, its operations, and its people so that the new employee is able to understand the relevance of his work within the context of the organization and develop effective interpersonal relationships. An orientation program should be aided by a variety of an organization's representatives over a period of one year. Key milestones of an orientation program follow.

1. First day:
   - Meet with the supervisor.
   - Attend a welcoming presentation given by the head of the organization, followed by a question-and-answer session.
   - Attend an orientation seminar that describes the business, its mission and goals, and its relevance to other entities, given by key division and department managers.
   - Read the workbook for new employees.
   - Tour the facility.
   - Meet with co-workers.

2. Remainder of first week:
    - Attend a one-on-one meeting with the supervisor. Topics to discuss at this meeting include:
        - The role of the group or project and the relationships with other groups and projects
        - Job responsibilities and performance expectations
        - Schedules, hours, time records, vacations, and absences
        - Work activities, policies, procedures, practices, and forms
    - Participate in one-on-one meetings with co-workers to learn what each person does and how they will work together.
    - Learn how to do the job and why it is done that way.
    - Negotiate a workplan with the supervisor and describe what the new employee should and should not do.
3. Remainder of first month:
    - Attend an employee benefit seminar that describes company policies, operational procedures, and various workplace issues, such as employee relations and conflict resolution.
4. Second through fifth months:
    - Meet with your assigned mentor on a periodic and "as-needed" basis. The mentor should show the new employee how to get things done, provide information, give advice, and help the new employee assimilate into the organization.
    - Attend biweekly progress reviews with supervisor. On a bimonthly basis, discuss progress with supervisor.
    - Attend monthly seminars on quality, productivity, and technology.
5. Sixth month:
    - Participate in performance review with supervisor.

3.2 Practices for Developing Individual Skills

Developing skills in personnel is important because technology changes rapidly and personnel must change with it to do their job efficiently and effectively. As Weinberg said [15], "When learning is finished, you're finished." In addition, skill development fosters loyalty and lowers turnover, which accounts for 20 percent of labor costs in most organizations [2].

Practice 3.7. Specify the number of days each year that people are expected to further develop their skills. The most common target is ten days each year, although as few as five and as many as fifteen days are almost as common. Because some people avoid training and others seek training they do not need, an organization must clearly define a role-based skills development program, as well as when and how personnel will further develop their skills.

Practice 3.8. Provide recent hires with on-the-job training. This training should discuss the institutional software engineering policies, practices, and procedures. Currently, most computer science departments of colleges and universities have weak curricula in practical software engineering. One researcher has indicated that the number of these institutions exceeds 85 percent [33], which is consistent with the comments of Practice 3.1. Because the education provided by these institutions of higher learning does not necessarily equip their graduates to develop quality software, graduates generally require significant on-the-job training. This training generally requires people to participate in courses on software review and inspection techniques, software configuration management, software metrics and measurement, complexity analysis and reduction, graphical user interface design, reusable software design, software sizing, planning, estimation, quality control, and risk analysis.

Practice 3.9. Train developers in the application domain. The most efficient way to do this is to develop a training curriculum that analyzes the application domains in which the developers work. Once they take such a training curriculum, the developers will better understand the concepts of these application domains, which will enable them to create better software [7, 34].

Practice 3.10. Relate skill development activities to the needs of individuals and projects. An organization should identify the training needs of each individual of its workforce to satisfy both current project and future technology needs [35]. The most sophisticated process involves assessing gaps in skills and identifying the development activities needed to close these gaps. Generally, a needs analysis should be done annually and become part of the overall training plan activity for the following year.

3.3 Practices for Rewarding Performance

Few people will stay with an organization for a long period unless they are fairly compensated for their services. This section identifies practices meant to reward people for doing quality work.

Practice 3.11. Reward outstanding accomplishments. An organization should reward people based solely on real employee contributions. If rewards are based on other factors, such as politics, lowered employee morale will result. Consequently, an organization should develop guidelines for recognizing and rewarding outstanding performance based on real contributions and communicate these guidelines to the workforce [27].

In addition, organizational power to reward and recognize people must be given to the specialist and scientist branches of the job classification hierarchy. This is to prevent people who are required to sign-off on work products from being threatened by managers who can leverage their control of the reward system. Thus, until senior specialists and scientists of each branch control the reward system for other members of their disciplines, an organization should expect either an inequitable reward system — one that caters to the personal whims of managers — or poor-quality software. Further, specialists and scientists are better able to reward other specialists and scientists because they better understand what they value, which is almost completely opposite that of managers.

Practice 3.12. Define individual performance goals and objectives with each employee. This helps to establish commitment by the employee to achieve these goals and objectives. In addition, the employee and manager should define measures for determining how well an employee has fulfilled each goal and objective.

3.4 Practices for Providing a Suitable Workplace

Environmental factors that influence personnel productivity and longevity include their office space, the people they work with, and the challenge provided by work assignments.

Practice 3.13. Provide small meeting rooms that can hold ten people. These rooms support important group activities, such as design and code inspections. One meeting room is generally sufficient to support a staff of about 30 people.

Practice 3.14. Provide private, noise-free office space for software professionals. IBM conducted cognitive studies on the impact of the office environment before building the IBM Santa Teresa Research Laboratory. A key goal of this new office space was to provide personal work areas that permitted intense concentration, screened distractions, and discouraged interruptions. IBM determined that this goal was best satisfied by the provision of private, enclosed, ten foot by ten foot offices [36]. When developing this laboratory, IBM sought the aid of software engineers to help define the requirements of the office space and make decisions affecting their work environments, which is a recommended practice of the People Capability Maturity Model® (Carnegie Mellon University, Pittsburgh, Pennsylvania) [27]. Several years after the development of the laboratory, it was shown that there is a strong correlation between spacious, quiet offices and productive people [27, 37]. For example, people working in quiet workspaces are one third more likely to produce *defect-free* work [2].

Practice 3.15. Control problem employees. Failure to deal with rogue employees has been a well-understood mistake for a long time [38]. At best, failure to deal with problem employees undermines the morale and motivation of a team. At worst, it increases turnover among the good developers and damages product quality and productivity. Thus, an organization should actively identify problem employees and deal with them appropriately. Following are a few common characteristics of problem employees:

■ They cover up their ignorance rather than trying to learn from others. As a result, they actively resist having others review their work.
■ They are territorial. They will claim that only they can do their assigned work, yet are too busy to do it. They will exclusively check out files from version control systems for long periods even though it prevents others from doing their work.
■ They complain about decisions that have been made and insist on revisiting them, usually in an attempt to convince others that their ideas were the right ones and should have been pursued.

Practice 3.16. Remove poor performers. Poor performers, as mentioned earlier, often are so unproductive that they actually represent a net loss. Even worse, the best performers of an information technology firm often quit because of their frustration with having to work with the less-talented individuals. The result of this situation is that the mediocre people of an organization tend to remain with it and its overall capability declines. Consequently, removing poor performers is often more valuable than adding good ones [39]. In fact, the best professional firms plan on removing the least talented among their workforces — sometimes as much as 10 percent each year. The consequence of these policies is that the caliber of the organization's employees gradually improves over time.

Practice 3.17. Challenge personnel. Because quality personnel like being challenged, an organization should occasionally assign them tasks requiring them to research an issue or perform some detailed analyses. When assigning tasks, it is best to assign several small challenges instead of one big one because the person performing several small steps in an incremental manner receives periodic reinforcement that encourages him to achieve more. Contrarily, the lack of challenge causes highly motivated people to become frustrated or, worse, bored. This dissatisfaction eventually will encourage talented individuals to find jobs elsewhere [30].

Practice 3.18. Motivate employees. Numerous studies have found that motivation has a larger impact on productivity and quality than any other factor [1]. Considering this, an organization should establish a full-fledged motivation program of central importance on every software project. However, because motivation is difficult to quantify and measure, it is often ignored.

Practice 3.19. Foster team cohesion. People who enjoy each other usually are more productive at work because they feel greater loyalty to each other and their employer and communicate better with each other [2, 30, 40]. Consequently, an organization should promote companionship through several organized and unorganized events. For example, at one place I worked, people went to lunch together a couple of times a week and had bagels together every Wednesday where they informally discussed problems and ideas. At another place, people seldom got together for lunch. At this organization, employees paid to participate in organizational Christmas parties. I paid once and arrived 15 minutes late. The only food that remained were potato chips, which, considering the cost of participation, cost me about $2.00 each 15 years ago. I never again participated in any function of that organization.

Consider that the first organization instilled camaraderie among its employees, which fostered cooperation and understanding among them, whereas the second organization did not. Of these two organizations, which one would you prefer to work for? Of these two organizations, which one do you expect to have greater loyalty among its employees? Of these two organizations, which one do you expect is more successful?

The first one was where I preferred to work; its employees had long tenure and it was more successful.

Practice 3.20. Do not allow software engineers to work overtime beyond 40 consecutive days. After 40 consecutive days, the performance of most people degrades significantly. Hence, requiring people to work overtime does not realize positive gains over the course of a project [16]. In addition, people performing the same work for extended periods tend to think in a constrained manner that causes them to see fewer options and alternatives [3], possibly resulting in poorer-quality software systems. On the other hand, it is possible for exceptional people to work excessive hours while remaining productive. This can occur if the person can quickly assimilate information and rapidly increase his knowledge of the domain and the problem being solved.

3.5 A Procedure for Hiring and Retaining Good People

An organization should use a formal procedure for hiring, retaining, and eliminating personnel. Such a procedure involves the iterative definition of a career hierarchy, the hiring of personnel, the establishment of a personal development plan for each individual, and periodic evaluation of the individual capabilities of an organization's staff. This procedure is briefly shown in Figure 3.2 and described in more detail below.

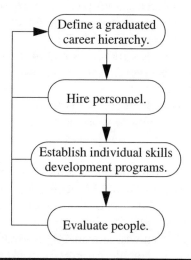

FIGURE 3.2   The personnel management procedure.

Step 1. Define a graduated career hierarchy. For each job title of the graduated career hierarchy, do the following:

- Associate minimal objective standards of computer science, software engineering, and domain knowledge with each job title. Quantify the knowledge in terms of the seven stages of expertise.
- Specify the detailed knowledge that is expected at each stage of expertise.
- Develop a checklist of questions that tests the various facets of this knowledge, as well as the answers to them.

Step 2. Hire personnel. For each candidate, do the following:

- Interview the candidate using the checklist developed in Step 1. The interview procedure should be held in a private room free of distractions [32] and last about one hour.
- Evaluate a portfolio of work provided by the candidate. Evaluation should be compared against the defined quality standards of the organization. If a portfolio of work is not available or the portfolio is seriously deficient when compared to the organization's defined quality standards, then the candidate should not be further considered for employment.
- Evaluate a presentation given by the candidate. This is primarily a subjective evaluation of the candidate's presentation skills and social interactions with others. If the evaluation is negative, then the candidate should not be given further consideration.
- Discuss the candidate with past mentors, supervisors, and associates. If these discussions are generally favorable, then the candidate is acceptable for hiring.
- Rank all acceptable candidates and hire the best one. However, when using this criteria, one might want to consider hiring the first acceptable candidate.

An alternative to this procedure is to hire a temporary employee and evaluate his quality of work and social interactions after three to six months.

Step 3. Establish a skills development program for newly employed people. This program should be developed to enhance the knowledge and skills that an employee needs to get to the next level in the career hierarchy identified in Table 3.1. It should indicate three advancement alternatives: advanced, normal, and minimal. Not making minimal acceptable progress toward the next level in the career hierarchy provides management with a simple way of identifying candidates for termination of employment.

Step 4. Evaluate people. Evaluate people using the criteria defined for the appropriate level of a job title. Such evaluation should be on an annual basis [32]. After an evaluation and under normal economic conditions, the following actions should be taken:

■ Outstanding performance should be significantly rewarded. For example, an organization should consider giving such individuals a raise double that given to a person whose performance is acceptable.

■ Acceptable performance should merit a cost of living increase plus one percent.

■ Unacceptable performance should merit a cost of living increase minus one percent.

■ Terminate personnel who do not satisfy the criteria to move to the next higher level after six years. This may sound harsh, and under the operating conditions of most organizations today, it is. However, if an organization specifies objective advancement criteria and communicates it to its staff, then the only reason for terminating people is that they do not have either the ability or desire to graduate to the next level. However, stagnation may be acceptable once a person becomes a senior scientist, senior architect, or senior manager.

3.6 Summary

This chapter has shown that people are the most significant factor in creating quality software. Unfortunately, industry would prefer to believe that all software engineers are interchangeable resources or components of a larger organizational architecture — each no different from the other. Dijkstra, for example, said [41]: "Industry suffers from the managerial dogma that for the sake of stability and continuity, the company should be independent of the competence of individual employees." Consequently, this belief has led to the overwhelming emphasis by organizations on the creation of software development processes, which have a lower return on investment than a defined process to hire, nurture, and retain the best people.

In view of this observation, this chapter has identified several practices and defined procedures for hiring, nurturing, and retaining talented people. These defined procedures advocate hiring knowledgeable employees and retaining them by providing a conducive work environment and a reward system based on objective criteria. This guidance, if followed, will result in a greater return on investment than anything else that an organization could possibly do. This guidance is contrary to the promotional practices followed by most organizations, which are based on personal associations, class status, and tenure. In conclusion, talented people are the primary element of a program to produce cost-effective, high-quality software.

References

1. Boehm, B.W., *Software Engineering Economics*, Prentice Hall, 1981.
2. DeMarco, T. and Lister, T., *Peopleware: Productive Projects and Teams*, Dorset House, 1987.
3. Humphrey, W.S., *Managing Technical People: Innovation, Teamwork, and the Software Process*, Addison-Wesley, 1997.
4. Paulk, M.C. et al., *The Capability Maturity Model: Guidelines for Improving the Software Process*, Addison-Wesley, 1994.
5. Weigers, K.E., *Creating a Software Engineering Culture*, Dorset House, 1996.
6. Curtis, B., Substantiating Programmer Variability, *Proc. of the IEEE*, 69, 846, 1981.
7. Curtis, B. et al., Software Psychology: The Need for an Interdisciplinary Program, *Proc. of the IEEE*, 74, 1092, 1986.
8. DeMarco, T. and Lister, T., Programmer Performance and the Effects of the Workplace, in *Proc. of the Int. Conf. on Software Engineering*, 1985, 268.
9. McConnell, S., *Rapid Development: Taming Wild Software Schedules*, Microsoft Press, 1996.
10. Mills, H., *Software Productivity*, Brown, 1983.
11. Sackman, H., Erikson, W.J., and Grant, E.E., Exploratory Experimental Studies Comparing Online and Offline Programming Performance, *Commun. of the ACM*, 11, 3, 1968.
12. Valett, J.D. and McGarry, F.E., A Summary of Software Measurement Experiences in the Software Engineering Laboratory, *J. of Systems and Software*, 9, 137, 1989.
13. Putnam, L.H. and Myers, W., *Measures for Excellence: Reliable Software on Time, within Budget*, Yourdon Press, 1992.
14. Sackman, H., *Man-Computer Problem-Solving: Experimental Evaluation of Time-Sharing and Batch Processing*, Auerbach, 1970.
15. Weinberg, G.M., *Understanding the Professional Programmer*, Dorset House, 1988.
16. Weinberg, G.M., *Quality Software Management: Systems Thinking*, Dorset House, 1992.
17. Gibbs, W.W., Software's Chronic Crisis, *Scientific American*, September 1994, 86.
18. Sheppard, S.B. et al., Modern Coding Practices and Programmer Performance, *IEEE Computer*, 12(12), 41, 1979.
19. Curtis, B., Krasner, H., and Iscoe, N., A Field Study of the Software Design Process for Large Systems, *Commun. of the ACM*, 31, 1268, 1988.

20. Yourdon, E., *The Decline and Fall of the American Programmer*, Yourdon Press/Prentice Hall, 1993.
21. Brooks, F.P., Jr., *The Mythical Man-Month: Essays on Software Engineering Anniversary Edition*, Addison-Wesley, 1995.
22. Brooks, F.P., Jr., No Silver Bullet: Essence and Accidents of Software Engineering, *IEEE Computer*, 20(4), 10, 1987.
23. Larman, C., *Applying UML and Patterns: An Introduction to Object-Oriented Analysis and Design*, Prentice Hall, 1998.
24. Bisant, D.B. and Groninger, L., Cognitive Processes in Software Fault Detection: A Review and Synthesis, *Int. J. of Human–Computer Interaction*, 5, 189, 1993.
25. Brooks, R., Towards a Theory of the Comprehension of Computer Programs, *Int. J. of Man–Machine Studies*, 18, 543, 1983.
26. Computer Science Accreditation Board, Computer Science Programs Accredited by the Computer Science Accreditation Commission of the Computing Sciences Accreditation Board, http://csab.org/~csab/acr-sch.html.
27. Curtis, B., Hefley, W.E., and Miller, S.A., People Capability Maturity Model, Version 2.0, Software Engineering Institute, Carnegie Mellon University, Technical Report CMU/SEI-2001-MM-01, 2001.
28. Rothman, J., *Hiring the Best Knowledge Workers, Techies, and Nerds: The Secrets and Science of Hiring Technical People*, Dorset House, 2004.
29. Page-Jones, M., The Seven Stages of Expertise in Software Engineering, *American Programmer*, July–August 1990.
30. Herman, R.E., *Keeping Good People: Strategies for Solving the Dilemma of the Decade*, Oakhill Press, 1997.
31. Levesque, J.D., *Complete Manual for Recruiting, Hiring, and Retaining Quality Employees*, Prentice Hall, 1996.
32. Mercer, M.W., *Hire the Best ... and Avoid the Rest*, AMACOM, 1993.
33. Jones, C., *Assessment and Control of Software Risks*, Prentice Hall, 1994.
34. Weigers, K.E., *Software Requirements*, Microsoft Press, 2003.
35. Mead, N., Tobin, L., and Couturiaux, S., Best Training Practices within the Software Engineering Industry, Software Engineering Institute, Carnegie Mellon University, Technical Report CMU/SEI-96-TR-034, 1996.
36. McCue, G.M., IBM's Santa Teresa Laboratory — Architectural Design for Program Development, *IBM Systems Journal*, 17, 4, 1978.
37. Wasserman, A.I., The Future of Programming, *Commun. of the ACM*, 25, 196, 1982.
38. Weinberg, G.M., *The Psychology of Computer Programming*, Van Nostrand-Reinhold, 1971.
39. Schulmeyer, G.G., *Zero Defect Software*, McGraw-Hill, 1990.
40. Gabriel, R.P., *Patterns of Software: Tales from the Software Community*, Oxford University Press, 1996.
41. Dijkstra, E.W., Computing Science: Achievements and Challenges, *ACM SIGAPP Applied Computing Review*, 7(2), 2, 1999.

Chapter 4

Project Management

Chapter 1 indicated that project mismanagement is a leading cause of software project failure. To reduce such failures, this chapter identifies several key practices for planning and managing projects and identifies a procedure for planning them.

Most projects significantly exceed their budgets and delivery dates, and many are cancelled before their completion [1]. A significant cause of these problems is poor project management. Bad project managers rarely match people with their work assignments, provide meaningful goals or necessary guidance, challenge their subordinates, or interact like collaborators or as equals [2]. In addition to mismanaging people, bad managers often do a poor job of planning, monitoring, and managing projects. This chapter addresses these issues by identifying several basic practices and a procedure for planning and managing projects that will help managers become more effective.

4.1 Practices for Planning a Project

This section discusses those practices that benefit the planning of a project.

Practice 4.1. Conduct feasibility studies. A substantial number of software development efforts are cancelled after years of development. I personally was involved in one project that was cancelled after spending more than $200 million dollars over four years. Capers Jones reports that the average cancelled project in the United States is about a year behind schedule and has spent twice its planned budget before being cancelled [3]. Hence, organizations should conduct a feasibility study to determine whether a project should be cancelled or continued early in the software development life cycle. The feasibility of a project should be based on both technical and nontechnical issues.

During the feasibility study, the project team should:

- Gain commitment from key decision makers and executive sponsors.
- Produce a vision statement for the project.
- Establish a business case for the product to be developed.
- Estimate project cost and schedule.
- Identify significant risks and how to mitigate those risks.
- Develop a detailed user interface prototype.
- Document key system needs.
- Generate a detailed software development plan.

To assess system feasibility, the following questions should be asked:

1. Is the system really needed?
2. What are the consequences if it is not developed?
3. How will the system help to achieve business objectives?
4. What critical processes will the system support?
5. How will the system affect other systems already installed or being developed?
6. What are the technology limitations that the development effort may face?
7. Can a useful system be built given the allocated budget?

Generally, it should take 10 to 20 percent of the total development schedule to study the feasibility of a project. Analyzing the feasibility of a project yields three benefits. First, cancelling doomed projects early saves a significant amount of money. Second, feasibility studies lead to more accurate funding requests [4]. Third, forcing the completion of 10 to 20 percent of a project before requesting additional funding focuses the effort on the critical upstream activities of a project, which significantly contributes to its success or failure. In sum, if a project is required to complete the most important upstream activities before proceeding with the downstream ones, overall project risk can be substantially reduced.

Practice 4.2. Develop a project schedule following a defined procedure. Following are the key activities that must be performed to produce a project schedule:

■ Produce a detailed program work breakdown structure that identifies clear, measurable objectives and responsibilities for each defined task.

■ Define entry and exit criteria for all tasks.

■ Analyze the dependencies and critical paths among tasks. This is important because the maximum number of personnel who can work on a task depends on the number of independent subtasks [5].

■ Assign people to perform each task. Assigning a task to someone who is to be hired or to be later determined indicates that a schedule is fictitious. In addition, hold the assigned person accountable for the completion of the task.

■ Include risk mitigation activities for each task of a project. Associate contingency factors with each risk.

■ Create concrete, specific, and measurable milestones [5]. One milestone should be the creation of the system architecture as part of the first incremental release to minimize the risk of architecture rework. Other milestones should include deliveries that package meaningful units of functionality and size for release to test groups and other evaluators (e.g., end users).

■ Create reasonably detailed schedules. If the schedule is in increments longer than a week (five workdays) per person, the schedule is not detailed enough. Letting people work without a schedule checkpoint occurring on a weekly basis implies that tasks can slip by more than a week without the project manager knowing it. However, no more than five levels of tasking should be defined. In addition, when creating a schedule, do not lose sight of its purpose — to facilitate product completion and delivery.

■ Develop schedules based on input from the people who will actually do the work. This helps create realistic schedules with reasonable milestones. If the schedule came from anywhere other than the people who will actually do the work, it most likely will be an inaccurate estimate.

■ Attempt to smooth the rate of change of the cost and utilized personnel when creating a schedule, while satisfying imposed milestone dates and other constraints.

Practice 4.3. Perform a risk assessment of a project following a defined procedure. Risk usually arises from deficiencies in schedule, cost, functionality, performance, reliability, and quality. Typical risks include:

■ Loss of data or loss of data integrity

■ Loss of access to network services, other computing devices, or products

- Unavailability of key staff and documentation
- Failure of partner or service providers that support, develop, or maintain software or equipment
- Loss of documents or software

Consequently, an assessment should analyze each of these types of risks and prioritize them based on the potential harm they might cause a project. Such an analysis should attempt to identify high-risk objectives and events that could increase or introduce risk. Each risk can be assessed in terms of the associated threat and vulnerability.

Each medium-impact and high-impact risk should be described by the likelihood of occurrence, its potential impact, potential mitigation strategies, and key action triggers or metrics that initiate mitigation. An assessment should also identify contingencies for each risk, as well as the impact and feasibility of each contingency. All risks to be mitigated should be summarized and reported, and an agreement should be reached on the planned mitigation activities.

Risk identification should be accomplished in facilitated meetings attended by project personnel most familiar with the area for which risks are being identified. A person familiar with problems from similar projects should participate in these meetings when possible. Risk identification should be updated at least monthly. Risk mitigation activities should be included in a project's schedule. All identified risks should be analyzed and prioritized by impact and likelihood of occurrence.

Typical actions to mitigate key risks include the following:

- Identify, negotiate, and track dependencies between organizations. Identify and negotiate each dependency, resolve need dates and delivery formats, and all parties should document and approve agreements. When groups cannot resolve an issue, there should be a documented process for resolving it.
- Manage the reuse of software. Analyze the full life-cycle costs, including maintenance, warranty, and licensing costs. Establish quantified selection criteria and acceptability thresholds for reusable artifacts and base all decisions on architectural and design definitions. Finally, revise reuse decisions as program conditions change.
- Ensure data and database interoperability. Define standards for database implementation and for the data elements that are included in databases. One standard should reduce unnecessary data redundancy as much as feasible. Another should require that data items be updated only once, and the changes should propagate

automatically. Finally, reexamine interoperability decisions as factors change.

Practice 4.4. Estimate the effort and cost of a software project following a defined procedure. The estimate of the effort and cost of a software project should follow from the estimates of the size of its artifacts. Personnel should derive these estimates based on experience with similar projects, when possible. They should provide breakdowns of monthly, quarterly, and yearly costs for the development effort. Personnel should use productivity data, when available, to estimate cost and document data sources and the rationales for using them. Cost estimates must include direct labor expenses, overhead expenses, travel expenses, and computer costs. Cost data should account for variables that can affect cost estimates, such as the geographic location of the workers, the stability of requirements, and the host environment. Developers should estimate these costs because estimates prepared by the people who do the work are more accurate than managers [6], although developers tend to be about 25 percent overly optimistic [7, 8]. Some heuristics to use to estimate the effort and cost of a project include:

- Estimate the size of critical or major work products and activities based on the size and complexity of the goals, objectives, defined work products, and problem constraints. To perform a reliable estimation, decompose a system to a sufficient level of granularity (see Practice 7.1) and then use historical data to estimate the size of the lower-level decompositions.
- The minimum estimated development time should use a maximum personnel growth rate of 30 percent per year because an organization cannot maintain effectiveness beyond this rate [9, 10]. Growing faster than this rate results in ineffective communication among personnel, resulting in lowered productivity. Similarly, the maximum estimated development time should not exceed 30 percent of the minimum development time because the cost and defect benefits are negligible beyond this point; the optimal point seems to be about 15 to 20 percent of the minimum [10].
- Base cost estimates on the Raleigh curve. Software development projects are composed of overlapping phases having a well-defined pattern of manpower versus time [11–13]. This pattern corresponds to a Raleigh curve [14], which has a long tail showing that 90 percent of the development effort is complete using only two thirds of the scheduled time. An explanation for this phenomenon is that a core

set of people is critical to the problem-solving process leading to a problem solution. These people structure the problem into an initial set of tasks and then assign new recruits to each task. Hence, the core group determines the pace of solving initial problems and later identified sub-problems. This determines the maximum rate at which one can add new people to projects. Thus, adding people too soon means that they will not be fully utilized, thus needlessly adding to project cost.

■ Explicitly identify all source code to be reused and estimate how much of it will be modified. This is important because software reuse is not free (see Section 10.2).

■ Do not use the number of source lines of code as a measure of size because it measures the solution and not the problem [15].

4.2 Practices for Managing a Project

This section discusses practices that help people to better manage projects. They primarily discuss how to organize a project and monitor the work being done.

Practice 4.5. Use metrics to manage a software project. Metrics information should be used as a primary input for making program decisions. Metrics should measure and track schedules, budgets, productivity, and quality. Adopted metrics should measure defect removal efficiency, percentage of development cost due to rework, defect leakage through inspections, and differences between initial estimates of software size and the actual size of delivered software.

In addition, use earned value systems to effectively control software development activities [16]. Earned value systems work by identifying a set of software development tasks, associating estimates of cost for each task, and associating an earned value with each task, which is generally equal to the estimated cost of performing the task. Then, as development proceeds, compute and review three metrics:

1. The Budgeted Cost of Work Scheduled (BCWS) to date, which equals the sum of the earned values for all tasks scheduled to be completed
2. The Budgeted Cost of Work Performed (BCWP) to date, which equals the sum of the earned values for all completed tasks
3. The Actual Cost of the Work Performed (ACWP) to date

After computing these metrics, one can evaluate them as follows:

- If the BCWP is greater than the BCWS, the development effort is ahead of schedule.
- If the BCWP is greater than the ACWP, the development effort is costing less than planned.
- If the BCWP is less than the BCWS, the development effort is either behind schedule, overrunning its budget, or both behind its schedule and overrunning its budget.

Furthermore, one can examine the trends to determine the accuracy of the proposed estimates and use that information to better plan the actual costs and effort to complete tasks. In sum, one should collect earned value on a frequent and regular basis consistent with the reporting cycle required by the work breakdown structure. For example, report the lowest-level schedules on a weekly basis, but report the highest-level schedules on a monthly basis.

Practice 4.6. Track milestones for large projects. Key milestones include the definition of requirements, design specifications, risk management and test plans, and completion of user documentation. Milestone reviews are extremely important sources of corrective action because they can limit major schedule delays by providing early warnings of impending problems. Failing to hold milestone reviews or to reset schedules following an unsuccessful milestone review indicates programmatic problems.

Practice 4.7. Establish a project office for large projects. Large projects are those whose size is expected to exceed 500,000 lines of code or involve 50 or more people. Such an office is responsible for overall schedule planning, cost estimating, and milestone tracking. Consequently, it should be equipped with planning, cost estimation, and quality estimation tools. In addition, the staff should have experience with management principles for large projects.

Practice 4.8. Use a hierarchical organizational structure for software projects. A hierarchical organizational structure is preferred to a matrix organizational structure because it tends to decrease the number of managers and the resulting communication overhead, both of which lower the productivity of people. In addition, organizations should have ten or more employees reporting to each manager because smaller spans of control decrease coordination difficulties between departments [13, 17], encourage mentoring of new team members, and ease the handling of peer reviews and formal inspections.

Practice 4.9. Collocate teams and the resources allocated to them. This is because the more distant team members are, the more difficult communication is among them [7, 17]. Similarly, the more distant the support resources, the more difficult it is to use them [18]. Electronic means of communication and collaboration can help if physical collocation is impractical, but face-to-face communication and resource usage should always be preferred. Without face-to-face communication, questions do not get asked, opportunities are lost, and development costs increase [19]. However, if one partitions a system into well-defined subsystems and has teams at different locations develop entire subsystems, the distributed development organization can be successful as long as periodic meetings are held to create a shared vision and understanding among the individual teams. Note, however, that this model of development is contrary to offshore development.

In offshore development, the software requirements and design are formulated at one location and the coding is done elsewhere. In this model, a shared vision and understanding is never created among the individual teams, which results in significant immediate and long-term costs. The immediate costs arise when the programmers have to communicate with the requirement analysts and software architects, who are in different time zones. Hence, this creates a development delay until a mutually acceptable time when both parties are awake and available to talk. Further, this form of communication is less efficient. Sometimes, both parties of a conversation must be able to draw diagrams on the same whiteboard and discuss them in real-time. Unfortunately, no technology exists today to make this happen when development occurs in geographically distributed locations. The long-term effect of such development is increased defects that result from less-effective communication, which results in increased costs, less reliable systems, and longer development or maintenance efforts. In sum, off-site development is inefficient and ineffective. Cockburn [19], for example, has stated that he has not been able to find a "methodologically successful offshore development project." However, there is no reason that entire projects cannot be moved offshore, including their management.

Practice 4.10. Assign personnel to projects who are experts in key technology areas. Each core technology should have an individual who can help others less knowledgeable of the technology. Such an individual need not be a technical lead or manager. Key technology areas include requirements engineering, architectural design, verification, and software tools and products.

Practice 4.11. Never add developers to a late project. Although one would expect that adding people to a project would increase the amount of work produced, when such additions occur near the end of a project, experience indicates that output is generally lowered [5].

Practice 4.12. Place an operational infrastructure into the work environment before the real work starts. Otherwise, everyone wastes a lot of time waiting for these critical items or converting everyone to use them. A critical part of this infrastructure is the software tools that personnel use to develop software. Hence, select and deploy an integrated tool suite to each computer that will support development activities before development actually begins. That is, the complete development environment should be available to practitioners on their first day of work.

4.3 A Procedure for Planning a Project

Following is a step-by-step description for planning a project.

> **Step 1.** Describe the purpose and scope of the project. Provide as much detail as is required to understand the nature of the project:
> - Identify the project's objectives.
> - Describe the importance of the project to the organization.
> - Describe the capabilities the project will provide to the organization.
> - Include any background information that is important to understanding the project.
>
> **Step 2.** Provide an overview of the development strategy selected for the project. Such a strategy might include prototyping the system, the use of commercial off-the-shelf software, or conversion of an existing system from one hardware and software family to another.
>
> **Step 3.** Create a series of iterations with one release per iteration. Assign a collection of needs, stories, use cases, or requirements to each iteration, as well as a start date.

Step 4. Describe the work breakdown structure required for the project. A work breakdown structure displays and defines the products to be developed or produced and relates the tasks to be accomplished to each other and to the end products. The work breakdown structure can be modified, if necessary, during the life cycle. Work elements requiring more than two weeks of calendar time should be subdivided until the largest bottom-level work element represents work that can be accomplished in an interval of at least one calendar week, but not more than two calendar weeks. This subdivision may appear arbitrary because, in some cases, the duration of a bottom-level task varies according to the number of resource units applied to it. In general, however, the bottom-level work elements should focus on tasks performed by a single individual. When that is done, the application of standard productivity rates can generally predict the expected duration of the work element and eliminate wide variation in work element duration.

A work breakdown structure dictionary provides detailed descriptions of each work breakdown structure element. Each work breakdown structure dictionary entry should contain a title that is the same as the work breakdown structure element it amplifies, a narrative describing the work represented by the element, the effort required (in person-hours), the most likely duration (in calendar days), and references to any special skills or resources required to accomplish the work. Work breakdown structure dictionary entries should be completed only for the lowest-level work breakdown structure elements.

Step 5. Identify the total amount of effort needed for each work breakdown structure element. Consider shared-resource categories, such as user representatives, suppliers, and consultants, as well as dedicated project team resources, such as programmer analysts and database analysts, when estimating. Use convenient units of measurement, such as person-hours, person-days, or person-weeks. Also estimate other types of consumable resources required for each work element, such as calendar duration, computer time, and significant supplies. Use caution when estimating human resources in person-months or person-years to specify exactly how many person-hours of direct project time one expects there to be in a person-month or person-year.

Estimating resource utilization effectively requires knowledge of the quantity of product or service to be produced or delivered in a work element, the expected productivity for each resource type to be employed, and the variances that are typical of these measures in project environments. Carefully and explicitly document assumptions made about resource availability, productivity rates, and quantities of output produced or services performed. Account for differences between the planned project environment and the project environments where the productivity rates were previously measured. A carefully maintained project history for a large number of projects is an invaluable aid in resource estimating. Industrywide productivity measures may also be helpful.

An alternative to this kind of bottom-up resource estimation process is a top-down approach. In the top-down approach, the gross estimate of product to be produced, such as function points of delivered application functionality, lines of source code, or pages of documentation, is multiplied by the aggregate expected productivity for the entire project team, giving total expected human resource requirements. Again, carefully maintained project history records and industry-wide averages can provide data useful for this computation. In addition, the total resource requirement can be subdivided into the work breakdown structure elements to provide numbers useful for checking the reasonableness of the bottom-up values.

Step 6. Develop the dependencies shared with other work elements for each work element. Record the dependencies in a precedence table and illustrate the dependencies using a network diagram. Use the work element durations from the estimates to help conduct a critical path analysis to determine the critical path schedule.

Next, factor in the expected availability of resources by resource type and adjust the critical path schedule to fit the availability of these resources. Generally, the scarcity of selected resource types will be a limiting factor on the actual scheduling of the tasks that need them and on all their dependent tasks as well. In addition, a reasonable growth and decline in the numbers of project resources by type over the life of the project is desirable, and the imposition of reasonable growth and decline rates can also limit the actual scheduling of the tasks. This process is known as resource leveling.

Factor in other project constraints as well, such as limitations on user review activities, lead times for purchasing, lead times for shipping, scheduling of approvals, and previously fixed milestone dates. It is possible that the defined set of tasks cannot be completed within the time frames specified by the fixed milestone dates and, if that happens, the planned set of tasks needs to be reviewed and pruned or the milestone dates adjusted.

If a scheduling tool is available and has optimization capabilities, use them to optimize the schedule to the optimization criteria, such as total duration or total resource utilization. Trade-offs can be discovered during iterative optimization runs. Exercise extreme caution when trading off resource utilization for duration because there are points in the trade-off curve where the benefit may not be worth the corresponding cost, and, more importantly, there may be limits beyond which the trade-offs cannot be made.

Step 7. Plan the addition of project resources and build a resource acquisition plan. Each type of resource should be considered in this resource acquisition plan. The plan should specify the source of the resources, the numbers of each, the start date for each, and the duration needed. It also should consider additional, associated resource requirements, such as office space, hardware and software, office equipment, other facilities, and tools. All acquired project resources will eventually be returned to their sources, and the details of the returns should be considered sooner, rather than later. A resource reallocation plan component of the resource acquisition plan should identify what resources will be returned and when they will be returned.

Step 8. Document the communication strategy for the project. Consider and document periodic status reports, newsletters, bulletins, problem reports, issue lists, status and review meetings, team meetings, and other forms of communication when creating the communication plan. Give careful thought to satisfying existing standards and following existing conventions. Also consider improving the communication process and ensuring that communication is simplified for all project team members and external entities.

Step 9. Identify and document standards and procedures for the project team. These standards and procedures may already be in place; if not, determine them now. These include technical standards, business-related standards, and quality assurance standards. Technical standards and procedures include naming conventions, inspection requirements, configuration management rules, security standards, documentation requirements, software tools, modeling techniques, and technical contractual obligations. Business-related standards and procedures include procedures for scope changes, requirements changes, costing, and sign-off standards. Quality assurance standards and procedures include review processes, testing procedures, and defect tracking requirements. Quality assurance standards may also address the use of metrics.

Step 10. Describe all types of project risk. Describe risks that might affect the ability to complete the project on schedule and within budget. Identify factors that contribute to these risks. Examples of such factors are the use of new computer hardware or software technology, uncertainty in the ability to define user functional requirements adequately, and a compressed development schedule. In addition, identify the approaches for mitigating the impacts of these factors.

Step 11. Describe personnel requirements and any known or proposed staffing requirements. Describe the number of people that are required, when they are required, and what their required skills are. If particular staff members have been selected or proposed for the implementation, identify them and their roles in the implementation.

Identify the training necessary to prepare staff for implementing and maintaining the system. Describe the type and amount of training required for each of the following areas, if appropriate, for the system:
- System hardware and software installation
- System support
- System maintenance and modification

Present a training curriculum listing the courses that will be provided, a course sequence, and a proposed schedule. If appropriate, identify which courses should be attended by particular types of staff by job position description. If training will be provided by one or more commercial vendors, identify them, the course names, and a brief description of the course content. If the training will be provided by internal staff, provide the course names and an outline of the content of each course. In both cases, identify the resources and support materials required by each course.

Step 12. Develop a project budget. Use standard costs and billing rates and the preliminary schedule to develop a project budget. Distribute the costs per accounting period and compare for reasonableness with the cost proposal data.

4.4 Summary

This chapter identified several key practices that project managers should follow to operate successful programs. First, project managers should identify the risk of each proposed project and determine if it is feasible. If a project is feasible, then its manager should define a project schedule, estimate the cost of the project, and, once approved, collect objective measures to manage it. Second, communication within a project should be maximized. This is achieved by locating the personnel of a project close to one another and organizing them within a hierarchical, separate management structure. Third, key technology experts should be involved in every project and all personnel should have access to an operational environment for developing software in an efficient and effective manner. Fourth, project managers should identify a vision for each project that emphasizes iterative, exploratory development. These key practices, as well as the others identified in this chapter, should be integrated into a procedure that project managers follow. One such procedure was identified in this chapter. Following it, project managers will have greater control over projects, which should lead to greater success.

References

1. McConnell, S., *Rapid Development: Taming Wild Software Schedules*, Microsoft Press, 1996.
2. Humphrey, W.S., *Managing Technical People: Innovation, Teamwork, and the Software Process*, Addison-Wesley, 1997.
3. Jones, C., *Assessment and Control of Software Risks*, Yourdon Press, 1994.
4. Boehm, B. et al., Cost Models for Future Software Life Cycle Processes: COCOMO 2.0, *Annals of Software Engineering*, Special Volume on Software Process and Product Measurement, Arthur, J.D. and Henry, S.M. (Eds.), J.C. Baltzer AG Science Publishers, 1995.
5. Brooks, F.P., Jr., *The Mythical Man-Month: Essays on Software Engineering Anniversary Edition*, Addison-Wesley, 1995.
6. Lederer, A.L. and Prasad, J., Nine Management Guidelines for Better Cost Estimating, *Commun. of the ACM*, 35:2, 51, February 1992.
7. DeMarco, T. and Lister, T., *Peopleware: Productive Projects and Teams*, Dorset House, 1987.
8. Van Genuchten, M., Why is Software Late? An Empirical Study of the Reasons for Delay in Software Development, *IEEE Trans. on Software Engineering*, 17, 582, 1991.
9. Stubberud, A.R., A Hard Look at Software, *IEEE Control Systems*, 9, February 1985.
10. Putnam, L.H. and Myers, W., *Measures for Excellence: Reliable Software on Time, within Budget*, Yourdon Press, 1992.

11. Daly, E.B., Management of Software Development, *IEEE Trans. on Software Engineering*, SE-3, 229, 1977.
12. Stephenson, W.E., An Analysis of the Resources Used in the SAFEGUARD System Software Development, *Proc. of the Int. Conf. on Software Engineering*, 312, 1976.
13. Putnam, L.H., A General Empirical Solution to the Macro Software Sizing and Estimating Problem, *IEEE Trans. on Software Engineering*, SE-4, 345, 1978.
14. Norden, P.V., Useful Tools for Project Management, in *Operations Research in Research and Development*, Dean, B.V. (Ed.), Wiley, 1963.
15. Weinberg, G.M., *Understanding the Professional Programmer*, Dorset House, 1988.
16. Boehm, B. and Huang, L.G., Value-Based Software Engineering: A Case Study, *IEEE Computer*, 36, 33, March 2003.
17. Grady, R.B. and Caswell, D.L., *Software Metrics: Establishing a Company-Wide Program*, Prentice Hall, 1987.
18. Gabriel, R.P., *Patterns of Software: Tales from the Software Community*, Oxford University Press, 1996.
19. Cockburn, A., *Agile Software Development*, Addison-Wesley, 2001.

Chapter 5

Configuration Management

Chapter 1 indicated that a common cause of software project failures is poor configuration management procedures. Thus, one cannot downplay the importance of a configuration management system because it is the foundation of a quality-oriented software engineering effort. Without a sound configuration management system, management cannot reliably plan and monitor development efforts. Likewise, without a sound configuration management system, developers cannot reliably produce software. To support both software managers and engineers, a configuration management system should capture all information relevant to a development project. This chapter identifies how to do this in a reliable manner.

A *configuration management system* establishes and maintains the integrity of software artifacts and their configurations throughout the software development life cycle [1]. The products managed by a configuration management system include the products delivered to an end user or customer and other artifacts produced or used that assist in the development of these products. A configuration management system includes the set of policies, practices, procedures, and tools that help an organization maintain its software. To support configuration management, several configuration management tools have been developed over the years (e.g.,

[2, 3]). However, no configuration management tool widely available today effectively supports all software configuration management best practices [4, 5] or adequately supports the entire software development life cycle.

The purpose of this chapter is to identify practices and procedures to successfully manage changes to software. The practices described in this chapter primarily resulted from introspection and by examining explicitly defined best practices [1, 6, 7] and implicitly defined practices arising from defined guidance [8–10]. The procedures defined within this chapter logically follow from these derived practices.

5.1 Practices for Managing Versions of Software Artifacts

This section discusses what artifacts should be placed under version management and the methods for manipulating them.

Practice 5.1. All source artifacts should be under configuration control. The benefit of placing all source artifacts under configuration control is that an organization can better control the development process, better maintain traceability between artifacts, and better perform impact analysis.

Practice 5.2. All artifacts used to produce an artifact of a delivery should be under configuration control. This typically means that libraries and other third-party products used to create the delivered artifacts of a delivery must be under configuration control. It is preferable that the build and installation process include the installation of these artifacts. Adoption of this practice improves the predictability of performing successful software builds after initial deliveries.

Practice 5.3. Work within managed, private workspaces. Each workspace should have a single purpose, such as providing a build and test area for a single developer or for a product release. People who develop artifacts within a workspace isolate their development activities from others and control the introduction of the changes of others into it. Working outside a workspace is, in effect, bypassing the configuration management system, which tends to cause many problems.

Practice 5.4. Save artifacts at the completion of intermediate steps of a larger change. Frequently saving artifacts helps to eliminate the loss of a large change if a hardware or other failure occurs. It also allows one to easily roll-back to a recent good state if one happens to have made a mistake during a change. That is, this practice ensures that software losses, if they should occur, will be small. This practice should be constrained when saving artifacts in a public workspace [5].

Practice 5.5. Regularly synchronize development with the work of others. A person's work in a team environment depends on the artifacts that others develop. Consequently, programmers should integrate the changes of others into their workspaces on a periodic basis [5]. However, a programmer should consider doing this in a new workspace instead of an existing workspace just in case defects exist in the artifacts contained in the public workspace. The benefit of this practice is that it reduces the effort required to fix incompatibilities within a public workspace during merge operations. In addition, it prevents the surprise of having unanticipated, large integration efforts from occurring immediately before a software release. That is, it permits managers to manage the development process by making several small schedule changes, if needed, instead of creating a few large, possibly unpredictable, perturbations to the schedule.

Practice 5.6. Define policies for branches, codelines, and workspaces. The type of policies that one must declare include the following:

1. Codelines:
   - Identify how many development codelines are available and name each one. Normally, there is only one development codeline; but for large systems it may be desirable to have one for each subsystem or other collection of software artifacts.
   - Identify how often development codelines must be integrated. (This is applicable only if more than one codeline is defined for a software product.)
   - Identify who can makes changes to a codeline, and under what circumstances [11].
   - Identify if parallel or non-parallel development is permitted for each codeline.
2. Branches:
   - Identify the necessary conditions for creating a branch.
   - Identify the necessary conditions for merging a branch back onto its source codeline.
   - Identify the maximum period that an artifact can undergo change without being saved within the configuration management system.

3. Workspaces:
   - Identify who can read and write artifacts of a workspace.
   - Identify who can add artifacts to a workspace or delete them from a workspace.

5.2 Practices for Controlling Changes to Software Artifacts

This section describes practices for controlling how artifacts are changed.

Practice 5.7. Document identified software defects. Documenting software defects helps to identify the quality of a product [1] and the components that are significantly flawed. An organization can categorize software defects in many ways: by type, source, severity of failure, etc. Thus, an organization should define or adopt a defect taxonomy that permits defects to be consistently and repeatably classified. Once this is done, a repository of reliable defect information will accumulate that will permit an organization to understand the nature of its defects, enabling it to improve its software development processes.

Practice 5.8. Create a defined process for requesting and approving changes. Controlling the process of requesting and approving change requests is the primary way to inject stability into software development efforts [1]. The benefits of controlling change are that an organization can ensure that it adds only necessary or beneficial features to a system. It also allows the organization to prioritize changes and schedule change in the most efficient or practical manner. Two key ideas of a formal change management process follow:

1. Use a change control board. A *change control board* controls the features that become part of a system by considering explicitly and consistently the performance, quality, schedule costs, and benefits of each proposed change [1]. Thus, a change control board reviews suggested changes, determines the ones to accept, prioritizes the accepted requests, and assigns the implementation of each one to a specific software release. To make the best decisions, the change control board should represent a cross-section of people from the client, development, and user communities. For example, project management, marketing, development, quality assurance, documentation, and user support personnel should participate on

change control boards. One person should make a final decision on each change request, under the advisement of others, which helps to avoid interproject politics. This, however, is only one scheme; there is no reason to disallow others.

2. Use change packages. A *change package* defines a unit of work, whether it is the repair of a defect, the addition of a new feature or capability to a system, or an original development activity [12]. Consequently, a change package should be traceable to a planned activity of a workplan or schedule. If it is not, the schedule is not an accurate reflection of the work a team is performing or when the team is performing it. The benefit of using change packages is that they aggregate collections of individual, yet related, changes, which helps to control the instability within a software system.

Practice 5.9. Apply defect repairs to existing releases and ongoing development efforts. Organizations often have fielded several releases of the same product that are being used by customers. These releases may be necessary to operate within several environments composed of varying operating systems, database systems, windowing systems, or other utilities. Additionally, some releases may update older releases but in the same operating environment. Regardless, each of these releases and internal development efforts may contain the same defect and the person repairing the defect should ensure that each release and internal development effort either does not have the defect or receives the repair. Alternatively, a change control board or another entity may decide which releases and internal development efforts should receive the repair. This practice simultaneously eliminates defects in multiple releases, yielding customer benefit. It also benefits ongoing development efforts, which improves personnel productivity and future product quality.

5.3 Practices for Building Software Systems

This section discusses ideas that affect how software products are built from source artifacts.

Practice 5.10. Use shared, static build processes and tools. It is rare that individual members of a project team use different build processes or tools. When they do, the results are often inconsistent and difficult to debug. Thus, an organization should avoid such an approach [5]. By controlling the build processes and tools, an organization encourages all its members to produce the same work products in the same manner. An additional benefit is that members can assist one another in tool use, which helps to reduce training costs.

Practice 5.11. Build software on a regular, preferably daily, basis. Increasing the frequency of software builds reduces the number of changed artifacts between builds, which reduces the number of potential flaws, or unwanted interactions, of each build [5, 11, 13]. Consequently, by increasing the frequency of software builds, an organization reduces the effort to find such incompatibilities because fewer artifacts are likely to have changed.

5.4 Practices for Releasing Software Systems

This section describes practices for releasing software products.

Practice 5.12. Maintain a unique read-only copy of each release. After each release, each version of each artifact comprising a release should be labeled with an identifier that helps to uniquely identify it. Alternatively, a configuration management tool can automatically name each release using one of many defined schemes. By protecting critical information in this manner, software engineers can easily identify artifacts that an organization used to produce a release. It also prevents software engineers from altering source artifacts and derived work products specific to a release after deployment.

Practice 5.13. A version manifest should describe each software release. A version manifest should identify all components that comprise a release, all open and closed problems, the differences between versions, relevant notes and assumptions, and build instructions. Because a version manifest explicitly identifies the specific version of each artifact that makes up a release, it permits a software development organization to better maintain and deploy systems.

Practice 5.14. Software artifacts that comprise a release should adhere to defined acceptance criteria. Typical acceptance criteria should include various metrics. For example, code metrics may include the use of code coverage criteria, various complexity metrics, and various sizing metrics. Most artifacts will have acceptance criteria that include a review or test process, if not both of them. Adoption of this practice will ensure that all artifacts adhere to a defined level of quality [5].

Practice 5.15. Configuration management tools should provide release updates. A release update augments an existing release to the current release state. The benefit of an update mechanism is that incremental releases can be practically deployed using slow telecommunication mechanisms, such as dial-up modems. The importance of this is that by providing such an update mechanism, an organization will provide better service to its customers.

5.5 Practices for Maintaining the Integrity of Software Artifacts

This section describes how an organization can ensure the integrity of the software it develops.

Practice 5.16. Use a software tool to perform configuration management functions. By definition, a configuration management tool provides:

- A history of each software artifact (i.e., version control)
- Configurations of larger aggregations of these artifacts (i.e., configuration management)
- A program to build derived artifacts, which are usually executable programs (i.e., build management)
- A mechanism to manage software changes (i.e., change management)
- Automation of software deployment, by maintaining an accurate record of its customers operating environments and the software they are entitled to use (i.e., deployment management)
- Management of various kinds of artifacts, such as requirements, architectural specifications, test plans, user documentation, and training materials

The use of a configuration management tool to control software development activities is beneficial for three reasons. First, it provides permanence for each software release, as well as a recovery mechanism for software artifacts. Thus, it helps to protect critical information. Second, it can enforce institutional policies, practices, and procedures. Third, it can automate the deployment of software and ensure the validity of such deployment.

Practice 5.17. Repositories should exist on reliable physical storage elements. An organization can enhance the reliability of a repository by using mirrored disk drives, RAID-1 or RAID-5 drives, redundant networks, and clustered servers. Adoption of this practice will yield highly available solutions and reduce the potential for significant loss of work products, which requires time and energy to replace.

Practice 5.18. Configuration management repositories should undergo periodic backups. These backups should be to nonvolatile storage devices. Several types of backups are possible (e.g., full and incremental). A configuration management plan must define the types of backups a software team will use, when an operator will perform each type of backup, the naming conventions for each one, and the manner of storing each backup. Backups may be stored remotely or locally and protected in various ways (e.g., fireproof vaults). Regular backups ensure the reproducibility of software, guarding against data and program loss.

Practice 5.19. Test and confirm the backup process. Most organizations back up their repositories, but seldom restore them. Thus, they have faith that the repositories will be accurately restored, but seldom validate that they are correctly saved and restored. This is a critical flaw in most configuration management processes. The benefit of performing this practice is to ensure that backups accurately capture the contents of repositories and that the restoration process can fully and accurately restore them.

5.6 A Procedure for Creating a Configuration Management System

Following is a procedure that an organization should follow to create a configuration management system that satisfies its needs.

Step 1. Acquire highly reliable and redundant physical storage and processing elements for the software repository.

Step 2. Identify the configuration management administrator, who is responsible for numerous tasks. The key tasks include:
- The creation of configuration management accounts and the assignment of capabilities to them
- The enforcement of defined configuration management policies and procedures
- The building of internal and external deliveries

Step 3. Define a backup procedure to regularly back up configuration management repositories to nonvolatile storage and periodically purge them of redundant or useless data. This procedure should identify when incremental and full backups are done.

Step 4. Define a procedure that verifies that the backup process functions correctly.

Step 5. Determine whether work must be authorized. If work must be authorized, then:
    Step 5a. Establish a change control board.
    Step 5b. Assign people to the change control board.
    Step 5c. Define rules for approving changes to artifacts.

Step 6. Identify the number of development lines. Typically, one is sufficient. If more than one development line is needed, then:
    Step 6a. Specify the frequency of the integration of each development line.

Step 7. Identify the number of new tasks that an individual can work on simultaneously.

Step 8. Identify the number of change requests or anomaly reports that an individual can work on simultaneously.

Step 9. Determine whether parallel development is permitted.

Step 10. Determine if branches can be created for tasks other than parallel development or the development of releases. If branches can be created, then:
    Step 10a. Identify who can create the branches.
    Step 10b. Specify under what conditions the branches can be created.
    Step 10c. Establish the criteria for determining when merges are performed.

Step 11. Determine who can create workspaces.

Step 12. Specify standard workspaces.

Step 13. Identify what information should be specified for each new development task, change request, and anomaly report. Consider performing the following as required actions for each change request and anomaly report:

■ Estimate the size of the change.
■ Identify any alternative solutions.
■ Identify the complexity of the change and the impact on other systems.
■ Identify when the need exists.
■ Identify the effect the change will have on subsequent work.
■ Estimate the cost of the change.
■ Identify the criticality of the change request.
■ Identify if another change request will solve this problem.
■ Identify the effort to verify the change.
■ Identify who will verify the change.
■ Identify whether the right people are available to work on the request.
■ Identify the impact on critical system resources, if this is an issue.
■ Identify the length of time that the change request has been pending.

Step 14. Select metrics to gather. Key metrics to collect on a periodic basis include the following:
■ Number of change requests submitted
■ Number of change requests reviewed and approved for resolution
■ Number of change requests resolved and length of resolution
■ Number of anomaly reports submitted
■ Number of anomaly reports reviewed and approved for correction
■ Number of anomaly reports corrected and length of correction
■ Number of artifacts changed
■ Number of artifacts changed more than once (these should be characterized by the number of changes and frequency of the changes)

Step 15. Acquire a configuration management tool that is able to manage software configurations, document identified software defects, and produce software releases.

Step 16. Automate the policies, practices, and procedures as much as possible.

5.7 A Baseline Procedure for Managing Software Configurations

Following is a baseline procedure for managing software that adheres to the recommended practices of this chapter.

Step 1. Purchase a disk storage system having RAID-1 capability.

Step 2. Specify the performance of nightly, weekly, and monthly backups. Weekly and monthly backups should be full backups, whereas nightly backups can be incremental from the last full backup. In addition, create a backup of each release. When a release is no longer supported, delete all versions of the software, except release versions, older than the versions of artifacts making up a release.

Step 3. Specify the use of the following backup verification process:
■ Select a computer to verify the process.
■ Install the development environment as specified according to system requirements on the verification computer.
■ Verify that the operating system, selected compilers, required libraries, and other tools used to build the application are the correct versions and are installed correctly on the verification computer.
■ Install the configuration management tool on the verification computer.
■ Restore the repository of the configuration management tool from a backup to the verification computer.
■ Ensure that the source and restored repositories are semantically equivalent.

Step 4. Specify the use of the following policies for a configuration management system:
■ Use only one development codeline.
■ Allow parallel development.
■ Permit developers to work on no more than two new tasks at the same time.
■ Permit developers to work on no more than two change authorizations at the same time.
■ All work must be authorized by an initial task assignment or change authorization.
■ Do not permit users to create branches.
■ Require that branches be created for each initial task assignment and change authorization. When an initial task assignment or change authorization is completed, require that the artifacts created or changed during such work be merged back into the development codeline.
■ A merge of an initial task assignment or change authorization is only allowed if the following criteria is satisfied:

- A regression test suite for the changed artifacts is created or augmented.
- The changed artifacts have achieved 100 percent statement coverage.
- The changed artifacts have achieved 80 percent decision outcome coverage.

■ Allow any configuration management administrator or developer to create a workspace.

■ Every month, identify the artifacts changed more than twice in the past three months.

■ Compute the following metrics on a weekly basis:
- Number of submitted change requests
- Number of submitted anomaly reports
- Number of change authorizations
- Number of completed change authorizations
- Average time to resolve each change authorization
- Number of artifacts changed
- Number of changed artifacts

■ Require that each initial development task and change authorization provide the following fields:
- Estimated size
- Estimated cost
- Estimated criticality
- Estimated system impact
- Estimated due date
- Person to perform the work
- Person to verify the work

Step 5. Identify the configuration management administrator, members of the change control board, and members of the development team.

Step 6. Acquire a configuration management tool that is able to manage software configurations, document identified software defects, and produce software releases.

This procedure tends to create codelines as shown in Figure 5.1.

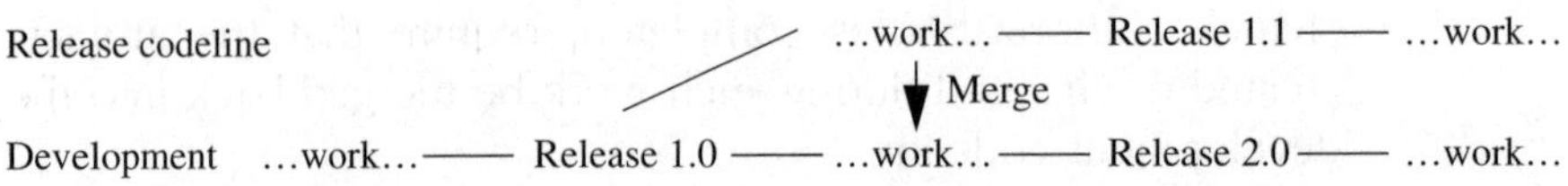

FIGURE 5.1   An example of development and release codelines.

5.8 Summary

A configuration management system is supposed to maintain the integrity of project artifacts. This chapter has identified several fundamental practices and supporting procedures essential to successfully doing this. These practices have emphasized the capture of all artifacts by a common configuration management system embodying several tools, whereby individuals change these artifacts in separate workspaces and periodically synchronize them with the work of others. However, each change is approved by a panel of key people having managerial and technical responsibility for a project and synchronized with the work of others once the changes have been demonstrated to work, or at least work as well as before each change.

Some of the practices identified in this chapter provide greater integrity of software artifacts than most defined configuration management systems. In addition, existing software process standards, such as the Capability Maturity Model® (Carnegie Mellon University, Pittsburgh, Pennsylvania) for Software [1], ignore many of these practices. However, these practices are essential for developing robust configuration management systems. In sum, the proposed configuration management procedure uses the proposed configuration management practices.

References

1. Paulk, M.C. et al., *The Capability Maturity Model: Guidelines for Improving the Software Process*, Addison-Wesley, 1994.
2. Tichy, W.F., Design, Implementation, and Evaluation of a Revision Control System, in *Proc. of the Int. Conf. on Software Engineering*, 1982, 58.
3. Rochkind, M.J., The Source Code Control System, *IEEE Trans. on Software Engineering*, SE-1, 364, 1975.
4. Kandt, R.K., Software Configuration Management Principles and Best Practices, in *Proc. of the Product Focused Software Process Improvement Conference*, Oivo, M. and Komi-Sirvio, S. (Eds.), Springer-Verlag, 2002, 300.
5. Wingerd, L. and Seiwald, C., High-Level Best Practices in Software Configuration Management, in *Proc. of the Int. Workshop on Software Configuration Management*, 1998.
6. Babich, W.A., *Software Configuration Management: Coordination for Team Productivity*, Addison-Wesley, 1986.
7. Jones, C., *Software Assessments, Benchmarks, and Best Practices*, Addison-Wesley, 2000.
8. Berlack, H.R., *Software Configuration Management*, Wiley, 1992.
9. Bersoff, E.H., *Software Configuration Management, An Investment in Product Integrity*, Prentice Hall, 1980.
10. Whitgift, D., *Methods and Tools for Software Configuration Management*, Wiley, 1991.

11. Berczuk, S.P. and Appleton, B., *Software Configuration Management Patterns: Effective Teamwork, Practical Integration*, Addison-Wesley, 2003.
12. Rigg, W., Burrows, C., and Ingram, P., *Ovum Evaluates: Configuration Management Tools*, Ovum Limited, 1995.
13. McConnell, S., *Rapid Development: Taming Wild Software Schedules*, Microsoft Press, 1996.

Chapter 6

Requirements Engineering

The engineering of requirements may be the most important activity of the software development life cycle. This is because requirements ultimately define what developed systems will be like and, possibly, how they will be developed. In addition, the largest number of defects that remain in delivered software is attributable to defective requirements and are the most costly of all defects to correct, costing as much as several orders of magnitude more than those introduced in the latest stage of software development. Consequently, this chapter describes numerous practices for generating good requirements that are incorporated into a defined procedure.

A *requirement* is a necessary, quantifiable, and verifiable capability, function, property, characteristic, or behavior that a system must exhibit to solve a real-world problem, or a constraint that it must satisfy or must be satisfied during the development of a system. *Requirements engineering* is the process of developing requirements. It consists of a structured set of activities that results in the production of a *requirements document*, which is a formal statement of the system requirements.

Requirements are generally imposed by multiple stakeholders from different organizations and at different levels of the operating environments where people work. Thus, requirements may be technical or nontechnical. *Nontechnical requirements* include agreements, conditions, and contractual terms. Examples include the identification of milestones, delivered products, delivery and milestone dates, and acceptance criteria. Technical requirements, on the other hand, are either functional or nonfunctional.

Functional requirements define the functional capabilities, or behavior, of a system. *Nonfunctional requirements* identify the constraints that a system must satisfy [1]. Nonfunctional requirements often identify CPU utilization, data, interface, memory, operational, performance, sizing, and timing needs [2]. Nonfunctional requirements specified less often identify availability, distribution, interoperability, maintainability, portability, reliability, reusability, robustness, safety, security, supportability, and usability needs of a system. Typical kinds of reusable requirements include those that constrain the system or system operations, identify the style of presentation, and reflect organizational policies. Because it is generally difficult to understand the impact of nonfunctional requirements on a system, satisfying them is generally more difficult than for functional requirements. Furthermore, many of these properties emerge over time, often when individual subsystems are integrated into a larger system.

Functional and nonfunctional requirements apply to a system, while *process requirements* specify how a system is to be produced. Typical process requirements specify the programming languages, database management systems, and other software tools that are to be used. Sometimes, requirements may be levied on the actual development process, such as "the contractor shall perform software inspections on every design document before coding begins."

Organizations with sound requirements engineering practices spend 10 to 15 percent of total project funds to develop requirements [3, 4]. Generally speaking, spending less than 10 percent of total project funds increases total mission cost because too many introduced defects must be corrected, whereas spending more than 15 percent of total project funds tends to yield modest gains in the quality of developed artifacts. Experience shows that projects that invest 10 percent or more of the total project development funds in requirements engineering achieve cost overruns of 0 to 50 percent, whereas those organizations that spend 5 percent or less exhibit overruns of 100 to 200 percent [4]. However, even if 10 to 15 percent of total project effort is allocated to requirements engineering, requirements engineers must use good practices and procedures to be efficient and effective. The benefits of a sound methodology for requirements engineering more than recoup the investment. These benefits include:

- Elimination of unneeded features
- Faster rework
- Less system training
- Fewer operational errors

- Lower development, maintenance, and operations costs
- Shorter schedules

6.1 Practices for Eliciting Requirements

Requirements elicitation is the process of identifying and consolidating various stakeholder needs [5]. Typical stakeholders of software systems include customers, operations personnel, regulators, software engineers, systems engineers, test engineers, and users. A *customer* is the individual or group who receives project deliverables and usually controls the resources for acquiring them. A *user* is an individual or organization that uses a system or the results produced by a system. A *stakeholder need* is a business or operational problem that should be eliminated or an opportunity that should be exploited. Following is a discussion of several important practices for elicitating requirements.

Practice 6.1. Identify and involve stakeholders. It is important to identify stakeholders because they have their own perspective, agenda, priorities, drivers, and unique information concerning their environment, project feasibility, and solution strategies [2, 4, 6–8]. By gathering and disseminating this diverse information, all the stakeholders can share a common vision, from which they can set realistic expectations and develop high-quality requirements [9, 10]. To develop high-quality requirements, requirements engineers must identify the stakeholder needs and involve them in the definition of a concept of operations and requirements. While doing this, requirements engineers must periodically ensure that operational concepts and requirements are consistent and feasible by integrating them and resolving conflicts as they arise [4, 5].

In sum, stakeholders should be involved in the definition of operational concepts and requirements for three key reasons:

1. Project failure often occurs because developers do not acquire a detailed understanding of the user's needs, and one way of overcoming this is by their active participation [3, 11].
2. Productivity is about 50 percent higher when there is a high level of participation by the customer in specifying requirements [12]. This is because frequent communication between stakeholders and developers improves the stability of requirements [13]. In fact, the frequency of communication with the stakeholders is more important than using a requirements definition methodology, inspecting requirements, or including stakeholders on requirements definition teams [13].

3. Stakeholder participation results in less rework, avoids the introduction of unnecessary features, and better satisfies the needs of the customers [4]. Without the participation of stakeholders, important needs may be ignored, and stated requirements may be incorrect, inconsistent, or ambiguous. Key stakeholders include actual users and system architects [8].

Practice 6.2. Identify the reason for developing a system. Identify the purpose for creating a new system [2, 8, 14]. The system purpose is the highest-level customer requirement that identifies one or more business needs [1]. All other requirements must support these needs. To identify the purpose of a system, consider the following questions. Has a new business opportunity arisen that necessitates a change? Will a new system improve the current operation? Will a new system implement new functionality? Have user needs, missions, objectives, environments, interfaces, personnel, or something else changed? What are the shortcomings of the current system, if one exists, that necessitate a new system? If no system exists, then justify why one is needed, as well as its proposed features. In sum, systems should solve only those problems that provide a business advantage [1].

Practice 6.3. Define a clear, crisp project vision. A vision statement should explain what a system will and will not do; describe the benefits, goals, and objectives that the system will satisfy; specify how it differs from competing systems; and identify who should care [4, 7, 15, 16]. Such a vision will help a team focus on creating an outstanding system with clear benefits. To determine whether a vision is clear, pick a few individuals from a variety of areas on a project and ask each one to briefly outline the project vision. If each person selected cannot immediately identify, in just a few sentences, the key goals and customers for the project, the project is in trouble. This may occur because the vision has not been well communicated to the team, or the team does not agree with or believe in the vision, or that it changes too frequently [7]. Whatever the cause, the lack of a shared project vision is a fundamental flaw because project personnel will lack the necessary guidance to assess the merit of features and prioritize the correction of defects. Thus, a project vision helps resolve issues before requirements are written and shortens the requirements review process.

Practice 6.4. Identify applicable operational policies. Operational policies provide guidance that constrains decision-making activities by imposing limitations on the operation of a system. Typical kinds of policies specify the required skills and characteristics of operational personnel, how they use a system, its operational modes, periods of interactive or unattended operations, and the type of processing it performs.

Practice 6.5. Identify user roles and characteristics. Accurately identify the general characteristics of the users and the way they interact with a system [5, 16]. General characteristics include the responsibilities, education, background, skill level, activities, and modes of operation of each user role. Formal and informal interactions among the various user roles also should be described, if they are relevant to the operation of a system. Especially important are the interactions among user groups, operators, and maintainers. Normally, users fulfill several roles, each requiring a common set of features.

Practice 6.6. Describe systems similar to the "to be" system. Such systems may be those that other organizations have developed or an existing system that is being replaced by a new one. Regardless, each description should be written using terminology understandable by a typical user. More specifically, it should be free of computer jargon. Graphical representations of any kind can be used as long as they concisely describe the behavior of a system and distinguish between automated and manual processes. Each description should include [2, 15]:

- The provided capabilities, functions, and features
- The adopted strategies, tactics, methods, and techniques
- The implemented operational modes, especially degraded and emergency modes
- Existing operating environment characteristics and interfaces to external hardware and software systems
- All system components and their interconnections
- All known current operational risk factors
- Actual performance characteristics, if known, such as peak and sustainable speed, throughput, and volume requirements

Practice 6.7. Identify all external interfaces and enabling systems. An *enabling system* is anything that a system needs to perform its mission but is external to it. Typical external interfaces include other software applications, databases, and hardware, such as input and output devices [16].

For each interface and enabling system, describe its purpose, source, format, structure, content, and method of support [4]. Use context diagrams to identify the external interfaces and enabling systems, and use arcs to indicate events, not dataflows [4, 16]. Defining external interfaces and enabling systems helps expose potential problems by revealing system boundaries, which are typically a major source of defects. When identifying external interfaces and enabling systems, a requirements engineer should determine how they can adversely affect a system across the interface, as well as how they can change it. For those that change, the risk associated with each change should be managed.

Practice 6.8. Define a concept of operations. An *operational concept* is a description of how a system is used and what it does in a typical day [2, 4]. Over time, a concept of operations should be refined to provide more detailed information. Operational concepts generally describe numerous scenarios, but seldom more than 50 of them.

Scenarios identify what a system does, how it operates or will operate, and how it is used or will be used. Each *scenario* identifies a specific situation that occurs in an operational environment. As such, a scenario is a description of one or more end-to-end transactions involving the system operating within its environment. Each transaction describes one or more actions and outcomes, of which exceptions are legitimate outcomes. In addition, each scenario should describe the state of a system before entering it, information about other activities occurring at the same time, the state of the system after completing the scenario, and the users who are interested in the functionality described by the scenario [2]. At a later time, the responsibility for performing the operations implied by the scenario will be assigned to a system component. Common scenarios should cover [4]:

- The development, verification, deployment, installation, training, operations, maintenance, upgrading, and disposal phases of the life cycle
- The viewpoints of all the stakeholders, including those of the developers, inspectors, testers, end users, customers, trainers, and maintainers
- Nominal operations and environments
- Off-nominal operations and environments, such as extreme and hazardous conditions
- The expected inputs and outputs, the non-occurrence of expected inputs and outputs, and the occurrence of incorrect inputs or outputs of all interfaces

Scenarios should be developed by the requirements engineers with the assistance of users [2]. The users identify weaknesses or flaws in the scenarios and the requirements engineers document these problems and ask questions about user actions, how tasks are performed, and what would happen if alternative approaches were taken.

Each scenario should be categorized along several dimensions. The relevance of the scenario should be defined as being either essential, desired, or optional. The technology risk associated with each scenario should be identified as being high, moderate, or low. Later, the analysts should identify the dependency among the scenarios, estimate the time and cost to realize each one, and assign them to development cycles. Further, analysts should assess the confidence they have in the estimated effort to implement each scenario as either high, moderate, or low. Those scenarios with the highest priority and greatest risk should be developed first. Guidelines for determining the proper granularity of a scenario follow.

- The estimated cost for realizing a scenario should use, at most, 5 percent of the available funds to develop all scenarios. If the scenario is larger than this, the scenario should be refined into two or more scenarios.
- The estimated cost for realizing a scenario should use at least 1 percent of the available funds to develop all scenarios. If a scenario is smaller than this, the analyst should consider whether its identification is constructive.

Several studies demonstrate the usefulness of scenarios. One experiment showed that 58 percent of requirements changes (defect corrections) were derived from analyzing scenarios and 28 percent of the questions that occurred while analyzing requirements could only be answered by analyzing scenarios [17]. In another study, scenarios and usability testing together reduced the number of usability defects by 70 percent and improved customer satisfaction [18]. In sum, operational scenarios elaborate the problem domain so that personnel better understand a planned system, thus eliminating the most common problem that occurs during the definition of requirements — not fully understanding the desired or necessary behavior of a system [19, 20]. As a result, this shared understanding of a "to be" system helps resolve requirement debates [21] and provides a basis for early requirements validation [2, 4]. In conclusion, some people assert that the most important thing to do in software development is to study potential user tasks, write down the results as scenarios, and identify and eliminate the gaps among them [18].

Practice 6.9. Emphasize the definition of vital nonfunctional requirements. When defining requirements, requirements engineers should pay particular attention to operational, performance, user interface, and site adaptation requirements because these are extremely vital to the successful operation of a system, and are often overlooked [4].

■ When operational requirements are defined for a system, an organization will spend less time training its users and its users will usually spend less time performing tasks.

■ When performance requirements are specified, project personnel can select appropriate hardware, technologies, and algorithms and validate a system's performance. Important performance requirements include the speed, availability, response time, and recovery time of various software functions [16].

■ When prototyping user interfaces, the number of omitted requirements before system development is reduced [18]. Hence, requirements engineers should identify screen formats, page layouts, the content of reports and menus, and the availability of programmable function keys [16].

■ When deployment requirements are defined, installing software at remote sites will be easier. Hence, requirements engineers should define the requirements for any data or initialization sequences specific to a given site, mission, or operational mode and specify those features that should be modified to adapt software for a particular installation [16].

Nonfunctional requirements are especially important when dealing with subcontractors. A contractual specification should specify various nonfunctional requirements, for example, covering guarantees about availability, mean time between failures, mean time to repair, throughput, etc. A failure to fulfill a nonfunctional requirement should be treated by the contracting organization as a breach of contract [22].

Performance requirements. Performance requirements specify the responsiveness of a system to specific events as a measurement of time or the number of events processed in a given period. Characterized differently, performance characterizes the timeliness of a system in providing a service. Note that this is different from speed, which attempts to minimize the average response time for delivering a service or several services. The performance of a system is primarily constrained by the resources used to fulfill system demands and the allocation of shared resources to satisfy them. That is, scheduling of system resources largely affects system performance.

Performance requirements should identify four types of concerns [23]:

1. *Latency* identifies how long it takes to respond to a specific event. A response window should be provided that identifies a minimum

and maximum latency. In addition, the expected average, best, and worst-case latencies should be identified. Sometimes, the precedence of event responses, whether partial or total, must be specified. Similarly, the variation in the time that a computed result is output is sometimes important. That is, it is possible to buffer responses before outputting them to a consumer.

2. *Throughput* identifies how many events can be processed over a period of time. It may be necessary to specify one or more throughput requirements for a particular resource but for different time periods. Similarly, the expected average, best, and worst-case throughput rates should be identified.

3. *Capacity* identifies how much demand can be handled (or work can be done) while satisfying latency and throughput requirements. That is, capacity identifies the maximum number of events that can be processed under ideal circumstances, without violating latency requirements. Thus, demand depends on the arrival pattern of events and the execution time for responding to them. Arrival patterns can be either periodic or aperiodic. Aperiodic arrivals can be sporadic, which is bounded by a minimum separation between events, or completely random. Utilization is the percentage of time a resource is busy, and peak utilization is the maximum utilization achievable while still meeting timing requirements.

4. *Modes of operation* affect the latency, throughput, and capacity requirements. A characteristic of a mode is the demand being placed on a system and the resources used to satisfy that demand. Anomalous modes of operation are especially important to identify. Two common modes are reduced capacity, where a system may have to operate when resources cease to function, and overload situations, where a system may sacrifice timing requirements of noncritical events.

Performance requirements should be defined for buses, networks, processors, and storage devices [24]. Table 6.1 identifies common topics of performance requirements.

Reliability requirements. There are several guidelines that one should use when designing software where a high level of reliability is desired. Some of these guidelines include:

- A system should permit the cancellation of current processing with a single action and revert to a known, consistent state from which it can safely resume.
- A system should permit unreliable, incorrect, or unsafe states to be exited and known consistent states to be entered with a single action.

TABLE 6.1 Common Performance Requirement Topics

Bus bandwidth	Maximum duration of masked interrupts
Maximum duration of non-preemptable sections	Network bandwidth
Number of task priority levels	Physical memory
Processor clock granularity	Processor speed
Scheduling discipline	Type of bus
Type of network	Virtual memory

- Two or more unique actions should be required to initiate any potentially hazardous function or sequence of functions.
- All information presented to the user by a system and all interactions between the user and a system should be clear, concise, and unambiguous.
- A system should confirm the entry of valid data or identify corrective actions taken.
- A system should inform the user when it does not perform requested actions.
- A system should continuously indicate that it is functioning, as well as its current status.
- A system should visually distinguish the significance of each error message.
- Watchdog timers should be used in a manner that does not permit an inner loop to reset a timer as part of the loop sequence.
- Software having extreme reliability requirements should be segregated from software that does not.
- Loops and other critical computations should not exceed a predefined constant maximum execution time.
- Executable code should not modify itself, nor should it grant access indiscriminately to other code.
- Program states should be represented by bit patterns that will remain unique given 1- or 2-bit errors.
- Parity checks, checksums, cycle redundancy checks, and other data verification techniques should be used to validate the transfer of data.
- Data transfer packets should have a predetermined format and content.
- Input and output data should be validated to adhere to predefined limits.

- Functions requiring two or more events to perform a critical function should receive them from different modules, ports, and processes or threads.
- The results of a program should not depend on its execution time or time of execution.
- All process and processor memory that is not used by an operational program should be initialized to a pattern that will cause the system to revert to a known, consistent state when executed.
- If a program is overlaid on another, then each one should occupy the same memory.

Usability requirements. There are several guidelines that one should use when designing software for usability. Common guidelines that increase the usability of a system [14, 25–27] include:

- A system should be effectively and efficiently used by a broad range of people under a variety of work conditions. To this end, the requirements engineer should come to understand the cognitive abilities, motivation, experience, and cultural background of the intended users. It may even be important to understand their vision and hearing abilities. Considering these issues will increase the number of people willing to use a system.
- A system should be easy to use and learn. Hence, new software systems should adopt existing standard tool processes or behaviors. For example, use File, View, and Edit menu items in a standard menu bar.
- A system should allow users to personalize it. Typically, systems permit users to adapt command bindings and short cuts. Sometimes, a system even provides a macro capability that captures command sequences so that they can be repeatedly applied. If a system is intended for international use, a system should permit users to alter text output and error messages so that they are presented in a preferred language.
- A system should minimize the required cognitive workload of its users. For example, a system should never require users to remember things or write down intermediate results. To minimize cognitive workload, a system should operate in a manner consistent with the way users perform their work.
- A system should validate all user input and verify that the necessary resources are available to perform the specified operations.
- A system should consistently present information to users. In addition, system output should be presented in a manner consistent

with the style of valid user input. Similarly, when different views of the same information are presented, the content of those views should be consistent with one another.

■ A system should permit users to reliably work on multiple tasks at the same time, and switch between them at will.

■ A system should predict the expected execution time of every task and provide continual feedback on them. For example, a system should indicate to users when activities are completed.

■ A system should record the interaction history between it and the user, and each interaction should be modeled as an atomic transaction. This provides the user with three key benefits. First, it permits the user to cancel a task during its operation without causing the occurrence of a side effect. Second, it allows the user to undo the results of tasks through the issuance of an undo command. Third, it provides a recovery mechanism that reduces data loss.

■ A system should allow the user to select and act upon arbitrary combinations of data.

■ The system should inform the user when important system events occur.

■ The system should provide informative and relevant guidance.

■ The user should be in control at all times. That is, the user should have the capability to influence ongoing computations.

■ The system should provide different user modes and roles.

■ The system should make necessary workflows explicit.

■ The command hierarchy for system menus should use the following guidelines:
  – Each service should be distinctly named using terminology familiar to the users.
  – The task names within each group should be ordered, based on frequency, a standard workflow pattern, alphabetization, or an existing standard.
  – Task groups should be limited to, at most, nine names due to limits of human cognition [28], and preferably to three subgroups of up to three items each [28].
  – The number of work events (click, drag, and keypunch) that a user must make to perform a task should be limited to minimize what the user must do to do a job.

Practice 6.10. Include specific quality targets in the requirements. An organization must define the minimum level of quality that is acceptable

[2, 4]. If not, it runs the risk of producing an inferior system that does not meet the needs of its customers. Similarly, organizations should define quality at least in terms of incoming defects after deployment, mean time between failures, and defect removal efficiency.

Practice 6.11. *Classify requirements using a multidimensional approach.* Segmenting requirements into key categories permits people to better understand their relationships, identify ambiguities and duplicates among them, and identify whether important types of requirements have been ignored [4]. In addition, structured requirements lead to more stable requirements, fewer design iterations, and better designs [29]. Several important categories are [30, 31]:

- Stakeholder views
- Operational scenarios
- Subsystems and system components
- Requirement types:
    - Functional system requirements
    - Nonfunctional system requirements categories (e.g., environment, safety, security, and performance, process)
- Requirement attributes (e.g., owner, source, status, priority, and revision date)
- Requirement cohesion

Practice 6.12. *Verify the source of a requirement.* It has been shown that between 5 percent and 43 percent of project requirements are defined by people not authorized to do so [32]. Thus, the source of the requirement statement must be verified as being a legitimate knowledge source to prevent the imposition of unneeded requirements [7]. Further, the verification and recording of the source of a requirement may help people understand why the requirement exists, as well as identify who to consult when help is needed [31].

6.2 Practices for Analyzing the Problem Domain and Application Needs

Requirements analysis is the process of identifying the appropriateness, completeness, quality, and value of a set of requirements. Following is a discussion of several important practices for analyzing requirements.

Practice 6.13. Develop conceptual models. A *conceptual model* is an abstraction used by a software engineer to understand a system before its construction [18]. Abstraction involves the selective examination of certain aspects of the real world and the desired system, usually at a reduced level of fidelity, that isolate important aspects while ignoring other, seemingly unimportant ones. Of course, what is and is not important at any time depends on the needs of the users of a conceptual model. By their nature, abstractions are incomplete and inaccurate. Hence, a good model of a system represents the aspects of a problem critical to its solution.

Although modeling is an ancient concept, correspondence modeling in the software profession is relatively new. *Correspondence modeling* involves building models so that there is a one-to-one correspondence between artifacts of the real world and those of the modeled world [33]. The field of artificial intelligence calls correspondence modeling model-based reasoning, whereas the software profession calls it object-oriented analysis and design. Several schemes are used to describe conceptual models, and many are based on the Unified Modeling Language [6].

The modeling process involves the following activities.

1. *The identification of the important concepts of the real world.* Examining the scenarios of the concept of operations helps identify these concepts, including the external interfaces and enabling systems. These concepts should be defined using the standard terminology of the problem domain and named using a single noun or an adjective and a noun.

2. *The identification of the relationships among the concepts.* To identify concept relationships, one should compare each pair of concepts and determine the relationship of one concept to the other. If related, one should determine if there is more than one relationship among a pair of concepts.

3. *The grouping into units of concepts that are closely coupled with one another.* Such units typically characterize a problem domain or an environment.

4. *The definition of the attributes of each concept, one for each unique type of feature.*

5. *The definition of the behaviors, or services, that each concept provides to other concepts.*

The benefits of developing a conceptual model are several. They can be used to:

1. Check system specifications
2. Identify development risks

3. Directly derive working systems
4. Form a basis for software reuse
5. Provide a general understanding of the modeled problem domain
6. Simulate system architectures

Practice 6.14. Record assumptions. Assumptions, once written, should be confirmed or corrected before too long [20]. If an assumption cannot be validated, it is a risk that must be analyzed and monitored [4] (see Practices 6.17 and 6.33).

Practice 6.15. Prioritize software requirements. Prioritizing requirements based on cost, dependency, and importance is beneficial because it helps select the most important requirements to implement, which may lead to a reduction in the number of implemented functional requirements, and can be used to define the capabilities of each software release or build [2–5, 18]. Three basic techniques are used to prioritize requirements:

1. Identify the absolute importance of each requirement one at a time. Unfortunately, this approach generally results in too many requirements being highly ranked.
2. Identify the relative value between every pair of requirements and use that information to rank priorities. The benefit of this approach is that its redundancy makes it less sensitive to errors and permits the measurement of the error. An approach based on this strategy is called the Analytic Hierarchy Process.
3. Identify the relative value between a random selection of requirement pairs and use that information to rank priorities. This is called the Incomplete Pairwise Comparison method and is a modification of the Analytic Hierarchy Process that eliminates half of the comparisons without adversely affecting the result [34–36].

One case study indicates that the pairwise comparison techniques are more accurate, efficient, and informative than the naive numerical assignment technique, and that there is greater consensus among analysts when they use them [37]. Hence, one should use the Analytic Hierarchy Process or the Incomplete Pairwise Comparison method to prioritize requirements.

The Analytic Hierarchy Process is a systematic procedure that decomposes a problem into smaller parts that eventually requires simple comparisons among each attribute pair to develop priorities among attributes of each level of a hierarchy [38, 39]. The process for prioritizing one set of attributes follows the following sequence of steps:

TABLE 6.2   A Matrix of the Analytic Hierarchy Process

	a_1	a_2	a_3	...	a_n
a_1	1	$r(a_1/a_2)$	$r(a_1/a_3)$	...	$r(a_1/a_n)$
a_2	$1/r(a_1/a_2)$	1	$r(a_2/a_3)$	...	$r(a_2/a_n)$
a_3	$1/r(a_1/a_3)$	$1/r(a_2/a_3)$	1	...	$r(a_3/a_n)$
...	...	...	...	...	...
a_n	$1/r(a_1/a_n)$	$1/r(a_2/a_n)$	$1/r(a_3/a_n)$	...	1

Step 1. Individually compare each pair of attributes and rate the importance of one element of each pair to the other. The algorithm for this operation follows.

```
for attribute i from 1 to n by 1
    matrix[i, i] = 1
    for attribute j from i + 1 to n by 1
        if the two attributes have equal importance
        then the relative importance is 1
        else if attribute i is more important than
                attribute j
        then identify the relative importance r of
            attribute i with attribute j using the
            following 4 values:
                3 for slightly more important;
                5 for strongly more important;
                7 for significantly more important; and
                9 for absolutely more important.
        else identify the relative importance r of
            attribute j with attribute i using the
            reciprocal of the 4 values described above.
        matrix[i, j] = r
        matrix[j, i] = 1 / r
```

The result of Step 1 is the construction of a matrix as shown in Table 6.2.

Step 2. Compute the priorities of each attribute. Formally, this is performed by computing the principal eigenvector of the matrix. An approximation to this can be found by computing p_i, as described in Equation 6.1, for each row i and then normalizing the resulting priority vector p by dividing each p_i by the sum of every p_i.

TABLE 6.3   Computation of Priorities from a Relationship Matrix

Relationship Matrix	Priority Vector (eigenvector)	Priority Vector (approximation)
$\begin{bmatrix} 1 & 5 & 3 \\ 1/5 & 1 & 1/3 \\ 1/3 & 3 & 1 \end{bmatrix}$	$\begin{bmatrix} 0.637(1) \\ 0.104(3) \\ 0.258(2) \end{bmatrix}$	$\begin{bmatrix} 0.470(1) \\ 0.219(3) \\ 0.310(2) \end{bmatrix}$

$$p_i = \sqrt[n]{\prod_{j=1}^{n} a_{ij}} \tag{6.1}$$

Table 6.3 shows the result of this procedure for a specific matrix based on the two methods for calculating priorities. Once a matrix has been computed for one set of attributes — that is, for one level — it can be repeated for each level of a hierarchy. Afterward, one can multiply the priorities of one level with those of the next, repeatedly, until a final prioritization has been performed.

Practice 6.16. Capture requirement rationales and discussions of them. The rationale for each requirement must explicitly state why a requirement is needed [4, 8]. When identifying the rationale, one often will find that the rationale is really the statement of a desired functional requirement, whereas the original statement is simply one realization that satisfies it [4]. So, identifying rationales is one way to find the true functional requirements of a system. In addition, documenting the rationale of a requirement may show that as many as half of the requirements are not necessary [8, 32]. Finally, documenting rationales allows other people to annotate a requirement with supportive or contradictory information that can identify unrecognized issues and offer alternatives [40]. In sum, the benefit of documenting the rationales of requirements is that they generally improve the quality of defined requirements, shorten the review of requirements and later change efforts, improve impact analysis, and capture corporate knowledge [4, 32].

Practice 6.17. Analyze the risks of each requirement. Common requirement risks include unknown or changed regulations and interfaces, missing requirements, and technical feasibility, cost, and schedule uncertainty. Consequently, when identifying requirements, engineers should identify requirements that do not have these risks, as well as identifying those requirements that could have significant impact [4]. When risk has been identified, project personnel need to perform feasibility studies and risk assessments.

Practice 6.18. Allocate requirements in a top-down manner. Allocate requirements to both system components and development cycles [4]. Allocating requirements to system components is the first step in planning the development of a system. Allocating requirements to development cycles is the second step, but this can be done only after requirements have been prioritized (see Practice 6.15).

6.3 Practices for Specifying Requirements

A *requirements specification* should establish an understanding between customers and suppliers about what a system is supposed to do, provide a basis for estimating costs and schedules, and provide a baseline for validation and verification [16]. Specifications are most often written in natural language because this is the only form of communication that is currently contractually binding [41]. The use of natural language, unfortunately, does not offer enough structure to produce good requirements. Hence, practitioners should adopt practices to improve the specification of requirements. Some of these practices follow. However, following these practices still does not guarantee that good requirements will be produced. The development of good requirements requires a lot of analytic thought. Attempting to specify a rationale for a requirement is one way to encourage such thought because when one identifies a rationale, the true requirement is often found (see Practice 6.16).

Practice 6.19. Define a glossary. A glossary uniquely defines the meaning of key words and phrases. This helps to precisely define requirements that are easier to correctly interpret [8]. An organization should maintain a standard glossary of terms common to its business.

Practice 6.20. Uniquely identify each requirement and ensure its uniqueness. Traceability should be both forward to higher-level requirements and backward to lower-level ones. Also, each requirement should be stated only once. Unfortunately, experience has shown that many requirements are duplicated.

Practice 6.21. Differentiate between requirement, goal, and declaration statements. A typical problem with requirements is that their authors use words other than "shall" to specify requirements — words that are not legally binding and seldom explicit [41]. To ensure clarity, requirements must use "shall" to specify contractually binding requirements, "will" to specify facts or declare purpose, and "should" to identify goals or non-mandatory provisions [4].

Practice 6.22. Use good writing style. Following are several rules for writing good requirements:

■ State only one requirement per requirement statement. When following this recommendation, changes to individual requirements are easier to analyze and trace. For example, "The system shall generate and deliver data to the spacecraft as specified in *document*" should be restated as "The system shall generate the data specified in *document*" and "The system shall upload the data specified in *document* to the spacecraft."

■ State requirements as active sentences. Sometimes, goals are stated, and it is not clear what is responsible for achieving it. Consider, for example, "The subsystem shall not be exposed to direct sunlight when the system is unpowered." This requirement statement does not identify the system component that is responsible for ensuring that the subsystem is not exposed to direct sunlight. It would be better rewritten as "The system shall ensure that the subsystem is never exposed to direct sunlight when the system is unpowered."

■ Always use a noun or definite pronoun when referring to a thing. The purpose of writing active sentences is to identify the thing that is responsible for satisfying a requirement. The use of indefinite pronouns negates this purpose. Hence, do not use them.

■ Use no more than one conjunction when writing requirements statements. When more than one conjunction is used, it is often difficult to understand the precedence among the conjunctions. This ambiguity, consequently, may result in an incorrect realization of a requirement.

■ Do not use negations within requirements statements. Negations are typically more difficult for people to understand and may cause the incorrect interpretation of a requirements statement. Another reason for avoiding negations is that it is often difficult or impossible to test such statements. For example, one should consider rewriting "The system shall provide *no* less than 4 MB of data storage in nonvolatile memory" as "The system shall provide *at least* 4 MB of data storage in nonvolatile memory."

■ Avoid using weak words and phrases. Such words and phrases are generally imprecise and allow the expansion or contraction of requirements beyond their intent [4]. Sometimes, these weak words and phrases occur when using indefinite pronouns and unqualified adjectives and adverbs. Many weak words end in "ly" (e.g., quickly, optionally, timely). Table 6.4 lists several weak words and phrases that people often use within requirements. Several examples of the use of weak words and phrases follow. A weak phrase that expresses a desired ability, but not a requirement is: "The system shall *be able to* acquire the *data* with an instantaneous field of regard variation of 3 mrad per second." Instead, this is better expressed as "The system shall acquire the *data* with an instantaneous field of regard variation of 3 mrad per second." An ambiguous requirement, is: "The subsystem shall *support* 21 potentiometers with an absolute angular range of 335 degrees." The use of *support* does not clearly identify the requirement. Will the subsystem provide these potentiometers? If not, will the subsystem provide power for them, measure their output, or provide physical space for them? This requirement also does not identify the range of values or the precision of the angular range. This requirement might be better expressed by the following three requirements: "The subsystem shall provide data storage for 21 potentiometers;" "The value of each potentiometer, measured in degrees, will be defined as any value between 0 and 335, inclusive;" and "The value of each potentiometer shall accurately represent six significant digits."

■ State the needed requirements without specifying how to fulfill them. Avoid specifying design decisions in requirements specifications unless the intention is to impose a constraint on the design activity [4]. Such a constraint is justified when using an external or enabling system, an existing product, or a desirable design practice. For example, requirements could specify the use of specific design frameworks and patterns to help create robust system architectures.

■ Write complete statements. A requirements specification should fully describe each requirement; hence, no requirement should be identified as *to be determined*. However, if an assumption must eventually become a requirement, then state it as a requirement, where the portion of the requirement that is assumed is enclosed in square brackets [4]. When such an assumption is made, the requirements specification must describe the conditions causing it, who is responsible for its elimination, and when it must be eliminated.

TABLE 6.4 Words and Phrases to Avoid Using within Requirements Statements

about	acceptable	accommodate	accurate	adequate	adjustable
affordable	analyze	and/or	applicable	appropriate	as a minimum
as applicable	as appropriate	average	be able to	be capable of	better
can	capability of	capability to	careful	deep	dependable
designed to	desirable	easy	economical	effective	efficient
essential	etc.	excessive	good	high quality	if practical
immediate	improper	including	instant	insufficient	known
less	low	major	maximize	may	minimize
minimum	neat	necessary	normal	not limited to	optimum
other	periodically	pleasing	possible	practical	process
proper	provide for	quick	reasonable	recognized	relevant
reputable	robust	safe	secure	significant	similar
simple	smooth	stable	substantial	sufficient	suitable
support	temporary	these	timely	typical	variable
various	when necessary				

"The flight software shall update the event timers [as needed] during EDL" is an example of an unfinished requirement. This requirement is incomplete and no one even assumed how often the event timers need updating. This lets the developer update them as often as he determines is appropriate, which may be never or continuously. A hypothetical completion for this requirement is "The flight software shall update each event timer every 10 milliseconds during EDL."

■ Write statements that clearly convey intent. A requirements specification should accurately and precisely reflect the intent of its author [4]. For example, the following statement illustrates a common type of problem: "The subsystem shall *be designed* to be used and operated at a single processor speed setting of 20 MHz." This statement places a requirement on the design of the system, although the intent was to level a requirement on the delivered system. This requirement would have been better written as "The subsystem shall use a processor clock cycle of 20 MHz."

Practice 6.23. Write consistent statements. Because requirements specifications must be consistent [2], requirements engineers should ensure that all quality requirements are compatible with one another and the characteristics of real-world objects. Heuristics for finding conflicting requirements include examining requirements that use the same data, the same type of data, and the same scales of measurement.

In addition, terminology must be consistently used in a requirements specification to achieve consistent statements. One way to achieve this is to use a standard dictionary of commonly used terms. Because experiments reveal that a small number of unique words are used when defining requirements [29], this would be easy to achieve and would lead to less ambiguous requirements that are more amenable to reuse. An organization could even take this one step farther by defining a concise language for defining requirements.

Practice 6.24. Define a verification method for each requirement. All requirements should be verified by analysis, demonstration, inspection, simulation, or test [4, 7, 42]. Identifying the verification method helps ensure that each requirement is verifiable and practical, and that resources are available to verify it. When functional tests are used, identify them in conjunction with the requirements definition to prevent their omission and to ensure that the functional tests validate the intent of the system requirements.

Practice 6.25. *Identify the relationships among requirements.* As each requirement is written, it should be linked to operational concepts or higher-level requirements and other work products [3, 4]. While doing this, requirements engineers should continually ask whether lower-level requirements satisfy higher-level requirements or whether any lower-level requirement dictates internal interfaces. Also, lower-level requirements should have explanations describing why a requirement is traced to multiple higher-level requirements or not traced to one requirement. In the latter case, a requirement that is not derived from a higher-level requirement may indicate that it does not meet business objectives or it could indicate an undefined higher-level requirement [4]. On the other hand, if a requirement is linked to several requirements, changing it will probably have a major impact on the resulting system. Hence, such requirements must be carefully assessed and monitored. Following are some common problems that have been observed in requirements documents:

■ Derived requirements do not follow from their parents. Therefore, it is important to link derived requirements to higher-level requirements so that the derivation can be validated. For example, in one requirements document, "The system mass shall not exceed 7.25 kg, including thermal control hardware" was linked to the derived requirement, "The subsystem shall respond to its functional and hardware faults."

■ Requirements are not elaborated. For example, the requirement statement, "The system software shall provide time management services" was never refined to identify the specific services to be provided.

■ Derived requirements seem inconsistent with higher-level requirements. For example, the source requirement, "The latency of the subsystem measurement delivery to the system flight software shall not exceed 50 msec" seems to be violated by the derived requirement, "The subsystem shall deliver measurements to the system not to exceed a latency of 20 percent of a 500-msec system cycle."

To identify these problems, requirements engineers should answer the following questions:

■ Are all functions, structures, and constraints traced to requirements, and vice versa?
■ Have the requirements been allocated to functions of the system?
■ Do the requirements indicate whether they are imposed or derived?

■ Have the derived design goals and implementation constraints been specified and prioritized?
■ Is each requirement uniquely defined?

Practice 6.26. Do not exclude higher-level requirements. For example, consider the following requirement: "All subsystem flight software shall be integrated by the Flight Software subsystem team." This requirement was derived from "The system shall perform integration and testing on all delivered hardware and software." Hence, the lower-level requirement wrongfully eliminates the testing requirement.

Practice 6.27. Write requirements that are independent of each other. Each requirement should be understandable on its own. If not, one increases the likelihood that a requirement may be misinterpreted because a reader of the requirement may have forgotten information specified in another requirement. That is, requirements should have no coupling among one another, except to represent derivation relationships.

Practice 6.28. Fully specify all requirements. A requirements specification should be complete [2]. It must describe all functionality of a system, all real-world situations that a system will encounter and its responses to them, and the responses to all valid and invalid inputs. In addition, those situations not encountered should not be described [41]. Following are several kinds of requirements that should be specified in a requirements document:

■ Specify a nominal value, precision, accuracy, and allowable range for all data elements and inputs. This ensures that applications do not violate interface requirements. It also prevents invalid data that is out of range or beyond the representational capability of the selected hardware.
■ Specify the minimum and maximum times that a process or thread should wait before the first input. If a software system has not received input within a reasonable amount of time after start-up, it most likely has not properly initialized itself and it should take corrective action to repair itself or notify an operator of the problem [43]. Similarly, if the time of receipt occurs too soon after start-up, proper initialization may not have occurred.
■ Specify time-out conditions and contingency actions for all input and output streams. One contingency action that should generally be specified is the length of a time-out. For example, a program

can buffer inputs to prevent sending excessive outputs. This, however, could result in either a short- or long-term buffer overrun. That is, a system could receive a nearly instantaneous high number of inputs or it could receive a sustained and higher than expected input rate that causes the accumulation of inputs. If a system does not properly handle these situations, catastrophic failures can occur.

■ Specify the minimum and maximum expected execution times for time-dependent computations and contingency actions for their violation. If a computation uses less time than expected, a failure may have occurred. If a computation has taken longer than expected, then the system may be in a deadlock situation or the system may be waiting for input from a defective component, module, or external system. In either case, something may have gone wrong, and adherence to this guidance tends to improve system reliability and safety.

■ Specify the conditions where software systems can return to normal processing load after encountering an anomaly. Adherence to this guidance prevents a system from reentering an anomalous situation. After detecting a capacity violation, for example, the system should not begin normal processing too quickly because the circumstances that caused the capacity violation may still exist and cause the system to violate the capacity limitation once again. Note that adherence to this guidance implies the identification of all expected anomalies before design begins.

6.4 Practices for Validating Requirements

Requirements validation attempts to demonstrate that artifacts satisfy established criteria and standards. For requirements engineering, validation attempts to show that requirement statements adhere to the specification practices identified earlier.

Practice 6.29. Assess the quality of each requirement. The assessment should indicate each violation of the practices identified in this chapter, which identify numerous important criteria for analyzing a requirement [8, 41, 44]. Following are some of them:

■ Ambiguity: the requirement should permit only one interpretation.
■ Completeness: all conditions regarding the applicability of a requirement are stated.
■ Conciseness: the requirement is simply stated.
■ Consistency: the requirement does not conflict with another one.

- Correctness: the requirement accurately states a user need.
- Feasibility: the requirement can be achieved within the existing constraints.
- Necessity: the requirement is essential to meet real user needs.
- Priority: the requirement is ranked to reflect its relative importance.
- Readability: the requirement should be easy to read and based on simple words and sentences.
- Traceability: the source of the requirement is identified and it can be traced to higher-level requirements, functional test cases, and either a subsystem or other architectural design artifact.
- Uniqueness: the requirement does not duplicate another requirement.
- Verifiability: the requirement can be verified (for example, a test could demonstrate the proper implementation of a requirement).

In addition, a requirements specification should include a sign-off sheet that indicates that the defined requirements represent the best understanding of the problem, that the described system will satisfy the customer's needs, that future changes will be made using the project's defined change process, and that such changes may require a renegotiation of cost, resource, and schedule [7]. If the document specifies the requirements of a system that is being internally developed, then the project managers, lead requirements analysts, and the lead software quality assurance person should sign the document. If the document is being developed for an external customer, then two representatives of that customer, having the authority to sign off on the requirements document, should do so.

Practice 6.30. Validate the completeness of the defined requirements. There are two key methods of doing this. First, correlate system functions with operations that create, read, update, and delete data. This will help identify key functions that have not been specified [7]. For example, a program may create, read, and update a datum without deleting it, which may indicate a defect in the specification. Second, identify sequences of events that may occur where no requirement is specified [45–47]. At the system level, these events are specified in the system context diagram. To identify incompletely stated requirements, use the following algorithm, where E is defined to be the set of elements e_1, e_2, e_3, ... e_n:

```
compute-sequences(set E)
    set S = null
    for all elements, e, in E do
        insert e into S
    for l = 1 to n
        for all s in S of length l do
```

```
            identify the response to s
            identify existing requirements that
             define the response to s
            if no existing requirement defines a
                response to s
            then derive an appropriate response and
                   have it validated by stakeholders
            if an existing subsequence has an
                equivalent behavior to s
            then mark s so that it cannot be expanded
                   into a longer sequence
      if l < n
           for all elements, e, in E do
               if s is not illegal or equivalent to
                   another subsequence
               then insert (s concatenate e) into S
   if a requirement is not traced to any sequence
   then one or more events have been omitted
         (assuming the requirement is necessary)
```

By following this algorithm, one could create a table similar to the one shown in Table 6.5. Of course, this assumes that one has defined the following four requirements, of which one or more could have been derived after discovering their omission:

1. If the first received event is an e_2, then print "illegal input."
2. If the last event was previously in the event history, then remove the previous event.
3. If the event history has all three types of events, then process the event history.
4. If the event history does not include the last event, then add the event to the event history.

Finally, note that this could be represented by a finite state machine, where the transitions are annotated with the requirement traces.

Practice 6.31. Inspect requirements using a defined process. People should review software requirements following a defined procedure to validate that the requirements accurately reflect the needs of the stakeholders [3, 5, 48]. This defined procedure should include asking the questions contained in a checklist. The review process should proceed in six basic steps [4]. Although this review process will not catch all defects,

TABLE 6.5 Canonical Sequences, Behaviors, and Requirement Traces

Sequence	Response	Equivalence	Trace
e_1	null		Req. 4
e_2	fail		Req. 1
e_3	null		Req. 4
e_1e_1	replace	e_1	Req. 2
e_1e_2	null		Req. 4
e_1e_3	null		Req. 4
e_3e_1	null	e_1e_3	Req. 4
e_3e_2	null		Req. 4
e_3e_3	replace	e_3	Req. 2
$e_1e_2e_1$	remove3	e_1e_2	Req. 2
$e_1e_2e_2$	remove2	e_1e_2	Req. 2
$e_1e_2e_3$	process		Req. 3
$e_1e_3e_1$	remove3	e_1e_3	Req. 2
$e_1e_3e_2$	process		Req. 3
$e_1e_3e_3$	remove2	e_1e_3	Req. 2

developers usually have the knowledge to interpret most requirements correctly [18].

Step 1. Review for editorial content. Two people should perform this task. Afterward, the author should resolve all identified issues.

Step 2. Review for goodness:
■ Two people should review the requirements using the identified practices. The chief architect should be one of the reviewers because he or she is the one person who has an intellectual understanding of the entire software system. The chief architect understands the interactions of the system components and is responsible for maintaining the conceptual integrity of the entire system, which is vital to achieve system quality. The lack of such a person or the unavailability of such a person for an inspection is an indication that the development effort has problems.

- The reviewers should use a defect-based inspection technique when requirements are created, have significantly changed, or a change affects the next cycle of development or a pending development effort.
- The reviewers and project manager or team leader must resolve requirement issues and document each resolution. Afterward, the reviewers should examine the changed requirements.
- If significant change is needed or the quality objectives are not met, then the requirements should be reviewed a second time. In this case, use two different reviewers.

Step 3. Review for content. All stakeholders should perform this task [3]. Afterward, the author should resolve every issue and document each resolution.

Step 4. Review for appropriateness all selected reused and third-party software. Personnel with intimate knowledge of such software should be the ones to review it [18]. Each requirement issue should be documented and resolved.

Step 5. Review for risk. Two senior engineers and managers should perform this task.

Step 6. Review for editorial content. Two people should perform this task.

6.5 Practices for Managing the Definition of Requirements

There are a few important practices that managers must perform. They primarily involve planning, monitoring interactions among people, and tracking development progress.

Practice 6.32. Use bilateral agreements. This is to ensure a common understanding of the requirements and to control requirement creep. Such agreements should identify the responsibilities of both the customer and supplier [4].

Practice 6.33. Monitor the status of software requirements following a defined procedure. The status of each requirement should be available, as well as the change activity for each one. Further, summary data should be collected for the total number of changes that others have proposed, approved, and added to the software requirements.

Practice 6.34. Measure the number and severity of defects in the defined requirements. These metrics help identify the quality of the requirements engineering activity so that the organization can improve it [4].

Practice 6.35. Control how requirements are introduced, changed, and removed. The average project experiences about a 25 percent change in requirements after the requirements have been defined for the first system release, which causes at least a 25 percent schedule slip [49]. If requirement volatility does not gradually decrease afterward, the project is out of control and most likely will fail. In addition, several studies have shown that requirements volatility contributes to the inefficient production of low-quality software [19, 50]. Consequently, requirements should be managed using a defined configuration management process that uses change control boards and automated change control tools that manage each requirement as a separate configuration item [2, 13, 17, 51]. Using a configuration management tool permits personnel to identify which requirements have been added, removed, or changed since the last baseline; who has made these changes; when they were made; and the reason for making them. In addition, by maintaining requirements in a configuration management tool, they can be traced to the artifacts that realize them.

6.6 A Procedure for Engineering Requirements

Requirements definition is a discovery process involving problem analysis and understanding [2]. *Problem analysis* is the activity where the requirements engineer learns about the problem to be solved, the needs of the users, and the constraints on the problem solution. As such, requirements engineering involves cycles of building up followed by major reconstruction [52]. As requirements are acquired, analyzed, and added to the requirements model, its complexity grows. At critical points, however, the requirements model should be simplified and restructured to reflect a new perception of the requirements problem. Thus, requirements do change, and the process of defining requirements is naturally iterative and opportunistic [2, 3, 5, 14, 40, 44, 53]. The critical points where change occurs are a result of critical, unexpected insights.

Notice that this behavior differs from the conventional notion of how requirements are defined. This behavior results when people are trying to cope with complexity, of which there are three kinds: (1) essential, (2) incidental, and (3) accidental.

1. *Essential complexity* represents the intrinsic understanding of a problem as indicated by a model. This type of complexity grows over time as the problem solution becomes more fully developed.
2. *Incidental complexity* involves the complexity created by the representational form. It often results because of a poor fit between the structure of the model and the real world. Consequently, it becomes increasingly more difficult to refine and extend a model. However, at crisis points, one can restructure a model to significantly reduce incidental complexity.
3. *Accidental complexity* represents the hidden knowledge of a model that becomes explicit only during reconceptualization that occurs during model restructuring at crisis points. After restructuring, it becomes part of essential complexity.

Thus, requirements engineering is not systematic; instead, it is driven by insight, which differs from conventional engineering descriptions. Consequently, requirements engineers should use several iterations to define a system so that existing requirements can be corrected, elaborated, refined, or removed during any iteration. Once the requirements for a system are fairly stable, the subsystem requirements should be defined, while monitoring any changes to the system requirements. In addition, each team specifying the requirements of a subsystem must also monitor the requirement definition process of those subsystems that impact the subsystem it is defining.

During each iteration, the following idealized general procedure should be used to engineer requirements [4]:

Step 1. Scope the system by defining needs, goals, objectives, mission or business cases, high-level operational concepts, customer requirements, constraints, schedules, budgets, authorities, and responsibilities.

Step 2. Develop an operational concept that describes how the system behaves and is used throughout its life.

Step 3. Identify interfaces between a system and the outside world, and clarify its boundaries, inputs, and outputs.

Step 4. Write the requirements.

Step 5. Capture the rationale of each requirement and expose assumptions and incorrect facts.

Step 6. Prioritize the requirements.

Step 7. Assess the verification statement of each requirement, identifying the verification technique and needed facilities and equipment.

Step 8. Format requirements and supporting information so that requirements are easily found.

Step 9. Define requirements according to system and subsystem divisions, ensuring that requirements are allocated to the appropriate level and are traceable to higher-level requirements.

Step 10. Baseline requirements after they are validated.

Step 11. Iterate as necessary and as time permits.

The inputs to the requirements engineering process often include [2]:

■ Existing information describing the systems to be replaced or external systems that must interact with the system to be developed
■ Description of the needs of stakeholders
■ Organizational standards
■ External regulations
■ General information about the problem domain

The outputs of the requirements engineering process include [2]:

■ A description of the requirements that stakeholders understand and have agreed on
■ In some cases, a detailed specification of the system functionality
■ A set of models that describes the system from different perspectives

The key users of requirements include [2]:

■ Customers, who specify and inspect the requirements
■ Managers, who use the requirements to bid on a system development effort and plan the development process

- Software engineers, who use the requirements to understand what the system is
- Test engineers, who use the requirements to develop validation tests
- Maintenance engineers, who use the requirements to better understand the system and the interrelationships between the subsystems

6.7 Summary

This chapter primarily sought to identify numerous practices that can improve the engineering of requirements and provide a standardized procedure for defining them. The potential impact of implementing these practices can be the construction of stable, precise, unambiguous, and correct requirements that have the potential for significantly reducing project development costs, primarily by reducing the amount of work that must be redone. The key practices may be summarized briefly:

- Clearly state a need for developing a proposed system.
- Use stakeholders in the requirements engineering process, both to achieve a better understanding of the problem domain and to review the correctness of the proposed requirements. Vital stakeholders include the expected users of a system.
- Develop a concept of operations that will describe how people and systems will use the new system.
- Develop a domain model from the concept of operations that describes the problem domain.
- Specify the various types of nonfunctional requirements, such as security requirements, in addition to the functional requirements. All these requirements should be clearly, consistently, and precisely written.
- Identify the rationale, involved risk, and verification method for each requirement.
- Prioritize the requirements.

Following these practices and the identified procedure should yield a significant reduction in the number of defects that remain in requirements specifications and increase the satisfaction of the stakeholders of the developed software systems.

References

1. Robertson, S. and Robertson, J., *Mastering the Requirements Process*, Addison-Wesley, 1999.
2. Kotonya, G. and Sommerville, I., *Requirements Engineering: Processes and Techniques*, Wiley, 1998.
3. Hofmann, H.F. and Lehner, F., Requirements Engineering as a Success Factor in Software Projects, *IEEE Software*, 18(4), 58, 2001.
4. Hooks, I.F. and Farry, K.A., *Customer-Centered Products: Creating Successful Products through Smart Requirements Management*, AMACOM, 2001.
5. Christel, M.G. and Kang, K.C., Issues in Requirements Elicitation, Software Engineering Institute, Carnegie Mellon University, Technical Report CMU/SEI-92-TR-012, 1992.
6. Booch, G., Rumbaugh, J., and Jacobson, I., *The Unified Modeling Language User Guide*, Addison-Wesley, 1999.
7. Weigers, K.E., *Software Requirements*, Microsoft Press, 2003.
8. Young, R.R., *The Requirements Engineering Handbook*, Artech House, 2004.
9. Grünbacher, P. et al., Repeatable Quality Assurance Techniques for Requirements Negotiations, in *Proc. of the Hawaii Int. Conf. on System Sciences*, 2003, 23.
10. Vitalari, N.P. and Dickson, G.W., Problem Solving for Effective Systems Analysis: An Experimental Exploration, *Commun. of the ACM*, 26, 948, 1983.
11. Humphrey, W.S., *Managing Technical People: Innovation, Teamwork, and the Software Process*, Addison-Wesley, 1997.
12. Vosburgh, J.B., Wolverton, R., Albers, B., Malec, H., Hoben, S., and Liu, Y., Productivity Factors and Programming Environments, in *Proc. of the Int. Conf. on Software Engineering*, 1984, 143.
13. Zowghi, D. and Nurmuliani, N., A Study of the Impact of Requirements Volatility on Software Project Performance, in *Proc. of the Asia-Pacific Software Engineering Conf.*, 2002, 3.
14. Blum, B.I., *Beyond Programming: To a New Era of Design*, Oxford University Press, 1996.
15. Institute for Electrical and Electronics Engineers, IEEE Guide for Information Technology — System Definition — Concept of Operations (ConOps) Document, IEEE Computer Society, IEEE Std. 1362-1998, 1998.
16. Software Engineering Standards Committee, IEEE Recommended Practice for Software Requirements Specifications, The Institute of Electrical and Electronics Engineers, IEEE Std. 830-1998, 1998.
17. Potts, C., Takahashi, K., and Antón, A.I., Inquiry-Based Requirements Analysis, *IEEE Software*, 11, 21, March 1994.
18. Lauesen, S. and Vitner, O., Preventing Requirement Defects: An Experiment in Process Improvement, *Requirements Engineering*, 6, 37, 2001.
19. Curtis, B., Krasner, H., and Iscoe, N., A Field Study of the Software Design Process for Large Systems, *Commun. of the ACM*, 31, 1268, 1988.
20. Potts, C., Invented Requirements and Imagined Customers: Requirements Engineering for Off-the-Shelf Software, in *Proc. of the IEEE International Symp. on Requirements Engineering*, 1995, 128.

21. Stark, G., Skillicorn, A., and Smeele, R., A Micro and Macro Based Examination of the Effects of Requirements Changes on Aerospace Software Maintenance, in *Proc. of the IEEE Aerospace Conf.*, 4, 165, 1998.
22. Szyperski, C., *Component Software: Beyond Object-Oriented Programming*, Addison-Wesley, 1998.
23. Barbacci, M. et al., Quality Attributes, Software Engineering Institute, Carnegie Mellon University, Technical Report CMU/SEI-95-TR-021, 1995.
24. Barbacci, M.R., Klein, M.H., and Weinstock, C.B., Principles for Evaluating the Quality Attributes of a Software Architecture, Software Engineering Institute, Carnegie Mellon University, Technical Report CMU/SEI-96-TR-036, 1996.
25. Bass, L. and John, B.E., Linking Usability to Software Architecture Patterns through General Scenarios, *J. of Systems and Software*, 66, 187, 2003.
26. Folmer, E., van Gurp, J., and Bosch, J., A Framework for Capturing the Relationship between Usability and Software Architecture, *Software Process Improvement and Practice*, 8, 67, 2003.
27. Pardee, W.J., *To Satisfy and Delight Your Customer: How to Manage for Customer Value*, Dorset House, 1996.
28. Miller, G.A., The Magical Number Seven, Plus or Minus Two: Some limits on Our Capacity for Processing Information, *Psychological Review*, 63, 81, March 1956.
29. Curtis, B. et al., Software Psychology: The Need for an Interdisciplinary Program, *Proc. of the IEEE*, 74, 1092, 1986.
30. Robinson, W.N., Pawlowski, S.D., and Volkov, V., Requirements Interaction Management, *ACM Computing Surveys*, 35, 132, June 2003.
31. Sommerville, I. and Sawyer, P., *Requirements Engineering: A Good Practice Guide*, Wiley, 1997.
32. Daneva, M., Lessons Learnt from Five Years of Experience in ERP Requirements Engineering, in *Proc. of the IEEE Int. Requirements Engineering Conf.*, 2003, 45.
33. Gabriel, R.P., *Patterns of Software: Tales from the Software Community*, Oxford University Press, 1996.
34. Carmone, F.J., Kara, A., and Zanakis, S.H., A Monte Carlo Investigation of Incomplete Pairwise Comparison Matrices in AHP, *European J. of Operational Research*, 102, 538, 1997.
35. Harker, P.T., Incomplete Pairwise Comparison in the Analytic Hierarchy Process, *Mathematical Modelling*, 9, 837, 1987.
36. Harker, P.T., Alternative Modes of Questioning in the Analytic Hierarchy Process, *Mathematical Modelling*, 9, 353, 1987.
37. Karlsson, J., Software Requirements Prioritizing, in *Proc. of the Int. Conf. on Requirements Engineering*, 1996, 110.
38. Satay, T.L., *The Analytic Hierarchy Process*, McGraw-Hill, 1980.
39. Satay, T.L., Priority Setting in Complex Problems, *IEEE Trans. on Engineering Management*, EM-30, 140, 1983.
40. Potts, C. and Bruns, G., Recording the Reasons for Design Decisions, in *Proc. of the Int. Conf. on Software Engineering*, 1988, 418.

41. Wilson, W.M., Rosenberg, L.H., and Hyatt, L.E., Automated Analysis of Requirement Specifications, in *Proc. of the Int. Conf. on Software Engineering*, 1997, 161.
42. Glass, R.L., *Software Reliability Guidebook*, Prentice Hall, 1979.
43. Leveson, N.G., *Safeware: System Safety and Computers*, Addison-Wesley, 1995.
44. Shaw, M.L.G. and Gaines, B.R., Requirements Acquisition, *Software Engineering Journal*, 11, 149, May 1996.
45. Prowell, S.J. and Poore, J.H., Sequence-Based Specification of Deterministic Systems, *Software — Practice and Experience*, 28, 329, 1998.
46. Prowell, S.J. et al., *Cleanroom Software Engineering: Technology and Process*, Addison-Wesley, 1999.
47. Prowell, S.J. and Poore, J.H., Foundations of Sequence-Based Software Specification, *IEEE Trans. on Software Engineering*, 29, 417, 2003.
48. Chudge, J. and Fulton, D., Trust and Co-operation in System Development: Applying Responsibility Modelling to the Problem of Changing Requirements, *Software Engineering Journal*, 11, 193, May 1996.
49. Jones, C., *Assessment and Control of Software Risks*, Prentice Hall, 1994.
50. Gibbs, W.W., Software's Chronic Crisis, *Scientific American*, 271:3, 86, September 1994.
51. Crnkovic, I., Funk, P., and Larsson, M., Processing Requirements by Software Configuration Management, in *Proc. of the EUROMICRO Conference*, 2, 260, 1999.
52. Nguyen, L., Armarego, J., and Swatman, P.A., Understanding Requirements Engineering: A Challenge for Practice and Education, School of Management Information Systems, Deakin University, School Working Papers 2002/10, 2002.
53. Boehm, B. and Egyed, A., Software Requirements Negotiation: Some Lessons Learned, in *Proc. of the Int. Conf. on Software Engineering*, 1998, 503.

Chapter 7

Design

The design of software is different from other engineering design tasks because software is not bounded by physical structures or laws. Consequently, the demanded functionality of software, to a large extent, is constrained only by what one can imagine. This unboundedness generally increases the complexity of the software design task, as well as derived software systems. However, four fundamental principles help manage this complexity: (1) the use of abstraction, (2) the maximization of cohesion, (3) the minimization of coupling, and (4) the creation of systems that correspond to reality. From these principles, several valuable software development practices can be derived, which, when adopted, significantly improve the quality of software systems. In addition, several metrics can be created to objectively and quantitatively measure the quality of software. This chapter discusses these principles, practices, and metrics and attempts to show that they respond to limitations of human cognition. Finally, these principles, practices, and metrics are incorporated into recommended procedures for architectural and detailed design.

Design is the activity of creating a solution that satisfies a specific goal or need. Software design is a design task that is eventually realized as a program or collection of programs. A *software design* is an artifact that represents a solution, showing its main features and behavior, and is the basis for implementing a program or collection of programs. Software design is different from other forms of design because it is not constrained by physical objects, structures, or laws [1]. As a result, software design tends to be much more complex than other forms of design because it is conceptually unbounded, whereas the capabilities of the human mind are bounded.

Further complicating the design task are the following characteristics of software design [2–5]:

- Tasks are generally ill-defined and suffer from incomplete and inaccurate specifications.
- There is seldom a predefined solution, although many solutions tend to satisfy the defined task.
- Viable solutions usually require broad and interdisciplinary knowledge and skill, some of which is based on rapidly changing technology.
- Task solutions often involve many components that have numerous contingent interactions [6].

When designing software systems, expert designers use a mostly breadth-first approach because it allows them to mentally simulate the execution of an evolving system to detect unwanted interactions, inconsistencies, weaknesses, and incompleteness of their designs [4, 7]. It appears that unbalanced detail is only introduced when an expert designer already has mental models of what is being built [5, 8], which requires little cognitive effort to invoke to solve problems [4]. Thus, design is opportunistically driven by known solutions [3], which increases performance by allowing a user to dynamically shift goals and activities [9].

In addition, exceptional designers structure problem formulations by discovering missing information, such as problem goals and evaluation criteria, and resolving many open-ended constraints [2, 4]. Hence, the challenge of design necessitates the use of a methodical approach [10] based on key principles and practices [11] to effectively and efficiently produce quality software designs. However, designers must occasionally deviate from a defined method in response to newly acquired information or insights.

This chapter advocates that software design is efficiently and effectively performed when one understands a small number of important software principles, practices, and procedures. *Software design principles* identify strategic approaches to the production of quality software designs, whereas *software design practices* identify tactical methods for producing quality software designs. *Software design procedures*, on the other hand, provide an organizational framework for designing software. The goal of this chapter is to identify the principles, practices, and procedures that skilled software designers follow. However, this chapter does not advocate that there is only one way to design software. Hence, the variations of a software design task may require one to tailor a baseline design methodology.

7.1 Fundamental Principles of Design

As already stated, software design is complex because there are no physical constraints on software and humans have cognitive limitations that affect what they can understand [6]. In addition, Dijkstra hypothesizes [12] that "the only problems we can really solve in a satisfactory manner are those that finally admit a nicely factored solution." In other words, he implies that we can only efficiently and effectively implement solutions to problems that by their very nature have little incidental complexity. That is, developing solutions to problems for which we do not have good representations — those that naturally fit the problem — will always be challenging.

Regardless, design principles exist that largely reduce the incidental complexity of many problem solutions. Fundamental design principles include separating design concerns, modeling real-world objects, and minimizing the interactions among cohesive design components. When applying these design principles, one should:

1. Plan for change, because it is inevitable [1, 13–15].
2. Plan for failure, because no nontrivial software system is free of defects.
3. Adopt a core set of ideas for each system design, because they will improve their conceptual integrity [16].

7.1.1 Separation of Concerns

There are two ways to separate design concerns: (1) by viewing only the important aspects of a software system (i.e., abstraction) and (2) by delegating individual responsibilities to modules (i.e., modularity). *Abstraction* is the act or process of focusing on the important aspects of a phenomenon and ignoring what is unimportant. There may be many different abstractions of a phenomenon, each providing a smaller view of the phenomenon that serves a specific purpose. Abstraction is one of the most vital activities of a competent software engineer, the purpose of which is to create a new semantic level where one can be absolutely precise [12] and work with concepts appropriate for solving a particular problem [17]. In fact, abstraction is such an important concept that the largest single productivity gain made in software development resulted when programmers switched from machine language to higher-level (more abstract) programming languages [18]. Unfortunately, people can only understand a very small number of levels of abstraction at any given time, or within any given context [12].

There are two common types of abstraction: (1) one that views a specific aspect, or perspective, of a problem and (2) another that views a problem at different levels of granularity. The *levels of granularity* view permits abstraction to occur in three ways [17]:

1. *Procedural abstraction* collects and names a sequence of descriptions that specify a behavior.
2. *Data abstraction* collects and names several descriptions of data.
3. *Control abstraction* names a sequence of control descriptions that structure control flow.

Until recently, software engineers seldom viewed software systems from different perspectives, although it is a fundamental idea that has been practiced for years by people who build or rely on database and knowledge-based systems. The levels of granularity view, on the other hand, has been extensively discussed in the software engineering literature. Knuth, for example, stated [19] that "a talent for programming consists largely of the ability to switch readily from microscopic to macroscopic views of a thing, i.e., to change levels of abstraction fluently." Similarly, Brooks said [20]: "The programming process is one of constructing mappings from a problem domain, possibly through several intermediate domains, into the programming domain." Finally, Wirth, states [21] that "the creative activity of programming … is … a sequence of design decisions concerning the decomposition of tasks into subtasks and of data into data structures." Later, he calls this "stepwise decomposition and refinement" process *structured programming* [10]. In the same article, he emphasizes that stepwise refinement and recursion is the basis of all problem-solving.

Although the use of abstraction is a highly effectively form of managing complexity, it should be understood that knowledge cannot be strictly categorized within a single hierarchy or multiple disjoint hierarchies. To some extent these hierarchies are tangled [6], and the points at which the intersections occur across the hierarchies tend to create problems. Gunter et al. [22] allude to this when they say that "software systems are highly 'multidimensional,' but the different facets of a system have an overlaid or interleaved structure … [and] it is difficult to get a handle on elements that cut across the natural spatial boundaries of a system."

Modularity is a measure of the decomposition of a system into modules adhering to a standard unit of measure. The unit of measure that is normally proposed for decomposing a system is a single design decision, and decomposition normally ends when a module addresses a single responsibility not practical for further decomposition [23]. Hence, modularity permits:

- Concerns to be separated by handling the details of each module in isolation
- The relationships among modules to be handled at another time
- Systems to be built quicker because [17, 23–25]:
  - Separate groups can work on modules, in parallel, with little need for communication
  - Defects are easier to localize
  - Drastic changes can be made to one module without affecting others
  - Systems can be studied one module at a time

Parnas, however, said [23] that "the effectiveness of a 'modularization' is dependent upon the criteria used in dividing the system into modules." That is, modularization should only be done when the code can be meaningfully decomposed. This is because modularization tends to increase coupling [26].

7.1.2 Coupling and Cohesion

Cohesion is a measure of the relative functional strength of a module [17]. That is, cohesion relates the closeness of the activities of one component or a group of components with another. A highly cohesive set of components indicates that they are highly related to each other [27]. Ideally, a cohesive module should do only one thing [17]. *Coupling*, on the other hand, is a measure of the relative independence between modules [17, 28]. To define loosely coupled systems, each module should perform one responsibility and provide a cohesive set of services [27].

An important goal of design, then, is to achieve high cohesion and low coupling. By maximizing cohesion and minimizing coupling, software systems are easier to understand, modify, and reuse because all the information to understand or change a component resides with the component and improves the locality of reference [7, 25]. Cohesion and coupling have been shown to be predictive of defect rates [29, 30]. For example, in one experiment, functions with the highest coupling/cohesion ratios had seven times more defects than the functions with the lowest ratios [31].

There are seven types of coupling, which are ordered below from the weakest to the strongest form:

1. *Indirect coupling* typically occurs when one object interacts with another object through a third component, usually a controller. Another form of indirect coupling occurs when using a data-driven style of computation.
2. *Data coupling* occurs when simple data is passed among modules. When using data coupling, shorter parameter lists are preferred to longer ones [25, 27].
3. *Stamp coupling* occurs when a portion of a data structure is passed among modules. When using stamp coupling, a smaller number of actual arguments are preferable to a larger number [27] because the only data that should be passed to a module is what it requires. Thus, it may be constructive to create structures solely to pass data to modules, which would prevent the communication of unneeded data to called modules.
4. *Control coupling* occurs when information is passed to a module that affects its internal control. This is undesirable because it requires the calling module to know the internal operation of the module being called [25, 27].
5. *External coupling* occurs when a module depends on the external environment.
6. *Common coupling* occurs when modules access common areas of global or shared data [25]. This form of coupling can cause one module to unintentionally interfere with the operation of another module. This also means that to understand the global information source, one must also understand all the modules that manipulate the information contained in it.
7. *Content coupling* occurs when one module uses information contained in another module [27].

There are eight forms of cohesion, which are ordered from weakest to strongest below [28]:

1. *Coincidental cohesion* occurs when unrelated components of a system are bundled together.
2. *Logical cohesion* occurs when components performing similar functions are put together (e.g., error handling).
3. *Temporal cohesion* occurs when components that are activated at a single time or time span are put together.
4. *Procedural cohesion* occurs when the elements in a component form a single control sequence.
5. *Communicational cohesion* occurs when all elements of a component operate on the same input data, produce the same output data, or operate on one area of a data structure.

6. *Sequential cohesion* occurs when the output of one element in a component serves as input for another element.

7. *Functional cohesion* occurs when each part of a component is necessary for the execution of a single function.

8. *Object cohesion* occurs when the functions of a common class of objects are aggregated with the class. In this scheme, interfaces are specified to reveal as little as possible about the inner workings of the object [23]. Thus, object cohesion supports *information hiding* and *encapsulation*. Experience also suggests that approaches based on object cohesion are superior for crafting resilient architectures [13]. Modern object-oriented programming languages are based on object cohesion, although the use of class inheritance reduces cohesion [28]. Consequently, when using class inheritance, one should consider augmenting inheritance mechanisms with rules or conventions that help control the coupling associated with inheritance [32].

7.1.3 Conceptual Modeling

A *model* is a set of plans or a pattern for building something. It is a simplification of reality and can be used to express ideas at different levels of precision. Booch, Rumbaugh, and Jacobson [13] indicate that "we build models of complex systems because we cannot comprehend such a system in its entirety." Hence, we build models to communicate the desired structure and behavior of systems to customers, check system specifications, simulate systems and system components, and educate software personnel [33–35].

The choice of a model, however, significantly influences the way a problem is solved. The best models have been shown to be connected to reality because they are expressed in terms of the problem domain — those entities, relationships, and operations familiar to system users [8]. These models are generally called conceptual models because they model the concepts of the real world. Thus, when developing a system, the software engineer should model the important concepts of the problem domain in sufficient detail so that the problem can be easily solved. Neighbors has stated this in another way [36]:

> *"The basic tenet of good design is that a system architecture should follow the decomposition of the system function. This technique breaks down when we stop modeling the objects and operations of the problem domain and start using known Computer Science abstractions to model the problem."*

Reinforcing this view, Stevens, Myers, and Constantine [25] state that "one of the most useful techniques for reducing the effect of changes on

TABLE 7.1   Common Concept Types

Containers of things	Processes
Events	Records of contracts, finance, and
External systems	work
Manuals, books, and other	Roles of people
documents	Rules and policies
Organizations	Specifications, designs, or
Physical or tangible objects	descriptions of things
Places	Things in a container
	Transactions and transaction line
	items

the program is to make the structure of the design match the structure of the problem, that is, form should follow function." Consequently, concepts typically included in a conceptual model are the items in Table 7.1 [11]. In conclusion, because conceptual modeling is driven more by the problem domain than by knowledge of the design process or by knowledge of software, it makes conceptualization and comprehension of design tasks easier and is, therefore, more natural for designers to use [8].

7.2 Practices for Designing Architectures

An *architectural design practice* is a customary action that a software engineer repeatedly performs to proficiently derive quality architectural designs. Following are several architectural design practices that positively affect the quality of architectural designs.

Practice 7.1. Reduce large systems into modules realized by 5,000 to 10,000 lines of source code. For most programmers, productivity rates drop off sharply when modules grow much larger than this size. More specifically, for each tenfold increase in system size, programmer productivity decreases by roughly 40 percent [37]. Thus, if software architects successfully decompose an application that is 500,000 lines of source code into 100 components of 5,000 lines of source code, assuming no additional cost for partitioning, the productivity of the programming staff would increase by about 700 percent. Additionally, software engineering teams would increase their ability to adhere to schedules from about 37 to 86 percent [37]. Thus, developing architectures composed of the right-sized modules at the lowest level of a system architecture is vital to the success of a development effort. Five to ten thousand lines of code is about the right size because it has been shown that the defect rate introduced into software of this size is relatively low and tends not to decrease when decomposed into smaller modules [31, 37].

Practice 7.2. Use different views to convey different ideas. Each type of view serves different goals. Some of these views include the following:

■ A *deployment view* describes the allocation of processes to hardware.
■ A *decomposition view* describes the decompositions among components.
■ A *dependency view* describes the dependencies among components.
■ An *activity view* describes the concurrency and interaction among asynchronous processes.
■ A *sequence view* describes how one or more components interact.
■ A *state view* describes the state of computation for individual objects.

Practice 7.3. Separate control logic from the functions that provide services. Common ways to specify and implement control logic include the use of functions, production rules, and finite state machines. However, the implementation of controllers using table-driven deterministic finite state machines is the only one discussed in this chapter. When using finite state machines as a basis for system design, a system is composed as a collection of passive service providers invoked by one or more active controllers. There are three key benefits of this approach:

1. Software professionals can easily understand, validate, and modify a system's behavior when controllers are the only active components in a system.
2. Controllers operate very efficiently when implemented using a table-driven approach.
3. The behavior of controllers can be changed when using a table-driven approach without modifying code when the tables are stored in a file or database.

In sum, using table-driven deterministic finite state machines provides a very flexible and reliable means for controlling software [23]. Following are some guidelines for designing finite state machine models:

■ Define transitions for every possible input of every state.
■ Define transitions within each state to handle cases where a time-out occurs.
■ Ensure that every state is reachable from its start state.
■ Prevent the occurrence of failures when transitioning to a risk-reducing state.

- Define both soft and hard failure modes when transitioning to a risk-increasing state [38].
- Ensure that state diagrams consistently process shared events [35].
- Specify the granularity of events and states based on system needs [35].
- Ensure that systems distinguish between activities and actions [35].

Pattern 1: *Hierarchical Control.* The *Hierarchical Control architectural design pattern* attempts to reduce complexity using hierarchical control to organize system functions. Each layer of the hierarchy includes controllers that provide similar types of functions. Each controller makes autonomous decisions and provides services to and requests services from other controllers. Communication between controllers can be imperative (e.g., issuing a command) or reactive (e.g., monitoring an event). System controllers operate concurrently and may possess, create, and manage one or more independent threads of control. Figure 7.1 illustrates an instance of a hierarchical design pattern.

When using this pattern, controllers should adhere to the following rules:

- Two controllers at the same level should only communicate through their common shared ancestral controller.
- A client controller should imperatively send messages to server controllers.
- A server controller should answer a client controller by signaling an event.
- A single controller should be responsible for allocating resources of the same type.

Pattern 2: *Workflow Manager.* The *Workflow Manager architectural design pattern* consists of a Task Manager and the components that fulfill requirements of the overall process, as illustrated in Figure 7.2. The Task

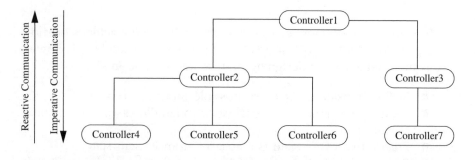

FIGURE 7.1   An illustration of a Hierarchical Control architectural design pattern.

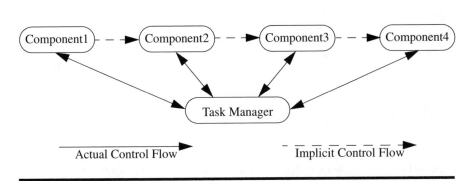

FIGURE 7.2   An illustration of a Workflow Manager architectural design pattern.

Manager provides the control facility for connecting each of the components involved in a workflow process. That is, it activates and sequences the components and exchanges data, as needed. The Task Manager contains a functional component profile, which is a collection of integration attributes for each component, and a task specifier, which defines the type of application and sequencing order. Together, they encapsulate the interactions of the workflow objects. In other words, a workflow manager is responsible for controlling and coordinating the interactions of a set of objects. It is an intermediary that receives messages from objects and forwards them to their intended recipients; thus, communication with a recipient is indirect and implicit. This approach prevents objects from explicitly referring to one another, which permits components to be easily added and removed from a system and their interactions to be changed. This pattern is often used when objects communicate with one another in complex ways or when a single behavior is realized by a collection of objects.

Pattern 3: *Event-Centered Architecture.* An *event* is something that has happened, is happening, or will happen. It is often an occurrence or observation of physical reality and represents an important change in the state of the world. A key aspect of a problem domain is its patterns of reoccurring events. Hence, one should structure systems around their responses to events. Doing so results in loosely coupled systems where no component has direct knowledge of another. This basic idea is called the *Event-Centered Architecture architectural design pattern*, which can be used to optimize the development and maintenance of entire families of software. Ideally, one should construct all members of a software family from the same reusable components that respond to the common set of reoccurring events of the problem domain. Architecturally, they should all be the same and only differ in their component mix or extensions. Thus, the common family architecture should consist of the essential

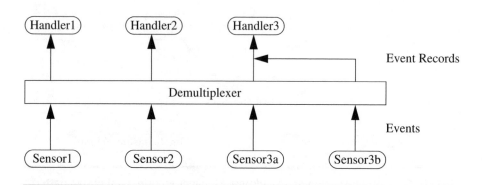

FIGURE 7.3   An illustration of an Event-Centered Architecture architectural design pattern.

components of a problem domain, subject to extension and specialization for a particular system.

There are three basic components of an event-centered architecture: (1) event sensors, (2) demultiplexers, and (3) handlers. An *event sensor* detects various source events. An *event demultiplexer* dispatches events to the proper event handlers, which process incoming events in a component-specific manner. To enable event processing, components must register with a central event dispatcher the event types they publish and subscribe. When an event sensor detects an incoming event, it sends it to the central event dispatcher. The central event dispatcher then compares it to the event types and dispatches it to the appropriate handlers, which process the event.

Event-driven applications using the Event-Centered Architecture architectural design pattern exhibit three basic characteristics. First, they asynchronously react to external events. Each event provides information to components of the modeled world. Second, since the system has no control over how events arrive, a controller orders the responses to them and detects illegal situations involving event arrival. Third, to overcome several limitations or constraints, controllers generally handle events very rapidly. Figure 7.3 illustrates an event-centered architecture.

Practice 7.4. Define and use common protocols for common operations. In general, common protocols reduce complexity by repeatedly using a core set of techniques for dealing with common kinds of problems, making it easier for software personnel to understand and develop systems. Several heuristics for defining object-oriented protocols follow [11]:

- Subclasses must adhere to the protocols of their superior classes [39].
- When one class contains or aggregates another, it should create, initialize, and destroy the contained or aggregated class.
- When one class contains the data used to initialize another class, it should create, initialize, and destroy the initialized class.
- When one class creates another one, it should initialize and destroy the used class.
- A controller class should handle the defined events of a problem domain relevant to a system. The class may represent an overall system, business, or organization, or an animate domain object that performs the work.
- Distribute the responsibility of a behavior that varies by class — using polymorphic operations — to each class. Such *divide-and-conquer* strategies reduce larger problems to smaller, more manageable ones.
- When member functions manipulate data, the data should belong to the class.
- When data is defined local to a class, the functions that manipulate it should also be local to the class.
- Assign a highly cohesive set of responsibilities for a group of classes to an artificial class to achieve low coupling and high cohesion. Similarly, assign a responsibility to an intermediate class to mediate between other classes or services. (See the description of Pattern 2.)

Some of these protocols can be generalized for non-objected-oriented representations, although these generalizations are not discussed because a desired practice is to model the real-world, which naturally fits with the object-oriented modeling paradigm.

Pattern 4: *Observer.* The intent of the *Observer architectural design pattern* is to define one-to-many dependencies between objects so that a change to one object triggers all its dependent objects, which allows them to react to object changes. The Observer architectural design pattern generally establishes these relationships using a publish-and-subscribe protocol.

A specific instance of this design pattern is the *Model-View-Controller pattern*, where a model represents the information of an application, a view visually represents the information, and the controller reacts to user input and internal events, effectively controlling the operation of the application. This means that the Model-View-Controller pattern encapsulates how the application responds to user input within the controller.

The benefit of this design pattern is that it decouples the representation and presentation of information from one another, as well as the processing of the information. Whenever the data of the model changes, the controller notifies the views containing the changed data. Thus, an application can associate multiple views to a model, each providing a different presentation of the same information.

Practice 7.5. Provide models of critical system-level concepts. Following are several useful concepts that should be modeled.

■ *Measurements.* The use of measurements ensures that applications do not violate interface requirements and prevents invalid data that is out of range or beyond the representational capability of the hardware [40]. Each measurement should specify the following attributes and functions:
  − The specific unit of measurement
  − A nominal value
  − The required precision
  − The required accuracy
  − A range of permissible assignments
  − A create function, which initializes the measurement
  − A release function, which frees the measurement for later reuse, if appropriate
  − A handle-exception function, which handles all exceptions that occur while executing a member function
  − Procedures for converting among measurements
■ *Clocks.* Clocks are often needed to schedule the start or end of an asynchronous activity. Each clock should specify the following attributes and functions:
  − An expiration time, which identifies when a clock should send an event to its listeners
  − A list of objects that desire to be notified when the clock expires
  − A create function, which synchronizes the clock and sets the initial expiration time
  − A release function, which frees the clock for later reuse, if appropriate
  − A handle-exception function, which handles all exceptions that occur while executing a member function
  − A synchronize function, which allows a clock to be synchronized with a master clock or some other time authority
  − A reset function, which allows a clock to reset its expiration time to some time in the future
■ *Data queues.* Using a data queue to store all sensor and user input provides a simple way to determine if information is unused, which

may be indicative of a requirement omission or a design defect. Each data queue should specify the following:

- A storage area
- The size of the storage area
- A `create` function, which initializes a data queue to be empty
- A `release` function, which frees the data queue for later reuse, if appropriate
- A `handle-exception` function, which handles all exceptions that occur while executing a member function (an important exception to handle is when a queue becomes full)
- `Enqueue` and `dequeue` functions, having the conventional meanings

▪ *Events*. Events represent the real-time, dynamic situations that occur during system execution and within the real world. An event should specify the following:

- The type of event
- The important attributes of an event
- Functions to access and manipulate the attributes of an event
- A `create` function, which, at a minimum, synchronizes a thread with the external world
- A `release` function, which frees the data queue for later reuse, if appropriate
- A `handle-exception` function, which handles all exceptions that occur while executing a member function

▪ *Threads*. Threads permit asynchronous processing to occur. Each thread, at start-up, must validate it has enough resources to start. In addition, there must be a health-monitoring thread that monitors the health of the other threads. A thread should specify the following:

- An indication of the actual process state, which is updated at start-up, after being resumed, and periodically thereafter
- A minimum time that a thread should wait before receiving its first input
- A maximum time that a thread should wait before receiving its first input
- A `create` function, which, at a minimum, synchronizes a thread with the external world
- A `release` function, which frees the data queue for later reuse, if appropriate
- A `handle-exception` function, which handles all exceptions that occur while executing a member function
- A `suspend` function, which temporarily halts the execution of a thread

- A resume function, which synchronizes the thread with the external world and resumes itself
- A terminate function, which permanently halts the execution of a thread
- A synchronize function, which synchronizes the internal model with the external world
- An execute function, which is the function that a thread executes

There are two special cases where threads should be used:
- To model critical operations, including atomic transactions
- To model input, output, and other event handlers

In general, a thread should be used for each critical operation or event handler. Alternatively, one could assign a thread to handle a class of critical operations or event handlers [41].

Critical operations should specify the following attributes:
- A minimum expected execution time
- A maximum expected execution time

Similarly, input, output, and other event handlers should specify the following attributes:
- A minimum expected arrival time
- A maximum expected arrival time
- A minimum valid value
- A maximum valid value

During processing, errors may occur. Common ways to handle such defects include:
- Record the error and isolate its source.
- Reduce the functionality of a software system.
- Change the operational behavior of a system. For example, use faster algorithms but with reduced accuracy.
- Halt or suspend a process or thread.

7.3 Practices for Adding Detailed Design Information

A *detailed design practice* is a custom that software engineers should repeatedly apply to satisfy fundamental design principles. Several such practices follow that positively affect software quality.

Practice 7.6. Use functions to encapsulate individual behaviors. That is, functions should hide implementation specifics from the rest of the code and each function should perform a cohesive set of operations fulfilling one purpose. Adoption of this practice contributes to improved quality and helps create programs that can easily monitor data access and evoke data-driven processing. Three specific instances of this practice are:

1. Isolate complex operations to a single routine.
2. Isolate the use of nonstandard language functions, which reduces the portability of code.
3. Isolate external code to individual routines [35].

Practice 7.7. Minimize the use of goto *statements.* In 1968, Dijkstra observed that program quality is inversely correlated with the density of goto statements [42]. His basic argument against the use of goto statements is that programmers use goto statements in an undisciplined manner. That is, they use them to jump into the middle of loops and to arbitrary locations in outer loops. In 1974, Knuth observed that goto statements are useful as long as their use is controlled [19]. He also said that the use of the goto statement often improves performance and sometimes more naturally allows the expression of an algorithm. His actual statement was [19], "we [Knuth and Floyd] found that there was no way to implement certain simple constructions with while and conditional statements substituted for goto's, unless extra computation was specified." Later, this statement was formally proven [43]. Knuth, however, never advocated the undisciplined use of the goto statement, because such use can dramatically increase the complexity of programs. He primarily advocated their use as a mechanism to exit an inner or outer loop, continue to the next loop iteration, or exit a function. The use of break and continue statements in many programming languages today satisfies most of these needs, but not all of them.

Thus, the controlled and systematic use of goto statements is appropriate as long as the rules governing their use are documented and do not reduce the ability of programmers to understand a program [19]. The following function, for instance, illustrates the controlled use of the goto statement:

```
boolean contains_negative?(double** a, int m, int n) {
    boolean r = false;
    for (int i = 0; i < n; i++)
        for (int j = 0; j < m; j++)
            if (a[i][j] < 0.0) {
                r = true;
                goto 1;
            }
1:  return r;
}
```

This function is probably the simplest and most easily understood algorithm for determining whether a matrix contains a negative number. Contrarily, an equivalent function that does not use a `goto` statement follows. Most people would consider this more difficult to understand, and certainly less efficient.

```
boolean contains_negative?(double** a, int m, int n) {
    boolean r = false;
    int i = 0, j = 0;
    while (!r && (i < n)) {
        if (a [i][j] < 0.0)
            r = true;
        if (j < m - 1)
            j++;
        else {
            j = 0;
            i++;
        }
    }
    return r;
}
```

Practice 7.8. Use program structuring techniques that optimize locality of reference. That is, it is always preferable to have data definitions be as close as possible to the statements that initialize and use them [44]. Therefore, it is preferable to define variables of a function in the innermost block of their use. For example, of the following two code fragments, the first one is preferable to the second because the first one localizes the initialization, test, and alteration of the variable, i, to a single block, whereas the second code fragment declares and initializes the variable in an outer block and uses it in an inner block.

```
for (int i = 0; i < n; i++) {
}
```

```
int i = 0;
... potentially lots of code ...
while (i < n) {
    i++;
}
```

Similarly, if one uses an object-oriented programming language, it is preferable to use class variables (or data members) instead of file or global variables. Likewise, it is better to use file variables instead of global variables because the existence of global data permits any part of a program to interact with or alter the behavior of any other program component through operations on the same data [45]. Moreover, the use of a few global variables dramatically increases the complexity of a program by increasing its coupling, which significantly reduces the ability of people to understand it. However, when global variables are needed, access to them should be encapsulated, as Practice 7.6 indicates, and protected from concurrent access using functions [39]. In conclusion, the benefits of this practice are simpler, easier to understand programs that have fewer defects.

Practice 7.9. Avoid creating and using redundant data. The problem with using redundant data is that a program must consistently maintain it. Unfortunately, it is easy for programmers to overlook this fact. However, the use of redundant data is often necessary to meet the performance requirements of a system. In these cases, programmers should use well-defined protocols (see Practice 7.4) for maintaining the consistency among the redundant data [39].

7.4 Practices Affecting the Design Process

Several process practices affect software designs. This section discusses several such practices that positively affect the quality of a software design.

Practice 7.10. Design and implement features that only satisfy the needed requirements. Because adding unneeded features to a system increases its complexity and are often sources of error [46], a software engineering team should be able to trace every major feature in a delivered software system back to a specific requirement. In addition, this tactic helps identify requirements that the application does not satisfy.

Practice 7.11. Periodically analyze and simplify software systems. As programmers repair defects, add new capabilities, and remove or change existing ones, the design of a software system can evolve into a state that is difficult to maintain [47]. Thus, people should periodically analyze designs and, if necessary, simplify them. Three heuristics for identifying when to improve a software system follow:

1. If it takes more time to understand a design than to design it, then redesign it.
2. If it takes more time to understand an implementation than to reimplement it, then reimplement it.

3. If an implementation has ten or more defects per thousand lines of code [48], then consider redesigning it before reimplementing it. This is because the probability of detecting a defect in a module is proportional to the number of defects already found in it [49]. In general, 20 percent of the modules of a software system account for 80 percent of the defects [50]. In extreme cases, less than 5 percent of code can account for more than 45 percent of the defects [51].

Practice 7.12. Create prototypes of critical components to reduce risk. Several reasons for prototyping follow:

1. It ensures that the users of a system will accept it. Thus, the purpose of a prototype is to acquire user comments about operational aspects of a system, including workflow and user interaction.
2. It identifies the difficult aspects of a system and potential methods for overcoming them.
3. It identifies missing requirements. The process of actually building a prototype and observing how it works encourages people to ask new and different types of questions, which only become evident when they actually see a system operate.
4. It permits the testing of alternative designs. For example, the performance characteristics of two designs can be compared.

Because the sole purpose of a prototype is to validate a prior decision or design, the software engineering team can ignore its defined software development processes. If so, software engineers seldom can cost-effectively scale such a prototype into a workable solution.

Practice 7.13. Use a notation having precise semantics to describe software artifacts. The key purpose of a design effort is to communicate a design to others — developers, testers, and customers — so that they will better understand how it is supposed to function. Using a precisely defined notation improves this communication. Unfortunately, there is no empirical evidence that indicates one specific notation is better than another one, although people do generally agree that formality lessens the ambiguity and vagueness of defined requirements.

Organizations currently use a number of notations, many of which are included in the Unified Modeling Language [13]. Following are three general heuristics about using graphical notations:

1. Create an activity diagram to model the behavior of interacting, concurrent activities.
2. Create a sequence diagram to model the behavior of interacting objects of a single activity.
3. Construct a state diagram to describe the dynamic behavior of an object.

Practice 7.14. Define and use criteria and weightings for evaluating software design decisions. Such criteria should consider the qualities described in Section 1.1. Using the relative merit of these criteria, designers can objectively estimate the quality of the final product, as well as intermediate artifacts and alternatives to them. However, a designer should defer making decisions as long as possible because he will continuously increase his understanding of the problem domain and the design activity, which will enable him to make better decisions and create better designs [52].

Practice 7.15. Record the rationale for each design decision. Although it is possible to capture the chain of reasoning that went into making a decision, examining the rationale — a summary statement of the chain of reasoning — is generally sufficient for others to understand the reasoning that underlies a design decision. However, once people review a design decision, they may desire to challenge or substantiate it, which means they should be able to add both supportive and contradictory evidence for a design decision or its rationale. In addition, people should be able to recommend alternatives to a design decision. Thus, it is essential that a record of the rationales of a design decision be maintained, as well as annotations to them [6]. Unfortunately, no integrated development environment provides a capability to capture design options and decisions or the rationale for choosing one option over another, although there are numerous formal decision management techniques that have been applied in other industries and significant research has been conducted in design rationalization [53–56].

Practice 7.16. Compute key design metrics. Several people have defined various metrics over the years that measure functional [57, 58] and object [59] complexity. Several others have attempted to identify which of these metrics are superior to others and how they correlate with one another [44]. The results indicate that some of these metrics are highly predictive measures of component quality. Some of these metrics include the following [17, 26, 58, 60]:

- A function should call, at most, nine other functions.
- A function should have, at most, five formal arguments.
- The depth of a class hierarchy should be less than seven.
- The depth of iteration statements should be less than five.
- The number of primitive branches in a function or module should be ten or less, assuming multi-way branch statements count as one primitive branch.

One complexity model relates the cognitive complexity of an artifact (c_p) to its internal complexity (c_i) and the internal complexity (c_j) of the functions it calls $(f(p))$ [61]. Equation 7.1 illustrates this relationship:

$$c_p = c_i + \frac{2}{3} \sum_{j \in f(p)} c_j \qquad (7.1)$$

It is important to note that all these measures reflect on the limitations of the human mind. Consider that people store information in their short-term memory as *information chunks*, whereby each information chunk is a collection of concepts that have strong associations with one another and much weaker associations with other concepts. Also consider that people can remember five to nine chunks of information in short-term memory, which corresponds to virtually every complexity measure that is predictive of defects [62]. The current consensus, however, is that this represents a compound capacity limit, which reflects a certain reasonable degree of chunking. Others have since suggested that a more precise capacity limit is only three to five chunks, which appears to be more accurate because extensive data supports this conclusion [63].

7.5 A Unified Framework for System Architectures

In 1969, Dijkstra indicated the importance for planning the development of families of programs when he said the following [64].

> *"Any large program will exist during its life-time in a multitude of different versions, so that in composing a large program we are not so much concerned with a single program, but with a whole family of related programs, containing alternative programs for the same job and/or similar programs for similar jobs. A program therefore should be conceived and understood as a member of a family; it should be so structured out of components that various members of this family, sharing components, do not only share the correctness demonstration of the shared components but also of the shared substructure."*

Today, this idea is called a software component framework. A *software component framework* is a dedicated and focused software architecture that uses a small and fixed set of important mechanisms, protocols, and policies that connect participating components of the framework [32]. A *software component* is a unit of composition with contractually specified *interfaces* and explicit context dependencies. A software component framework, then, is a reusable design and partial implementation of a common class of applications. A framework shares many characteristics of a library although it differs in a few important ways.

- A framework provides integrated functionality for a specific problem domain. Because a framework closely models a specific problem domain, its reusability is significantly larger than with a library.
- A framework provides a collaborative infrastructure. That is, the framework determines which methods to invoke in response to system events. An application developed with a library, on the other hand, invokes methods within the library.
- A framework provides an incomplete, but working application. Programmers develop applications by instantiating and specializing existing framework components, which provide default behaviors.

Thus, a framework constrains the architecture of a system by defining the overall system structure, including classes, class responsibilities, object collaboration, and system control. In conclusion, software component frameworks:

- Encourage reuse and enhance reliability because of known component limitations and failure modes [36]
- Create a common language for discussing future needs and extensions to components and component frameworks
- Help overcome omissions in nonfunctional requirements because a software component framework should have already considered such issues

The features of the framework that I now propose include the following, which share the characteristics of a *blackboard system architecture* [65, 66] and Patterns 1 through 4:

- Information is partitioned into independent processing elements, which may be transformed from one level to another using strategies involving procedures, finite state machines, and rule-based systems. Transformation between levels is opportunistic and can be done in a bottom-up (data-driven) or top-down (goal-driven) fashion.

- Processing elements communicate with one another by adding events to event queues. A processing element can only communicate with processing elements that are its parents or children.
- Interfaces describe the attributes and behaviors of concepts, as well as the input and output specifications for each behavior. Classes, on the other hand, provide realizations of these interfaces.
- Relations are defined as first-class objects within memory models.

Figure 7.4 illustrates a processing element of this framework. It shows that a processing element is composed from several types of artifacts. These artifacts comprise an event queue, memory, a controller, and several components. Each component of a processing element provides one or more services. The controller invokes these services to satisfy its objectives. Some of these objectives may be in response to the needs of other processing elements. In this case, other processing elements post events in the event queue of the processing element, which the controller processes according to its scheduling algorithm. Hence, all processing by a processing element is completely controlled by a controller, with the exception that the event queue has a public interface that other processing elements can invoke to add events to an event queue. In addition, because the processing elements operate asynchronously, the access to the data queue is synchronized. Memory, on the other hand, is updated only by the controller of a processing element and represents all information known by the processing element. Memory can represent the current state or can represent the current state and the history of states, depending on the memory model that is used. Similarly, memory may or may not be

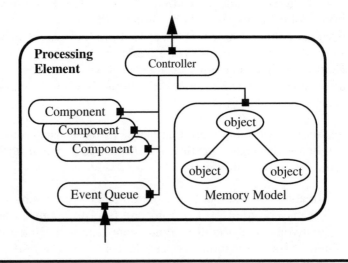

FIGURE 7.4   An illustration of a processing element.

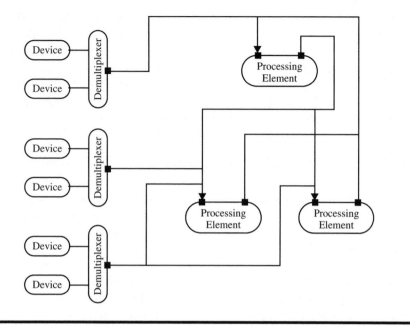

FIGURE 7.5   An illustration of the unified framework for system architectures.

transaction oriented. Items contained in memory are represented as collections of interrelated objects. These relationships are represented as objects themselves.

Figure 7.5 illustrates the framework. It shows two levels of a processing network. The top-level processing element can modify the data queues of the two lower-level processing elements that, in turn, can modify the data queue of the top-level processing element. Thus, asynchronous, bi-directional communication among any two processing elements is possible. Similarly, several demultiplexers can place events in the event queue of each processing element, as long as each demultiplexer adheres to the processing element's interface specification, which specifies what kinds of events can be posted on an event queue. These events are created in response to raw events produced by external devices. Thus, each demultiplexer maintains a registry of processing elements that have subscribed to the events that they provide. In conclusion, this architecture reduces the number of problems that arise from the use of shared memory and concurrent processing.

7.6 A Procedure for Designing Software

Mills originally proposed the Chief Programmer Team as an approach to software development in the mid-1970s. The *Chief Programmer Team* is a highly functional team where the chief programmer designs a system, specifies all subsystems, and codes its critical components. This approach proved to work well for projects whose size is a maximum of about 100,000 source lines of code and for small groups of six to nine people [67].

Following is a proposed approach for designing software called the *Chief Architect Team*. It is similar to the Chief Programmer Team approach and another approach proposed by Gomaa in 1986 [67]. This approach is based on the insight that using a small number of designers to decompose a large system into right-sized modules increases its conceptual integrity; increases the productivity of the personnel designing it, as well as the whole team; and increases schedule predictability [16]. This insight is based on the observation that the best software engineers are one to two orders of magnitude better than the worst ones. Consequently, an organization should use its best software engineers to decompose systems into small modules with well-defined interfaces.

In this approach, the chief architect concentrates on designing and validating the overall system architecture. This implies that the chief architect defines the interfaces of all subsystems and simulates their behaviors by executing all applicable functional test cases by defining stubs for each module that respond appropriately to each input. Using this approach, the system architecture can be completely validated before the entire design is completed, which is contrary to current practice.

In a like manner, the design and implementation of each subsystem is performed by its own development team that has a subsystem architect that performs the same function as the chief architect, but of narrower scope at the subsystem level. Continuity between the system design and the subsystem designs is ensured by including the subsystem architects in the system design team and through reviews of the system design. Although the chief architect may suggest how to design subsystems, subsystem designs are the responsibility of the subsystem architects. Thus, any design that satisfies a subsystem specification is acceptable.

The process of decomposing a system may continue through many levels of detail, although more than five would most likely be incomprehensible, until the lowest-level of composition is estimated to be 5,000 to 10,000 lines of source code. Once units have been decomposed to this estimated level of detail, their implementation can be assigned to other members of the team. Although these programmers may be less talented or less experienced than the architects, the constraints of the prior design tasks minimize the impact of any differences in individual programming skill. In addition, productivity is further increased in two ways. First, because architects decompose systems into modules with well-defined interfaces, communication among project personnel is significantly reduced. Second, because interface defects have been eliminated by the simulation of the architecture, all defects experienced by a programmer should be local to the module he or she is developing. In conclusion, the Chief Architect Team proposes the continuous design, decomposition, and verification of a system as it evolves.

7.7 Summary

Design, by its very nature, is challenging; software design even more so because the artifacts being designed are conceptual rather than objects of the real world. To overcome the challenge of software design, several core practices should be followed. First, architects should decompose software systems into small modules that manipulate models of the problem domain. Such modeling helps create natural system boundaries that reduce module coupling and increase module cohesion. Second, architects should define strict behavioral interfaces for every module of the system that separate internal control logic from the specification of the provided services. These specifications should provide detailed descriptions of the formal parameters, return values, pre- and post-conditions, and possible error conditions of each function provided by each interface, as well as the underlying assumptions of each interface. Third, models of critical concepts of an application domain should be provided to developers through a common software component framework. One general-purpose, high-level architecture was proposed. Fourth, architects should create appropriately sized specifications. Such specifications should include a description of the entire decomposition of the system into its various components and the interactions among the modules. Such specifications should be produced and verified following the Chief Architecture Team approach to design.

References

1. Parnas, D.L., Designing Software for Ease of Extension and Contraction, *IEEE Trans. on Software Engineering*, SE-5, 128, 1979.
2. Curtis, B., Krasner, H., and Iscoe, N., A Field Study of the Software Design Process for Large Systems, *Commun. of the ACM*, 31, 1268, 1988.
3. Goel, V. and Pirolli, P., The Structure of Design Problem Spaces, *Cognitive Science*, 16, 395, 1992.
4. Guindon, R., Designing the Design Process: Exploiting Opportunistic Thoughts, *Human–Computer Interaction*, 5, 305, 1990.
5. Vitalari, N.P. and Dickson, G.W., Problem Solving for Effective Systems Analysis: An Experimental Exploration, *Commun. of the ACM*, 26, 948, 1983.

6. Shrobe, H.E., Dependency Directed Reasoning for Complex Program Understanding, Artificial Intelligence Laboratory, Massachusetts Institute of Technology, Technical Report 503, 1979.
7. Curtis, B. et al., Software Psychology: The Need for an Interdisciplinary Program, *Proc. of the IEEE*, 74, 1092, 1986.
8. Rosson, M.B. and Alpert, S.R., The Cognitive Consequences of Object-Oriented Design, *Human–Computer Interaction*, 5, 345, 1990.
9. Thomas, J.C. and Carroll, J.M., The psychological study of design, IBM T. J. Watson Research Center, Research Report RC7695, 1979.
10. Wirth, N., On the Composition of Well-Structured Programs, *ACM Computing Surveys*, 6, 247, 1974.
11. Larman, C., *Applying UML and Patterns: An Introduction to Object-Oriented Analysis and Design*, Prentice Hall, 1998.
12. Dijkstra, E.W., The Humble Programmer, *Commun. of the ACM*, 15, 859, 1972.
13. Booch, G., Rumbaugh, J., and Jacobson, I., *The Unified Modeling Language User Guide*, Addison-Wesley, 1999.
14. Gabriel, R.P., *Patterns of Software: Tales from the Software Community*, Oxford University Press, 1996.
15. Martin, R.C., *Agile Software Development: Principles, Patterns, and Practices*, Prentice Hall, 2003.
16. Brooks, F.P. Jr., *The Mythical Man-Month: Essays on Software Engineering Anniversary Edition*, Addison-Wesley, 1995.
17. Pressman, R.S., *Software Engineering: A Practitioner's Approach*, McGraw-Hill, 1992.
18. Brooks, F.P., Jr., No Silver Bullet: Essence and Accidents of Software Engineering, *IEEE Computer*, 20, 10, 1987.
19. Knuth, D.E., Structured Programming with *go to* Statements, *ACM Computing Surveys*, 6, 261, 1974.
20. Brooks, R., Towards a Theory of the Comprehension of Computer Programs, *Int. J. of Man–Machine Studies*, 18, 543, 1983.
21. Wirth, N., Program Development by Stepwise Refinement, *Commun. of the ACM*, 14, 221, 1971.
22. Gunter, C., Mitchell, J., and Notkin, D., Strategic Directions in Software Engineering and Programming Languages, *ACM Computing Surveys*, 28, 727, 1996.
23. Parnas, D.L., On the Criteria to Be Used in Decomposing Systems into Modules, *Commun. of the ACM*, 15, 1053, 1971.
24. Ghezzi, C., Jazayeri, M., and Mandrioli, D., *Fundamentals of Software Engineering*, Prentice Hall, 1991.
25. Stevens, W., Myers, G., and Constantine, L., Structured Design, *IBM Systems Journal*, 13, 115, 1974.
26. Beizer, B., *Software Testing Techniques*, Van Nostrand Reinhold, 1990.
27. Hohmann, L., *Journey of the Software Professional: A Sociology of Software Development*, Prentice Hall, 1997.
28. Sommerville, I., *Software Engineering*, Addison-Wesley, 1992.
29. Shneiderman, B., *Software Psychology*, Little-Brown, 1980.

30. Succi, G. et al., Practical Assessment of the Models for Identification of Defect-Prone Classes in Object-Oriented Commercial Systems Using Design Metrics, *J. of Systems and Software*, 65, 1, 2003.

31. Selby, R.W. and Basili, V.R., Analyzing Error-Prone System Structure, *IEEE Trans. on Software Engineering*, 17, 141, 1991.

32. Szyperski, C., *Component Software: Beyond Object-Oriented Programming*, Addison-Wesley, 1998.

33. Blum, B.I., *Beyond Programming: To a New Era of Design*, Oxford University Press, 1996.

34. Kang, K.C. et al., Feature-Oriented Domain Analysis (FODA) Feasibility Study, Software Engineering Institute, Carnegie Mellon University, Technical Report CMU/SEI-90-TR-21, 1990.

35. Rumbaugh, J. et al., *Object-Oriented Modeling and Design*, Prentice Hall, 1991.

36. Neighbors, J.M., The Evolution from Software Components to Domain Analysis, *Int. J. of Software Engineering and Knowledge Engineering*, 2, 325, 1992.

37. Jones, C., *Software Assessments, Benchmarks, and Best Practices*, Addison-Wesley, 2000.

38. Leveson, N.G., *Safeware: System Safety and Computers*, Addison-Wesley, 1995.

39. Hunt, A. and Thomas, D., *The Pragmatic Programmer*, Addison-Wesley, 2000.

40. Karr, M. and Loveman, D.B., Incorporation of Units into Programming Languages, *Commun. of the ACM*, 21, 385, 1978.

41. Shumate, K. and Keller, M., *Software Specification and Design: A Disciplined Approach for Real-Time Systems*, Wiley, 1992.

42. Dijkstra, E.W., Go To Statement Considered Harmful, *Commun. of the ACM*, 11, 147, 1968.

43. Lipton, R.J., Eisenstadt, S.C., and DeMillo, R.A., The Complexity of Control Structures and Data Structures, in *Proc. of the ACM Symp. on the Theory of Computing*, 7, 1975, 186.

44. Nikora, A. and Munson, J., Determining Fault Insertion Rates for Evolving Software Systems, in *Proc. of the Int. Symp. on Software Reliability Engineering*, 1998.

45. Wulf, W. and Shaw, M., Global Variables Considered Harmful, *SIGPLAN Notices*, 8, 28, February 1973.

46. Wirth, N., A Plea for Lean Software, *IEEE Computer*, 28, 64, 1995.

47. Winograd, T., Beyond Programming Languages, *Commun. of the ACM*, 22, 391, 1979.

48. McConnell, S., *Rapid Development: Taming Wild Software Schedules*, Microsoft Press, 1996.

49. Fenton, N.E. and Ohlsson, N., Quantitative Analysis of Faults and Failures in a Complex Software System, *IEEE Trans. on Software Engineering*, 26, 797, 2000.

50. Weinberg, G.M., *Quality Software Management: Systems Thinking*, Dorset House, 1992.

51. Myers, G.J., *The Art of Software Testing*, Wiley, 1979.
52. Paulk, M.C. et al., *The Capability Maturity Model: Guidelines for Improving the Software Process*, Addison-Wesley, 1994.
53. Freeman, P. and Newell, A., A Model for Functional Reasoning in Design, in *Proc. of the Int. Joint Conf. on Artificial Intelligence*, 1971.
54. Kandt, R.K., Pegasus: A Software Design Tool, in *Proc. of the Hawaii Int. Conf. on System Sciences*, 2, 650, 1985.
55. Kandt, R.K., A Tool to Support Competitive Argumentation, *J. of Management Information Systems*, 3, 54, Spring 1987.
56. Moran, T.P. and Carroll, J.M., *Design Rationale: Concepts, Techniques, and Use*, Lawrence Erlbaum, 1996.
57. Halstead, M.H., *Elements of Software Science*, Elsevier North-Holland, 1977.
58. McCabe, T.J., A Complexity Measure, *IEEE Trans. on Software Engineering*, SE-2, 308, 1976.
59. Henderson-Sellers, B., *Object-Oriented Metrics: Measures of Complexity*, Prentice Hall, 1995.
60. Fairley, R., *Software Engineering Concepts*, McGraw-Hill, 1985.
61. Davis, J.S., Chunks: A Basis for Complexity Measurement, *Information Processing and Management*, 20(12), 119, 1984.
62. Miller, G.A., The Magical Number Seven, Plus or Minus Two: Some Limits on Our Capacity for Processing Information, *Psychological Review*, 63, 81, March 1956.
63. Cowan, N., The Magical Number 4 in Short-Term Memory: A Reconsideration of Mental Storage Capacity, *Behavioral and Brain Sciences*, 24, 87, 2001.
64. Dijkstra, E., Structured Programming, in *Classics in Software Engineering*, Yourdon, E.N. (Ed.), Yourdon Press, 1979, 43.
65. Nii, H.P., Blackboard Systems, Knowledge Systems Laboratory, Stanford University, Report No. KSL 86-18, 1986.
66. Hayes-Roth, B. et al., A Domain-Specific Software Architecture for Adaptive Intelligent Systems, *IEEE Trans. on Software Engineering*, 21, 288, 1995.
67. Gomaa, H., Software Development of Real-Time Systems, *Commun. of the ACM*, 29, 657, 1986.

Chapter 8

Programming

Once a detailed design specification for a software module has been produced, it can be programmed. Programming, however, is an error-prone process, that can be improved by following a small number of generic practices. These practices largely revolve around defining policies and standards that are known to reduce risk and eliminate common types of defects generally introduced into code. This chapter identifies five key practices for improving the quality of code and the speed of creating it.

The act of programming produces the primary products — executables — of a software development effort. All prior activities culminate in their development. Following are some practices that programmers should follow to rapidly develop, maintain, and evolve software.

8.1 Practices for General-Purpose Programming

Following are several programming practices suitable for most types of programming.

Practice 8.1. Use the highest-level programming language possible. The reasons for doing this follow [1]:

1. The complexity of software systems is growing quicker than our ability to develop software solutions [2]. For example, productivity

of computer personnel increased about 6 percent per year during the 1990s, whereas the growth in NASA mission software is about 25 percent per year.

2. Productivity is constant in terms of program statement size. That is, writing ten lines of code in assembly language requires as much work as writing ten lines of code in C++ [3, 5]. Another way of looking at this is that by using high-level programming languages, programmers "shrink" the size of the programs they write [5]. As a consequence of this, Brooks has said that the advent of high-level programming languages had the greatest impact on software productivity because there was at least a factor of five improvement in productivity [3, 6]. Similarly, there is a factor of at least six among high-level programming languages [5].

3. The use of high-level programming languages results in more reliable software [4, 7].

To get a better idea of how important it is to reduce the size of existing software systems, consider that understanding 1 million lines of source code is equivalent to understanding the characters, coordinated interactions, plots, subplots, etc. of 100 novels, when assuming that the complexity of one computer instruction is equivalent to one short sentence [8]. On the other hand, several practical factors should influence the selection of a programming language, such as general information about technology trends, organizational information technology strategies, customer restrictions on programming language selection, the experience of the development team with each programming language under consideration, and the features of a programming language, such as its capability to interoperate with external systems.

Practice 8.2. Use integrated development environments. Generally, such suites include a compiler, a make utility, an editor, several inspectors, a profiler, and a debugger. More recently, integrated development environments include tools to model software designs and implement graphical user interfaces. Together, these products can significantly increase programmer productivity once the programmers know how to properly use the environment. Brooks, for example, has stated that interactive facilities at least double productivity [3].

Practice 8.3. Adopt a coding standard that prevents common types of defects. Coding standards are controversial because the choice among many candidate standards is subjective and somewhat arbitrary. Standards are most useful when they support fundamental programming principles.

Consequently, it may be easier for a software team to adopt a standard for handling exceptions than for identifying the amount of white-space to use for each level of indentation. Thus, an organization should always ask itself whether a coding standard improves program comprehension characteristics. Following are several detailed practices that should be considered for inclusion in a programming standard:

1. Internal documentation:
   ■ Specify the amount of white-space that should be used and where it should appear. One should consider adding white-space before and after loop statements and function definitions.
   ■ Identify the amount of white-space that should be used for each indentation level. One study showed that program comprehensibility was significantly improved when two to four spaces were used for each level of indentation [9].
   ■ Physically offset code comments from code when contained on the same line.
   ■ Use comments to explain each class, function, and variable contained in source code. Comments should account for about 10 percent of the source code [5]. However, Brooks says that it is possible to over-comment, so use discretion when commenting [10]. Consider using comments to describe:
     – Key interactions that a function has with other functions and global variables
     – Complex algorithms used by every function, including references to important source materials
     – The type of exceptions, anomalies, or errors that can occur within a function and how the system handles them
     – The data type of every variable (whether it is a formal parameter, global variable, local variable, or member variable) and valid values that they can assume
     – The data type of every return value of a function, if it exists, and the values they can assume
     – The behavior and effect of iterative control flow statements and interior block statements
   ■ Provide working examples in the user documentation or tutorial materials. Examples often provide the necessary detail to understand a concept. A software engineering team should describe these examples step by step. In addition, plan to include a significant amount of clear and concise graphic material in all user manuals.

2. Variable definition and use:

   ■ Declare variables as specifically as possible. This will prevent the assignment of more generic values to them, which may not be appropriate.

   ■ Initialize all variables when declared because some software engineers may not know how a compiler initializes default variables. The only legitimate reason for not initializing a variable where it is declared is if the initial value depends on some computation occurring first.

   ■ Declare no more than one variable per statement. In some languages, not every programmer thoroughly understands the grammar, which can cause misunderstandings. Even when they do, it is easy to make interpretive mistakes. Thus, single-variable declarations are less confusing and encourage programmers to associate a brief description with each one.

   ■ Do not use similarly named variables within the same lexical scope. Adoption of this guidance reduces the confusion that programmers may have regarding the purpose and applicability of variables.

   ■ Consistently use clear and easily remembered names for labels, variables, functions, and classes. A useful variable name, for example, can help identify the intent of a variable or the type of information it contains. One common naming convention distinguishes between formal parameters, local variables, global variables, and member variables (for object-oriented languages). Another one distinguishes the type of a variable within a variable name. The problem with this approach, however, is that if the variable type changes during development, then the variable declaration and references to it must also change. Adherence to this guidance makes programs easier to understand.

   ■ Follow a uniform scheme when abbreviating names. Add the abbreviations and their expanded prose to a glossary used by the entire organization.

   ■ Do not use local declarations to hide declarations at greater scope. Not following this guidance usually causes confusion for readers other than the author.

   ■ Never use a variable for more than one purpose (e.g., in one case an error, and all others the answer). Not following this guidance generally makes it difficult for readers to understand the meaning or purpose of a variable.

3. Control flow:

   ■ Do not assume a default behavior for multi-way branches. A multi-way branch, for example, may test all but one of the valid values and assume the specification of the last value because the other tests failed. Instead, programmers should write code to test each value and upon failing all tests, cause an exception.

■ Do not alter the value of an iteration variable within a loop because distributing the logic that manipulates the loop variable makes the code difficult to understand.

■ Use recursion, when applicable. Recursion is a simple way to express algorithms that tend to perform the same operations on hierarchical substructures or when dividing large problems into common ones of smaller size. This often improves the ability of a reader to comprehend code.

4. Function:

■ Explicitly define input and output formal parameters. In some languages, programmers can specify that functions cannot alter actual parameters. When these languages are used, programmers should use this feature to indicate the actual parameters that are free of side effects. Adherence to this guidance improves the readability of code and prevents the introduction of future defects.

■ Use assertions (e.g., pre- and post-conditions) to verify the accuracy and correctness of input and output formal parameters [11]. The use of pre- and post-conditions helps programmers detect defects closer to their origin [7]. Pre-conditions should verify each actual parameter and the external state that affects the function. Post-conditions should validate that a function performs all desired side effects and returns valid results. Programmers also should consider using assertions to test several other situations, such as invariant loop conditions, array access, and complex arithmetic computations. By adopting this practice, programmers will greatly reduce the time they spend debugging and maintaining programs because their programs will be more reliable and better tested.

5. Operations:

■ Make all conversion of data explicit, especially numeric data. This practice helps indicate to the reader of code that the programmer is cognizant of what he or she is doing, which reduces the effort of reviewing and debugging code.

■ Do not use exact floating-point comparison operations. Because floating-point operations can lead to loss of accuracy, programmers should specify inexact logical comparisons between floating-point numbers that identify the required accuracy.

■ Avoid using operators in potentially ambiguous situations. Therefore, explicitly identify operator precedence assumptions when not using basic mathematical operators, and use parentheses liberally in expressions involving mixed operators. Similarly, avoid using the assignment operator in a place where it can be easily confused with the equality operator.

6. Exception handling:
   - Process all exceptions so that personnel can more easily detect their cause. Exception handlers should create an exception report that includes the time an exception occurred and a trace of the function calls leading to an exception. In addition, exceptions causing an application to terminate or a system to reboot should save buffers and other data identifying the program state. Without saving the program state, software engineers will have few clues for diagnosing these kinds of severe errors.
   - Log important system events, including exceptions. An example of an important event is the recording of internal data and control flow information for use during auditing activities. Logging should include detailed information on what actions completed successfully or unsuccessfully and when events occurred. In addition, an organization should specify the defined logging retention time for each type of event. It may be advisable to have an exception automatically create a failure report. The primary benefit of creating event logs is that personnel can use them to identify and diagnose unique and reoccurring problems. In addition, they can use logs to identify software artifacts having significantly more defects than other artifacts.

7. Maintenance:
   - Isolate the use of nonstandard language functions. Most programming languages contain nonstandard extensions that are useful in specific environments but hinder the migration of code to other platforms. Thus, if software developers use nonstandard extensions, they should build routines that encapsulate those extensions. Following this guidance permits developers to better quantify the difficulty of porting code to other environments.
   - Isolate complex operations to individual functions. Software is easier to understand if programmers can localize inherent computational complexity to one routine, or a small number of routines. In addition to enhancing program understandability and adaptability, this guidance makes it easier for people to diagnose software failures because more natural inspection points are available to them.

8. Operational:
   - Do not permit any compilation to produce warnings. Because such warnings are indicative of various anomalies such as

uninitialized variables and unreachable code, programmers must eliminate the cause of these warnings before releasing code.

■ Optimize software only after it works, is complete, and only if required to achieve performance goals. Because some optimizations tend to make reading code more difficult, premature optimization sometimes causes the introduction of defects.

Practice 8.4. Prototype user interfaces and high-risk components. Prototyping helps control mid-project feature bloat and tends to lead to smaller systems because prototypes identify those features that are without merit or show little benefit and should not be implemented. In addition, user interface prototyping helps identify necessary features that software engineers might otherwise overlook. The benefits of prototyping are that it reduces development efforts by 45 to 80 percent [12], improves operational behavior, and reduces development risk because it allows programmers to explore methods for achieving performance and other requirements. It also helps an organization develop a system that meets the needs and expectations of its users. In conclusion, a project plan should indicate when a software development team should develop prototypes, and it should indicate the specific purpose of each prototyping effort.

Practice 8.5. Define critical regions. A task that interrupts an interdependent operational sequence before it is completed can leave a program in a vulnerable state, resulting in inconsistent and inaccurate results. Therefore, computer systems often must execute such an operational sequence as a single uninterruptable transaction. Such a transaction is called a *critical region*. Once a process begins executing a critical region, only it can execute until it leaves the critical region [13]. Critical regions help prevent the occurrence of *deadlocks*, which occur when a process is waiting for an event that will never occur [13]. This commonly occurs when one process desires a resource that is exclusively held by another, but unwilling to give up its exclusive access.

Possibly the best approach to eliminate concurrency problems is to define a risk management plan that defines rules to help prevent their occurrence and identifies test procedures to detect their existence or absence. Because the process of efficiently synchronizing programs and making code reentrant is a challenge for many computer programmers, an organization should have its best people address these issues. These people should have the most experience creating these types of programs, plus understand the theory of operating systems, programming languages, and formal languages.

8.2 Summary

This chapter identified five important programming practices that I have found effective in efficiently producing quality software. They are based on the use of very-high-level programming languages, coding standards, software tools, prototyping, and the definition of critical regions within code. Most of these practices occur before the programming phase of a software life cycle and many of them must be subjectively made. Consequently, one should follow a formal process for making such decisions, a process that identifies the parameters that affect the decision-making process and the impact that each one has on an outcome.

References

1. Hunt, A. and Thomas, D., *The Pragmatic Programmer*, Addison-Wesley, 2000.
2. Paulk, M.C. et al., *The Capability Maturity Model: Guidelines for Improving the Software Process*, Addison-Wesley, 1994.
3. Brooks, F.P., Jr., *The Mythical Man-Month: Essays on Software Engineering Anniversary Edition*, Addison-Wesley, 1995.
4. Wasserman, A.I., The Future of Programming, *Commun. of the ACM*, 25, 196, 1982.
5. Jones, C., *Software Assessments, Benchmarks, and Best Practices*, Addison-Wesley, 2000.
6. Brooks, F.P., Jr., No Silver Bullet: Essence and Accidents of Software Engineering, *IEEE Computer*, 20, 10, April 1987.
7. Glass, R.L., *Software Reliability Guidebook*, Prentice Hall, 1979.
8. Putnam, L.H. and Myers, W., *Measures for Excellence: Reliable Software on Time, within Budget*, Yourdon Press, 1992.
9. Miara, R.J. et al., Program Indentation and Comprehension, *Commun. of the ACM*, 26, 861, 1983.
10. Brooks, R., Towards a Theory of the Comprehension of Computer Programs, *Int. J. of Man–Machine Studies*, 18, 543, 1983.
11. Rumbaugh, J. et al., *Object-Oriented Modeling and Design*, Prentice Hall, 1991.
12. Gordon, V.S. and Bieman, J.M., Rapid Prototyping: Lessons Learned, *IEEE Software*, January 1995.
13. Bustard, D.W., Concepts of Concurrent Programming, Software Engineering Institute, Carnegie Mellon University, Technical Report SEI-CM-24, 1990.

Chapter 9

Verification

An important quality of good software is that it is free of defects. This chapter identifies two complementary techniques for finding defects: (1) inspections and (2) testing. An inspection is a structured review process that is applicable to a variety of artifacts. Testing, on the other hand, is applicable solely to code or some other form of operational specification. This chapter proposes the application of a verification procedure based on software inspections, functional tests, structural tests, and a variety of system tests.

A *defect* is a product anomaly that causes a program to do something unexpected [1]. Because it is currently impractical and financially prohibitive to deliver defect-free software for anything other than trivial programs, an organization should use an efficient and effective defect-detection approach. The benefit of such an approach should be significant because defect detection and correction activities, which are generally practiced inefficiently and ineffectively, consume about 50 percent of the labor to create software [2] and as much as 75 percent of total software life-cycle costs [1].

It is the premise of this chapter that one can make defect detection efficient and effective by planning an orderly approach for finding defects based on software inspection and testing. Inspection and testing focus on verifying that software does what it is supposed to do, or what its stakeholders expect it to do. The primary difference between the two techniques is that testing involves dynamic execution of code by machine, whereas inspection involves the static analysis of a variety of software artifacts by people.

The proposed approach uses best practices integrated into defined procedures, tailored for finding specific types of defects at the earliest possible stage in the software development life cycle. It specifies the inspection of all artifacts, the functional and structural testing of software designs and code, and various forms of system testing affecting delivered artifacts and their deployment. To support this approach, procedures are identified for performing software inspections, executing test suites, and planning a verification activity. Furthermore, a baseline verification procedure is provided that quantifies the thoroughness of a test effort.

9.1 Inspections

Michael Fagan introduced the software inspection technique in 1976 [3]. As originally conceived, it defined a formal, detailed review process applicable to any type of artifact. It specifically defined entry and exit requirements, participant roles and behaviors, measurement activities, and follow-up actions. Evidence suggests that software inspections are cost-effective techniques for removing defects. For example, the introduction of software inspections at Jet Propulsion Laboratory was a major success [4]. During 1988 and 1989, the institution conducted 300 software inspections. During these inspections, the inspection teams typically found four major defects and twelve minor defects in each document or code whose average length was 38 pages, which is consistent with an observation that inspections tend to find 0.5 to 1 defect per work-hour [5]. The total time expended for each software inspection was 28 hours, but each inspection saved $25,000 (or about $50,000 today). Assuming an average hourly cost of $150 for senior professionals, this implies a benefit-cost ratio of better than 10 to 1. However, the effectiveness of inspections can vary widely [6–11], although software inspections typically find 45 to 60 percent of all defects [12–14].

Inspections differ from walk-throughs and other review processes primarily in their formality. That is, walk-throughs and other peer review processes are practiced with varying regularity and thoroughness, which contribute to inconsistent results [3]. Another distinction is that software inspection techniques emphasize the identification and correction of defects, whereas other review processes generally serve other needs, such as establishing buy-in among senior executives, exploring design alternatives, evaluating conformance to standards and specifications, and educating other personnel. As a result, inspections tend to be superior to walk-throughs and other peer-review processes for finding defects [5].

9.1.1 Practices for Inspecting Artifacts

The following practices can enhance inspection efforts.

Practice 9.1. Provide explicit training in software inspection techniques. Such training should provide guidance on how to look for defects. For example, in one study, instructing individuals in program inspection techniques reduced the number of post-release defects to about 10 percent of the baseline average, at significantly reduced cost [15].

Practice 9.2. Require that the appropriate people inspect artifacts. Chief architects should inspect requirements documents and code because they understand the interactions of the system components and are responsible for maintaining the conceptual integrity of entire systems, which is vital to achieving product quality [16]. The lack of such a person or the unavailability of such a person for a code or requirements inspection is an indication that the development effort has problems. For example, code inspections, from a chief architect's perspective, should seek to determine whether programmers correctly followed the design specification and, if not, what effect it will have on the implementation. A requirements inspection, on the other hand, should attempt to identify whether the defined requirements are consistent, unambiguous, and provide a solid foundation for software design. Similarly, chief programmers should inspect architectural designs for simplicity, low coupling, high cohesion, and adherence to applicable standards. Finally, the appropriateness of other individuals to act as inspectors should be based solely on their ability to find defects, not on their experience or quality assurance capability [17]. The best way to determine the ability of a person to find defects is to use a small sample inspection to separate the better inspectors from the less-capable ones.

Practice 9.3. Use a checklist-based inspection technique. During a checklist-based inspection, several questions are provided to each inspector, which they must answer when inspecting an artifact. These questions should be tailored to find specific types of defects [18–21], usually those that commonly occur in the applications produced by an organization that cannot be detected by automated tools. This technique is not only efficient and effective, but inspectors prefer to use checklist-based inspection techniques instead of alternative inspection techniques [8].

Practice 9.4. Use two people to inspect artifacts. Several studies have attempted to determine what constitutes an effective team size for inspections and found that two-person inspections are, or are among, the most effective [9, 22–26]. Note that the author of an artifact should not be included in the count of the number of inspectors.

Practice 9.5. Conduct meeting-less inspections. Software inspections were originally proposed to use inspection meetings, where inspectors discussed identified defects [3]. Such meetings were supposed to have a synergy effect that occurred among personnel, but recent experience indicates that little synergy actual occurs [8, 27, 28]. More specifically, it has been shown that 75 to 95 percent of all defects are found during the preparation for an inspection meeting [29–31]. In addition, recent research has shown that meeting-less inspections can be performed using electronic support at least as well as without them [31]. One study even demonstrated that inspections using group support software was significantly better than paper-based inspections [32]. In this study, inspectors found 40 percent more defects using group support software when the inspection rate was 200 to 300 source lines of code per hour and 20 percent more defects for rates of 300 to 400 source lines of code per hour. Other reasons for not using inspection meetings are that they are difficult to coordinate [20] and operate inefficiently because evidence indicates that few inspectors actually listen to the conversations that occur in them [33].

9.1.2 A Procedure for Inspecting an Artifact

Three types of people are involved in an inspection: (1) authors, (2) administrators, and (3) inspectors. *Authors* present artifacts and respond to questions during overview meetings. They also change artifacts in response to identified corrective action items. *Administrators* schedule overview meetings, develop checklists, provide checklists to inspectors, identify corrective action items, and ensure that corrective action items are resolved. *Inspectors* examine artifacts and identify potential defects. A description of the inspection process follows.

> **Step 1.** Plan the inspection. During the planning stage, the task manager selects an administrator. Thereafter, the administrator:
> - Instructs the authors to collect and develop the necessary presentation materials
> - Determines who should participate in the inspection
> - Reviews the presentation material against inspection entry criteria and halts the inspection if the entry criteria are not satisfied

- Tailors the applicable checklists for each inspector
- Selects the meeting time
- Provides the artifact, presentation material, and relevant checklist to each inspector

Step 2. Hold an overview meeting. During the overview meeting, the author describes the artifact to the inspectors and explains everything they need to know to effectively examine it. All inspectors should attend the presentation.

Step 3. Inspect the artifact. Each inspector independently examines the artifact using their assigned checklists and notes all suspected defects. Although detecting defects is the primary concern of each inspector, inspectors also may make suggestions that authors may not have considered. Inspectors should have at least three days and generally no more than five days to inspect the presentation material.

Step 4. Review the inspection notes. During the review of the inspection notes, the administrator and author decide on the disposition of each suspected defect. Afterward, the administrator creates corrective action items, which are assigned to the author.

Step 5. Revise the inspected artifact. The author revises the artifact according to the corrective action items.

Step 6. Verify resolution of the corrective action items. After the author resolves each corrective action item, the administrator verifies that they have been resolved as planned.

9.2 Testing

Testing cannot show that software is free of defects [34], but it can identify their existence. Thus, the purpose of testing is not to show that a program works, but to find its defects. Following are several practices for testing software.

9.2.1 Practices for Testing Code

Practice 9.6. Generate functional test cases from defined scenarios. These scenarios represent common transactions that reflect the tasks that the users will carry out [2]. These test cases should be included in a regression test suite.

Practice 9.7. Use a code coverage tool. The reason for using a code coverage tool is that it provides quantitative evidence on how thorough a test effort is. Weigers illustrates the value of a code coverage tool when he said [35]:

> *"Good programmers testing without benefit of a coverage tool are only achieving about 80 percent code coverage, while average programmers are getting 50 to 60 percent, and poor program-mers are hitting less than 30 percent. Test strategies that empha-size only the functional behaviors of the software may cover the requirements adequately, but this is no guarantee that the inter-nal structure of the program has been thoroughly exercised."*

Practice 9.8. Perform basis path testing. Basis path testing independently tests each conditional predicate of a module [36]. That is, the outcome of each condition that can affect control flow is independently tested. Thus, basis path testing localizes a defect to a single subpath of a module because there are no interactions between decision outcomes. A further benefit of this approach is that the size of the testing effort is predictable before testing begins, whereas other techniques are predicated on examining the ongoing progress of a test effort (e.g., [37]). In basis path testing, the required number of test cases for a module is exactly its cyclomatic complexity, which is computed by counting the number of conditional predicates of a module plus one (each separate case of a case statement counts as one). In sum, basis path testing is an effective, efficient, and quantifiable software testing technique that catches about two thirds of all defects [2].

Consider the following function, which computes the factorial of a number, and its associated flow graph, shown in Figure 9.1. The cyclomatic

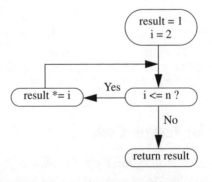

FIGURE 9.1 The flow graph of the factorial function.

TABLE 9.1   Structural Test Cases for the Factorial Function

Input Value (n)	Output Value	Technique
1	1	Basis path testing, boundary value testing
2	2	Basis path testing
3	6	Boundary value testing

complexity of this function is 2, indicating that two edges exist in the flow graph: one test case is required for the condition 2 <= n and another one when 2 > n. Hence, n equals 1 and n equals 2 are two valid inputs that will transverse every edge of the control flow graph of the Fibonacci function, as shown in Table 9.1.

```
void factorial(int n) {
    int result = 1;
    for (int i = 2; i <= n; i++)
        result *= i;
    return result;
}
```

Now consider the following function, which computes the greatest common denominator of two numbers, and its associated flow graph, shown in Figure 9.2. Its cyclomatic complexity is 3; hence, there are three required test cases. In general, there are many possible sets of test cases

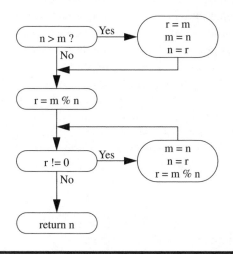

FIGURE 9.2   The flow graph of the gcd function.

TABLE 9.2   Structural Test Case for the gcd Function

Input Value (m)	Input Value (n)	Output Value	Technique
4	5	1	Basis path testing, boundary value testing
5	5	5	Basis path testing, boundary value testing
5	4	1	Basis path testing, boundary value testing

that can be chosen when multiple decision outcomes are involved. One of these satisfies the following conditions: n <= m and r == 0; n >= m and r != 0; and n > m and r != 0. For the selected test set, the chosen input value pairs are specified in Table 9.2.

```
int gcd(int m, int n) {
    int r;
    if (n > m) { r = m; m = n; n = r; }
    r = m % n;
    while (r != 0) { m = n; n = r; r = m % n; }
    return n;
}
```

Note that many people have suggested breaking up complex modules into smaller modules, as measured by cyclomatic complexity. This is not necessarily a good thing for two reasons. First, decomposing a module into multiple modules may not make sense because it may be difficult to decompose the larger module into smaller ones, each having specific responsibilities. Thus, decomposition may turn out to be arbitrary and not very meaningful. Second, decomposing a module into more modules actually increases the testing effort. Consider, for example, how one might decompose the greatest common denominator function. An example of one such decomposition follows; its flow graph is shown in Figure 9.3. Note that this decomposition requires writing four test cases to satisfy the basis path testing technique, instead of three test cases as in the original version.

```
int gcd(int m, int n) {
    if (n > m) return gcd0(n, m);
    else return gcd0(m, n);
}
```

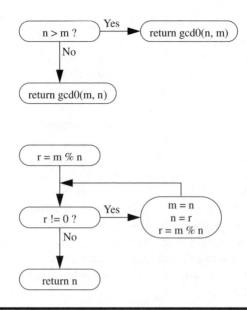

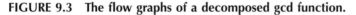

FIGURE 9.3 The flow graphs of a decomposed gcd function.

```
int gcd0(int m, int n) {
    int r = m % n;
    while (r != 0) { m = n; n = r; r = m % n; }
    return n;
}
```

Also note that many people claim that object-oriented programming requires more testing than imperative programming. More specifically, they claim that derived classes must test all inherited methods. This is true only if people violate good design and programming practices by associating different semantics to the methods having the same names.

Practice 9.9. Examine the boundary conditions affecting the control flow of a program. Test predicate variables in a condition by testing the two values one unit of measurement from the specified value. For example, if a predicate is x == 1, where x is an integer value, test cases should be written so that x is bound to 0 and 2 when the condition is executed. For the factorial function of Figure 9.1, checking the boundary conditions would yield the two test cases corresponding to n equals 1 and n equals 3. By choosing the input values wisely for basis path and boundary value testing, one can reduce the total testing effort. For this example, there are three unique test cases — n equals 1, 2, and 3 — that satisfy the structural testing procedures identified by Practices 9.8 and 9.9, which are shown in Table 9.1. For the greatest common denominator function of Figure 9.2, three boundary value conditions occur, which are satisfied by the wise selection of the inputs for basis path testing.

Furthermore, examine loop statements, which are a special case of boundary value testing, using the following heuristics.

- Execute each loop statement zero, one, and two times. This is more-or-less performing boundary value testing of the initial step of the iteration variable. In addition, it has been shown that executing a loop twice can detect some unique initialization problems.
- When using nested iteration statements, select a constant value for all iteration variables except the one being tested, vary it as previously described, and then repeat this process for the remaining nested iteration variables. This heuristic reduces the number of required test cases.

Practice 9.10. Verify data and file usage patterns of a program. That is, check that a program opens files before it operates on them and that it closes files before it terminates. Similarly, verify that a program declares and initializes data before it operates on the data, and that it reclaims all data before it terminates.

Practice 9.11. Verify that invalid and unexpected inputs are handled, as well as valid and expected ones. People often detect numerous defects when they use a program in proper but unexpected ways. Consequently, test cases containing unexpected and invalid inputs often find greater numbers of defects than do test cases containing valid input. In addition, an important class of inputs — command languages and data formatting protocols — should be rigorously tested. Useful heuristics include (1) executing repeated rewrite rules to find limitations in buffer sizes; (2) violating syntactic rules; (3) reversing syntactic tokens and other forms; (4) creating the null program; (5) creating null expressions (e.g., {}); (6) examining code for missing, wrong, and too many delimiters; and (7) checking code for field value errors. One might consider writing a syntax checker that mutates valid input strings in defined ways, which requires a formal definition of the syntax.

Practice 9.12. Verify all critical timing modes and time-out conditions. A critical timing mode occurs whenever execution timing is mission critical, consisting of (1) a fixed number of tasks, threads, or event-handlers running concurrently on a critical processor; (2) a fixed allocation of functions to tasks, threads, or event-handlers; and (3) fixed priorities and frequencies for each task, thread, or event-handler.

Practice 9.13. Verify that systems work in a variety of configurations —as many as practical. Use the same hardware and software environments that the deployment sites will use during the integration test. The benefit of this is that an organization will detect defects unique to host environments of the field sites before it deploys software to them.

Practice 9.14. Verify the accuracy of the documentation. This includes verifying the correctness of the software installation procedures. Following this practice is important because documentation defects represent 10 to 25 percent of all delivered software defects [2, 38].

9.2.2 Testing Heuristics

One should consider the financial return and risk associated with the adoption of any verification technique. I assume that the cost of thoroughly testing mission-critical software outweighs the potential risk. That is, it might cost $3 million to achieve 100 percent decision test coverage of mission-critical software, whereas the loss of a mission might cost $250 million. That is why the Federal Aviation Administration requires all of its mission-critical software to undergo modified condition/decision coverage testing, which basis path testing efficiently satisfies. In non-mission-critical software, one should compare the cost of removing a typical defect to the cost of leaving one in. Of course, this implies that an organization has a quality metrics program that measures the cost and value of removing a defect for a given point in a project. Further, because all types of defects do not pose the same risk, an organization should wisely select those it will attack. Following are some heuristics for tailoring a verification procedure:

- Test modules that have changed. Experience indicates that changing code is a more error-prone process than writing new code. In fact, programmers introduce about two thirds of coding defects while changing software [39].
- Test complex modules. Complex modules usually have more defects than less complex ones. Two effective techniques for measuring complexity follow:
  - Compute the cyclomatic complexity of each module. Those having a cyclomatic complexity greater than ten have 21 percent

more defects per source line of code than those with values at or below ten. Further, 23 percent of these functions account for 53 percent of the software defects [2].

– Count the number of tokens in the source code of a module [2]. On a proportional basis, those modules having a greater number of tokens are more likely to have defects than modules composed of a smaller number of tokens.

■ Test modules that have proven highly defective. The probability of detecting a defect in a module is proportional to the number of defects already found in it. In general, 20 percent of the modules of a software system account for 80 percent of the defects [40]. In an extreme case, 4 percent of a system's modules produced 47 percent of the defects found by users [10].

■ Test the most frequently called modules and those consuming the most resources. Because these modules provide most of the system functionality, thoroughly testing them will yield the greatest true value to the user. Consider using this heuristic when functional testing is not performed, or not performed well.

■ Test low probability paths. This is because they are generally the ones most ignored [2].

9.2.3 A Procedure for Testing a System

The testing techniques that I have advocated, such as basis path testing, are algorithmic in nature. That is, one can write programs to partially or wholly implement these techniques. This was a deliberate attempt to tell the reader *how* to test software, instead of telling the reader *when* to test it. Most testing techniques, as practiced, emphasize unit, integration, system, and acceptance testing, which are based on milestones. For example, when a programmer codes a module, he should test it afterward. When a test team integrates several modules together, it should test them. When the entire system is integrated, then the test team should test it. Finally, when the product is ready for delivery to the customer, the customer should test it. In all four cases, it is unclear how testing is done because no clearly identified algorithms or procedures are specified. Simply creating test cases, scripts, or scenarios does not guarantee that any of these four forms of testing is efficient or effective.

Alternatively, this book identifies such algorithms and procedures and captures test cases in one regression test suite. The implication of this is that each level of testing is performed every time a system is built, which is daily. Hence, unit-, integration-, and system-level testing is done every day! This form of continuous testing uses basis path testing and boundary testing to perform unit- and integration-level testing and functional test cases, derived from operational concepts, to perform system-level testing. This form of continuous testing finds problems immediately, instead of being delayed until a specific form of milestone testing is done.

Following is the recommended procedure for testing code, whose testing effort can be quantified before testing begins:

Step 1. Collect existing scenarios. A Concept of Operations document should have been generated during mission conceptualization or requirements definition. Within it, or within the requirements specification, one should find descriptions of individual scenarios.

Step 2. Develop functional test cases for each scenario. The functional test cases should test every normal and alternative sequence of operations for each scenario. In addition, the alternative sequence of operations should document all critical timing modes and time-out conditions.

Step 3. Verify that functional tests are developed for all timing and error handling requirements. Do not assume that all nonfunctional requirements are included within scenarios. Many of these will be developed after a concept of operations is defined and will not be described by a scenario.

Step 4. For each module:
  Step 4a. Pick the most important functional path through the module to test, called the baseline path. This forms one test case. It is important to start this way because 16 percent of all software defects are functional defects of one kind or another [2].
  Step 4b. Change the outcome of a decision of the baseline path that has not already been changed, while keeping as many of the other decision outcomes the same. Any decisions that are not part of the baseline path can be taken arbitrarily, although it is preferable to select the most useful functional path.
  Step 4c. Repeat this process for all other paths. At the conclusion of this process, a module test suite is produced that tests all paths in a linearly independent manner.
  Step 4d. Generate test cases that modify each decision outcome involving a comparison operation by the smallest possible increment and decrement. This will detect situations where, for example, a < operator should have been used instead of a <= operator, as well as other *off by one* issues.

Step 5. Verify the performance requirements. An organization should use performance and logic simulators to perform this practice [16], as well as software test beds.

Step 6. Verify the stress requirements. Verification that software properly handles excessive volumes of data for short periods of time is normally called *stress testing*. Stress testing is particularly important for programs that operate under varying loads, or are real-time or process-control programs.

Step 7. Verify the capacity requirements. Verification that software properly handles excessive volumes of data for long periods of time is normally called *capacity testing*. Capacity testing exercises the maximum planned capacity for system resources (e.g., storage, buffer, tape, etc.).

Step 8. Verify the reliability requirements. Ensure that the mean time between failures and the mean time to correct failures satisfies the defined requirements, as well as satisfying any other reliability requirements.

Step 9. Verify that the system properly handles incorrect input. This form of testing is often overlooked and can cause unpredictable results.

Step 10. Verify all critical timing modes and time-out conditions. Use formal verification methods to perform this activity [41].

Step 11. Verify that the system works in a variety of configurations. The configurations that should be tested are those that fairly represent the most important customers and largest market segments.

Step 12. Verify the accuracy of the documentation. Also ensure that it is easy to read and that it emphasizes task-based learning strategies. This helps to improve the accuracy of documentation and eliminate documentation defects, which represent 10 to 25 percent of all software defects [2, 38].

9.3 A Procedure for Planning the Verification Procedure

Following is a procedure for planning a verification procedure. It is comprised of several steps:

Step 1. Identify verification goals. These goals should be derived from the section of the software requirements document that discusses the desired product quality attributes and their relative importance. A goal should describe a specific, measurable outcome that is strict enough to keep critical defects out but lenient enough to disregard trivial ones. Some goals can be used to determine when to proceed to the next phase of software development.

Step 2. Identify the techniques that can address each goal. Identify those techniques that are mandated by standards or other requirements applicable to the project. Based on this, identify the minimal set of techniques that satisfies the goals, while achieving an acceptable level of risk.

Step 3. Identify the tools that automate activities of the selected techniques. A criterion for preferring one tool to another should be tool interoperability. When selecting a tool suite, consider asking the following questions. What are the costs of the tools and the acquisition times for each one? What is the availability of documentation and training for each tool? What is the effectiveness of each tool? Specific tools that one should consider using include:

■ Code auditors that examine source code and determine whether prescribed programming standards and practices were followed
■ Control structure analyzers that identify the control branches and paths used by test coverage analyzers
■ Cross-reference generators that list the functions and methods that use data elements and call other functions and methods
■ Data flow analyzers that examine source code to detect when data access does not follow a logical sequence of creation, initialization, use, and destruction
■ Interface analyzers that examine the consistency of the information flow among functions and other components
■ Symbolic evaluators that symbolically execute programs to generate expressions that describe the cumulative effect of computations
■ Test coverage analyzers that execute programs and report the amount of the code that was executed

Step 4. Evaluate and select various software tools. Before evaluating software tools, define criteria and a weighting for each tool category. The benefit of using software tools is that their use can make an organization twice as productive as those that do not use them and, more importantly, such organizations deliver software with seven times fewer defects [42]. Table 9.3 identifies the types of defects that these tools typically detect.

TABLE 9.3   Common Types of Coding Defects Detected by Software Tools

Data truncation during variable assignment	Multiply initialized variables
Different numerical types in arithmetic operations	Non-arithmetic data types in arithmetic operation
Exact floating-point comparisons	Non-integer array references
Illegal array references	Undeclared variable types
Illegal division by zero	Unhandled underflow or overflow exceptions
Illegal memory addresses	Uninitialized variables
Implicitly initialized variables	Unreachable code
Inconsistent data type comparisons	Unused enumeration items
Incorrect variable lengths	Unused variables
Mixed data type comparisons	

Step 5. Identify the responsibilities of project personnel and support groups. External project groups that one should consider include the software quality assurance and independent verification and validation organizations.

Step 6. Identify the available computing resources. This should include the available machines, access methods, support utilities, and technical support.

Step 7. Identify the budget and schedule and allocate them to the artifacts to be developed. In addition, discuss the acquisition of training and computing resources.

Step 8. Identify the artifacts that project personnel will inspect and test. If it is not practical to inspect and test each artifact, then the plan should identify criteria for prioritizing those artifacts that will be inspected and tested before internal and external deployment. For example, what should an organization do if it decides not to achieve 100 percent decision outcome coverage? It should use four heuristics to focus its verification activities:

■ Identify the size of the development team. The larger the team, the more important it is to verify the interfaces between modules.
■ Verify software that is the most critical. There are two types of software: critical and non-critical. Critical software can cause loss of life or catastrophic failure. Non-critical software is everything else.
■ Verify artifacts that have changed because experience indicates that changing code is a more error-prone process than writing

new code. In fact, programmers introduce about two thirds of coding defects while changing software [39].

■ Verify complex modules because they usually have more defects than less complex ones. This has resulted in the following important proposals, which have all proven to be good indicators of complexity: measure the cyclomatic complexity of a module, count the number of operators and operands of a module, count the number of tokens in a module, and count the source lines of code in a module.

Step 9. Specify how defects will be tracked and reported. During any defect detection activity, the organization must categorize identified defects by number, defect type, severity class, and point of occurrence in the software development life cycle so that it can later analyze the cause of defects and take specific actions to prevent their reoccurrence. One way to do this is to conduct periodic causal analysis meetings to discuss the causes of defects and then use this knowledge to change development processes for the remainder of a project [2].

Step 10. Specify an automated regression test strategy to consistently repeat software tests in different environments and configurations. Such automation helps verify that new changes have not broken or adversely affected previously working features and functionalities. It also reduces the testing effort and improves the quality of a program over time, because no one can ever forget or lose the test cases.

9.4 A Baseline Procedure for Verifying Software Systems

Figure 9.4 shows the first part of the idealized software development procedure for one cycle of development. During the verification phase, the following activities should be performed by the designated personnel.

■ The chief architect and a senior tester should inspect each new or changed scenario and requirement using the inspection procedure identified in Section 9.1.2.
■ The chief programmer and a senior tester should inspect the architectural design when it is created and each time it is changed using the inspection procedure defined in Section 9.1.2.

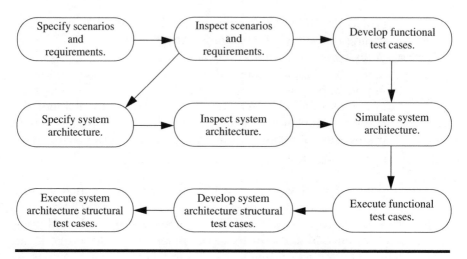

FIGURE 9.4   Phase 1 of the software development procedure.

■ Once the test team has defined the functional test suite and the design team has defined the architecture and produced a simulation of the system, it should develop a structural test suite for the architectural design as defined in Section 9.2.3.

■ Software Quality Assurance personnel should periodically collect the following metrics:

Requirements coverage =

$$\frac{\text{Number of requirements traced to functional test cases}}{\text{Number of requirements}} \qquad (9.1)$$

System architecture statement coverage =

$$\frac{\text{Executed SLOC of system architecture}}{\text{Total SLOC of system architecture}} \qquad (9.2)$$

System architecture edge coverage =

$$\frac{\text{Executed decision outcomes of system architecture}}{\text{Total decision outcomes of system architecture}} \qquad (9.3)$$

Figure 9.5 shows the second part of the idealized software development procedure for one cycle of development. During this phase, the following activities should be performed by the designated personnel:

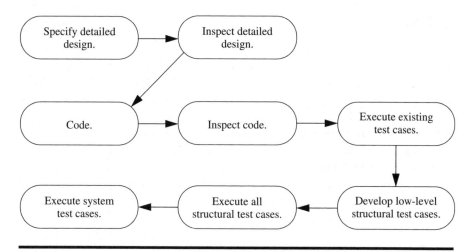

FIGURE 9.5   Phase 2 of the software development procedure.

- Programmers should apply quality assurance tools that verify that code adheres to quality requirements. Typical tools that should be used include static analyzers and other tools that find memory allocation anomalies.
- The chief programmer and another programmer should inspect each new or changed code module using the inspection procedure defined in Section 9.2.3 to find defects not detectable by automated tools or the planned test suite.
- Programmers should test each module using the test procedure identified in Section 9.2.3 to satisfy defined quality requirements. It is recommended that reusable code achieve 100 percent statement coverage and 80 percent decision outcome coverage. For mission-critical software, 100 percent decision outcome coverage should be required.
- Software Quality Assurance personnel should periodically collect the following metrics:

$$\text{System statement coverage} = \frac{\text{Executed SLOC of system}}{\text{Total SLOC of system}} \quad (9.4)$$

$$\text{System edge coverage} = \frac{\text{Executed decision outcomes of system}}{\text{Total decision outcomes of system}} \quad (9.5)$$

9.5 Summary

This chapter has identified numerous practices and procedures to reduce the number of defects in delivered software. It has advocated the use of both software inspection and testing because they have proven effective, efficient, and complementary to one another [9, 43, 44]. Inspection techniques help find defects in the earlier stages of the software development life cycle, whereas testing techniques have residual benefits that accrue over time because test suites can be reapplied in the future at no extra cost. This residual benefit is especially important when an organization produces reusable code. Finally, the recommended approach is consistent with what others have recommended [35, 36].

References

1. Myers, G.J., *Software Reliability: Principles and Practices*, Wiley, 1976.
2. Beizer, B., *Software Testing Techniques*, Van Nostrand Reinhold, 1990.
3. Fagan, M.E., Design and Code Inspections to Reduce Errors in Program Development, *IBM Systems Journal*, 15, 182, 1976.
4. Bush, M.W., Improving Software Quality: The Use of Formal Inspections at the Jet Propulsion Laboratory, in *Proc. of the Int. Conf. on Software Engineering*, 1990, 196.
5. Ackerman, A.F., Buchwald, L.S., and Lewski, F.H., Software Inspections: An Effective Verification Process, *IEEE Software*, 6:3, 31, May 1989.
6. Fagan, M.E., Advances in Software Inspections, *IEEE Trans. on Software Engineering*, 12, 744, 1986.
7. Gilb, T. and Graham, D., *Software Inspection*, Addison-Wesley, 1993.
8. Laitenberger, O., El Emam, K., and Harbich T.G., An Internally Replicated Quasi-Experimental Comparison of Checklist and Perspective-Based Reading of Code Documents, *IEEE Trans. on Software Engineering*, 27, 387, 2001.
9. Myers, G.J., A Controlled Experiment in Program Testing and Code Walkthroughs/Inspections, *Commun. of the ACM*, 21, 760, 1978.
10. Myers, G.J., *The Art of Software Testing*, Wiley, 1979.
11. Porter, A.A. et al., Understanding the Sources of Variation in Software Inspections, *ACM Trans. on Software Engineering and Methodology*, 7, 41, 1998.
12. Basili, V.R. and Selby, R.W., Comparing the effectiveness of software testing techniques, *IEEE Trans. on Software Engineering*, 13, 1278, 1987.
13. Biffl, S., Freimut, B., and Laitenberger, O., Investigating the Cost-Effectiveness of Reinspections in Software Development, in *Proc. of the Int. Conf. on Software Engineering*, 2001, 155.
14. Briand, L. et al., Using Simulation to Build Inspection Efficiency Benchmarks for Development Projects, in *Proc. of the Int. Conf. on Software Engineering*, 1998, 340.

15. Rifkin, S. and Deimel, L., Program Comprehension Techniques Improve Software Inspections: A Case Study, in *Proc. of the Int. Workshop on Program Comprehension*, 2000, 131.

16. Brooks, F.P., Jr., *The Mythical Man-Month: Essays on Software Engineering Anniversary Edition*, Addison-Wesley, 1995.

17. Biffl, S. and Halling, M., Investigating the Influence of Inspector Capability Factors with Four Inspection Techniques on Inspection Performance, in *Proc. of the Int. Symp. on Software Metrics*, 2002, 1.

18. Miller, J., Wood, M., and Roper, M., Further Experiences with Scenarios and Checklists, *Empirical Software Engineering*, 3, 37, 1998.

19. Parnas, D.L. and Weiss, D.M., Active Design Reviews: Principles and Practices, *Proc. of the Int. Conf. on Software Engineering*, 1985, 215.

20. Porter, A., Votta, L., and Basili, V., Comparing Detection Methods for Software Requirements Inspections: A Replicated Experiment, *IEEE Trans. on Software Engineering*, 21, 563, 1995.

21. Porter, A. and Votta, L., Comparing Detection Methods for Software Requirements Inspections: A Replication using Professional Subjects, *Empirical Software Engineering*, 3, 355, 1998.

22. Bisant, D. and Lyle, J., A Two-Person Inspection Method to Improve Programming Productivity, *IEEE Trans. on Software Engineering*, 15, 1294, 1989.

23. El Emam, K. and Laitenberger, O., Evaluating Capture-Recapture Models with Two Inspectors, *IEEE Trans. on Software Engineering*, 27, 851, 2001.

24. Kusomoto, S. et al., A Promising Approach to Two-Person Software Review in an Educational Environment, *J. of Systems and Software*, 40, 115, 1998.

25. Neu, H. et al., Simulation-Based Risk Reduction for Planning Inspections, in *Proc. of the Fourth Int. Conf. on Product Focused Software Process Improvement*, Springer, 2002, 78.

26. Porter, A. et al., An Experiment to Assess the Cost-Benefits of Code Inspections in Large Scale Software Development, *IEEE Trans. on Software Engineering*, 23, 329, 1997.

27. Johnson, P. and Tjahjono, D., Does Every Inspection Really Need a Meeting?, *Empirical Software Engineering*, 3, 9, 1998.

28. Laitenberger, O. and DeBaud, J.M., An Encompassing Life-Cycle Centric Survey of Software Inspection, *J. of Systems and Software*, 50, 5, 2000.

29. Eick, S.G. et al., Estimating Software Fault Content before Coding, in *Proc. of the Int. Conf. on Software Engineering*, 1992, 59.

30. Humphrey, W.S., *Managing the Software Process*, Addison-Wesley, 1989.

31. Vermunt, A., Smits, M., and Van der Pijl, G., Using GSS to Support Error Detection in Software Specifications, in *Proc. of the Hawaii Int. Conf. on System Sciences*, 1988, 566.

32. van Genuchten, M. et al., Using Group Support Systems for Software Inspections, *IEEE Software*, 60, May/June 2001.

33. Aurum, A., Petersson, H., and Wohlin, C., State-of-the-Art: Software Inspections after 25 Years, *Software Testing, Verification and Reliability*, 12, 133, 2002.

34. Parnas, D.L., van Schouwen, A.J., and Kwan, S.P., Evaluation of Safety-Critical Software, *Commun. of the ACM*, 33, 636, 1990.

35. Weigers, K.E., *Creating a Software Engineering Culture*, Dorset House, 1996.
36. Watson, A.H. and McCabe, T.J., Structured Testing: A Testing Methodology Using the Cyclomatic Complexity Metric, National Institute of Standards and Technology, NIST Special Publication 500-235, 1996.
37. Musa, J.D. and Ackerman, A.F., Quantifying Software Validation: When to Stop Testing?, *IEEE Software*, 6, 19, May 1989.
38. Boehm, B.W., *Software Engineering Economics*, Prentice Hall, 1981.
39. Nikora, A.P., Software System Defect Content Prediction from Development Process and Product Characteristics, Ph.D. dissertation, Computer Science Department, University of Southern California, 1998.
40. Weinberg, G.M., *Quality Software Management: Systems Thinking*, Dorset House, 1992.
41. Holzmann, G., *The SPIN Model Checker: Primer and Reference Model*, Addison-Wesley, 2003.
42. Grady, R.B. and Caswell, D.L., *Software Metrics: Establishing a Company-Wide Program*, Prentice Hall, 1987.
43. McConnell, S., *Rapid Development: Taming Wild Software Schedules*, Microsoft Press, 1996.
44. So, S.S. et al., An Empirical Evaluation of Six Methods to Detect Faults in Software, *Software Testing, Verification and Reliability*, 12, 155, 2002.

Chapter 10

Remaining Quality Practices and Issues

This chapter briefly discusses three critical aspects of a successful software development activity: (1) the creation of user documentation, (2) software reuse, and (3) techniques for defect estimation.

This chapter discusses some important issues that did not seem to fit well with previous chapters or that demand chapters of their own. The first topic of this chapter discusses how to write good documentation for users of software systems. This is especially important because the effectiveness of a software system is largely related to the ability of its users to use it. Hence, this chapter identifies many practices for writing user documentation that will help users effectively and efficiently learn how to use a software system. The second topic of this chapter discusses the reuse of software. More specifically, it describes why reuse is important, its relationship to abstraction, and the common approaches to software reuse. Finally, this chapter identifies several techniques for estimating the number of defects that remain in software, which is important to measure so that one can build a product that meets its quality requirements.

10.1 Practices for Writing Useful User Documentation

The degree of satisfaction with documentation is critical in explaining customer satisfaction with a product because it affects perceptions of a product's usability, capability, performance, reliability, installability, and maintainability [1]. To improve customer satisfaction with documentation, an organization should perform numerous practices when documenting a system. These practices are listed below and have been derived from numerous publications [2–7].

Practice 10.1. Orient the documentation around descriptions of real tasks. Such descriptions reflect the way that people actually do their work. To focus on real tasks, consider adopting the following advice:

- Identify how a work product satisfies the needs of its target audience. For example, if the audience consists of the users of a product, then the documentation should identify how they would use it. On the other hand, if the target audience consists of programmers, then the documentation should describe how the product works and is structured internally.
- Write documentation in a brief, action-oriented manner using the terminology of its users. This permits the reader to imagine performing the actions described in the documentation.
- Provide a practical reason for the information and describe its significance. The reader must understand the relevance of the information for a particular task.
- Order the presentation of information to reflect the order of its use. If one should learn a concept before one is able to perform a task, then it should be presented first. Such an ordering facilitates learning. Reference information, on the other hand, should be presented in a manner that will permit the reader to rapidly retrieve it.
- Use titles and headings that clearly convey the task. That is, one should be able to read a heading and know what information will be discussed in the following section. These headings should produce a table of contents permitting its readers to go directly to the section relevant to the task at hand.
- Exploit the user's prior knowledge and experience.

Practice 10.2. Organize the presentation of information. Readers can better understand the material when they understand its organization. This permits them to easily find the appropriate material when they need it. Consider the following advice:

- Identify how the components fit together. The document should tell the reader what is going to be said, followed by saying it, and then conclude by verifying what was said. Along the way, the writer needs to constantly inform the reader where he is by showing the progress from the initial state to the desired state.

- Emphasize the main points and focus less on secondary ones. In addition, the key points should be identified first — in the heading, in the introduction, and in the first sentence of each paragraph. Contrarily, give little attention to secondary information.
- Discuss ideas in a contiguous manner. That is, avoid referring to other sections of a document or other documents. Everything that a reader needs to understand a topic should be presented as a contiguous sequence of material, whether expressed as a sequence of sentences, paragraphs, or sections. A writer should consider that reference to other material is characteristic of the `goto` statements of a programming language.
- Present similar topics in the same manner using the same level of detail, notations, and formatting.

Practice 10.3. Provide an overview of the information of each major section of a document. An overview identifies what information the reader will be seeing shortly, and the sequence of its presentation. Following is some information that will make this easier:

- Provide introductory sections for chapters and major headings that describe the purpose and content of the information that immediately follows.
- Create an index of predictable entries for each topic. Such entries should include common phrases and synonyms for each topic, as well as subentries that provide more precise information.
- Emphasize significant words and phrases. When emphasizing significant words and phrases, use either an italicized or bold-face font.

Practice 10.4. Clearly present information. If the material is not clearly presented, the reader will find it difficult to understand. Following is some advice about how to clearly present information to people:

- The material should be written in a manner readable by the intended audience. Thus, it is important to quantify the education and training of the expected reader. Simplicity is a desired goal; therefore, avoid involved, complex sentences. For example, sentences should be short and contain few prepositional phrases or compound constructions [8].

- When presenting a collection of information, item groups should always be seven or less.
- Use words economically to convey information. The quantity of words is unimportant although the amount of information is.
- Whenever a term is used for the first time, immediately define its meaning and include it in a glossary or index.
- Use technical terms only when they are necessary and appropriate, and be consistent in their use. Similarly, avoid acronyms unless they are commonly understood by the intended audience.
- Provide realistic examples — analogies, narratives, and scenarios — to illustrate ideas. Furthermore, one can use a series of examples to identify specific instances of a general rule or to test the reader's understanding of a general rule.

Practice 10.5. Use visual techniques to effectively convey information. When presenting technical information, use charts, diagrams, figures, and tables to convey that information. However, excessive use of these techniques leads to the production of incoherent documents that either tire or bore the reader. Remember that the underlying reason for using visual techniques is to attract and motivate readers by using a better presentation medium than simple, unstructured text.

Practice 10.6. Provide accurate information. This advice applies not only to the primary text, but also to references and index entries. To improve accuracy, consider the following guidelines:

- Use correct grammar, spelling, and punctuation.
- Ensure that contradictions do not exist in a document, whether they are explicitly or implicitly stated. That is, it is possible for one statement to implicitly contradict or be implicitly contradicted by the implications of other statements.

Practice 10.7. Provide complete information. Similarly, only present the information that is needed — extraneous information may confuse the reader. Therefore,

- Provide only as much detail as is necessary. That is, inform the reader what is needed to perform a task, but no more. When writing, focus on the primary audience, and do not attempt to provide information of interest to readers who are not members of this group.

■ Discuss everything that you said you would. Often, an introduction will identify several issues that will be addressed by the immediately following section, only to have it ignore some of those issues. This can be very frustrating to the reader.

■ Emphasize and reinforce important points as often as necessary to avoid forcing the reader to jump to other sections of the document.

10.2 Reusability

The software crisis is a result of there being a demand for quality software that exceeds what can be provided with current technology. Software reuse is a promising idea that may help alleviate this undesirable situation by using previously developed artifacts to develop new software. Although the goal of a reuse program is to provide a significant return on investment, such return may be difficult to achieve. For example, it has been said that the cost of developing reusable software is often twice that of creating an equivalent nonreusable component, and the cost of integrating reusable software is often one third the cost of developing software [9]. Thus, for simple products, reuse is generally beneficial once an artifact has been reused three times; whereas for complex products, artifacts often must be reused 13 times before returning a benefit [9]. Although the return on investment generally takes some time to recover, the improved quality of reused artifacts is immediately apparent. For example, 98 percent of modules reused without modification are defect free; and when defects are found in a module, rarely are any found after three reuses [9]. On the other hand, the reuse of software with modification has not been very successful because a description of how a module works is seldom provided, causing its adaptation to be difficult [10]. When provided, the cost of providing such a description negates any immediate benefit [11, 12]. Thus, the creation of reusable artifacts should only be considered when one repeatedly constructs similar systems.

When one builds a reuse repository, one should ponder the following questions [10, 11]:

■ How are artifacts classified to enable their reuse?
■ How does one efficiently retrieve an artifact of interest from a reuse repository?
■ How does one determine the suitability of a retrieved artifact for an immediate need?

- If a retrieved artifact does not meet the immediate need, how can one change it to meet the need?
- What are the consequences of changing an artifact?

In addition, one should understand that the following factors have been shown to significantly affect the reusability of software [9, 11, 13]:

- The use of abstraction
- Low coupling among modules
- High cohesion among modules
- Small module size

10.2.1 *The Relationship between Abstraction and Reuse*

An *abstraction* is a succinct description that suppresses unimportant details and emphasizes important information [14]. Abstractions permit users to effectively locate, understand, compare, and select the appropriate artifacts from a repository. Without abstraction, people would have to painfully search through a repository of reusable artifacts trying to determine what each artifact did and how to reuse the appropriate ones. Hence, abstractions are essential to effectively reuse software artifacts.

There are three parts of an abstraction: (1) a hidden part, (2) a variable part, and (3) a fixed part [14]. The hidden part hides the details of an abstraction realization that are not visible in the abstraction specification. Within an abstraction realization, the variable part represents its variant characteristics, whereas the fixed part represents its invariant characteristics. Thus, an abstraction specification with a variable part allows alternate realizations. Furthermore, when representations are layered, a realization at one level is the specification of the immediately lower level.

In sum, the abstraction specification typically describes *what* the abstraction does, whereas the abstraction realization describes *how* it is done. For an abstraction to be effective, its specification must express all of the information that is needed by the person who uses it. This may include space and time characteristics, precision statistics, scalability limits, and other information not normally associated with specification techniques. This is the reason why describing an artifact to be successfully reused may be more time consuming than newly developing the artifact. This is also the reason why frameworks that provide the infrastructure for a small number of large-grained components work. However, large components are more specific and, hence, one needs more of them to choose from to satisfy different requirements. Regardless, the issue is not whether an organization should develop and use small or large components. Instead, the issue is how many components can be contained in a reuse repository so that they can be effectively reused. This appears to be about 1300 components per problem domain, which is based on human cognitive limitations and empirical evidence from other industries [11].

10.2.2 Approaches to Reuse

The generation of reusable components can occur during any phase of the software life cycle. There are, however, only a limited number of techniques in common use today for reusing these components. The deep-structure approaches require people to have knowledge of the internal structure of artifacts and their interrelationships, whereas the surface-level approaches embody such knowledge in a higher-level language that people easily understand.

- Deep-structure approaches:
    - The *scavenging* or *inheritance* approach attempts to reduce workload by copying as much as possible from similar systems that have already been developed [14, 15]. The abstractions used in scavenging are mostly informal and often only exist in the developer's mind. In this approach, the practitioner is involved with all parts of the abstraction and, therefore, nothing is hidden from him, which requires him to become intimate with the details of a realization before he can use or edit it. In practice, the effectiveness of this approach is restricted by its informality because there is no way to effectively share fragments among many different programmers. Although this approach sometimes is better than writing code from scratch, it is generally a poor choice because it often results in the costly development of unreliable software.
    - The *library* approach occurs when a programmer uses a file containing several components linked at compile time or loaded at execution time. Because the behaviors are static and published, the library approach is better than the scavenging approach. However, this approach unduly burdens each and every user, who must understand the interfaces of the reused components as well as other tools such as linking loaders [10].
- Surface-structure approaches:
    - High-level languages use abstraction to succinctly and more naturally express program intent. In this approach, reuse is so easy that most programmers do not think that reuse is actually occurring. The primary limitation to this form of reuse is that a large amount of effort must go into designing a language for reuse [14].

- The *domain-specific programming language* approach advocates the reuse of analysis and design, which is then embodied in a programming language that generates code in a target language. This approach is better than the ones already discussed because it acknowledges that the programming effort of a project consumes only about 15 percent of the labor resources of a project [15]. The difficult part of a project, as everyone knows, occurs during the analysis, design, and verification phases. The domain-specific programming language approach embodies the results of these phases into a language tailored for solving problems of a specific problem domain, which significantly eases future work. Hence, it is often the best way to solve programming problems [16].

In sum, the effectiveness of a reuse technique can be evaluated in terms of its *cognitive distance*, which is a measure of the intellectual effort required to use a technique. Cognitive distance is reduced using as few higher-level abstractions as possible — at the knowledge level — to reduce the effort of transforming an initial concept of a software system to representations contained in the reuse repository [10, 14, 17]. Hence, software reuse generally occurs because domain and component knowledge lies in the minds of the people assigned to a project. That is why personnel capability and domain knowledge, as identified in Table 1.1, seem almost interchangeable.

10.3 Defect Estimation Techniques

Typical organizations find 85 percent of their defects, whereas the best ones find more than 99 percent of them. One author claims that an organization achieves the shortest schedules, uses the least effort, and obtains the highest user satisfaction when it finds about 95 percent of all defects, which is when product delivery should occur [18]. However, to achieve 95 percent defect detection requires extensive testing. Unfortunately, because the cost of finding defects increases dramatically once the defect density level drops below one per thousand lines of source code, the costs of removing 90 to 95 percent of all defects become very high [19]. However, for mission-critical modules, this kind of extensive testing is necessary to achieve acceptable levels of reliability.

Several defect estimation techniques have been proposed over the years. Following are some of the more common ones. Some of these have proved very accurate in specific cases, although it would be foolish to strictly rely on a single technique or ignore human intuition about the likelihood of the number of remaining product defects.

10.3.1 Historical Techniques

Historical techniques establish upper and lower bounds for defects based on historical evidence. Based on this information, an organization can estimate the number of remaining defects in a module, D_1, using Equation 10.1, where l is the number of source lines of code for the module, d is the typical number of defects per source line of code, and D_d is the number of detected defects.

$$D_1 = (l \times d) - D_d \qquad (10.1)$$

The basic assumption of this approach is that the detection of too many defects indicates a poorly written artifact, whereas too few defects indicates a poorly reviewed artifact. Unfortunately, if this assumption is not valid, a high-quality artifact may be needlessly reinspected and a poor-quality artifact may not be reinspected although the inspection was poorly performed.

10.3.2 Halstead's Technique

Halstead's technique, shown in Equation 10.2, computes the remaining defects of a module as follows. First, compute n_1,* which is the number of distinct operators (e.g., keywords) in a program, and n_2, which is the number of distinct operands (e.g., data objects) in a module. Then, compute N_1 and N_2, which are the total number of operators and operands in a module. Next, estimate the number of remaining software defects, D_2, using Equation 10.2, where D_d is the number of detected software defects. The benefit of this technique is that defect estimation is directly related to software size and requires no additional work. One experiment showed that this technique is accurate to within eight percent [21].

$$D_2 = \frac{\left(N_1 + N_2\right)\log\left(n_1 + n_2\right)}{3000} - D_d \qquad (10.2)$$

---

* Halstead defines n_1, n_2, N_1, and N_2 in *Elements of Software Science* [20].

10.3.3 Detection Profile Method

This is a curve-fitting model that plots the detected defects versus the number of verification personnel who identified each detected defect [22]. The defects are sorted in decreasing order with respect to the number of personnel who identified the defect. Then, either a linear or exponential regression line is plotted through the data and its intercept estimates the number of remaining defects. The linear regression line is a lower-bound estimator and the exponential one is an upper-bound estimator. One study claims that the linear estimator works fairly well, although the exponential one overestimates way too much [23]. Another study claims detection profile estimators are superior to capture-recapture methods [24]. Regardless, detection profile methods are not very effective for small teams, especially when they are composed of four or less people.

10.3.4 Capture-Recapture Techniques

Capture-recapture techniques were originally proposed to estimate the size of animal populations. Animals were first captured over a period, tagged, and then released back into the wild. Later, people would go back to the same area and capture some more animals. The total number of animals captured for each period was recorded, as well as those animals captured a second time (as indicated by the tags). Later, Mills proposed the use of a capture-recapture model in 1972 for predicting the number of defects in software [25], but such techniques received little attention until recently.

As presented here, capture-recapture techniques compute the number of the remaining defects of a module based on the defects found by two distinct groups for a defined period.* For example, at the end of a defined period, assume that each group finds some defects. Let us call the number of defects found for reach group m_1 and m_2. In addition, let m_{12} denote the common defects found by both groups. Based on this information, the basic technique calculates the number of remaining defects, D_3, as shown in Equation 10.3. For example, if group 1, m_1, found 20 defects, group 2, m_2, found 30 defects, and they both found 8 defects in common, which is m_{12}, then this technique would estimate that 33 defects remain.

$$D_3 = \frac{m_1 \times m_2}{m_{12} - \left(m_1 + m_2 - m_{12}\right)} \qquad (10.3)$$

---

* Capture-recapture techniques can actually be used for any number of reviewers, although the more complicated formulae do not yield significantly different results.

The Chao (Chapman) estimator [26], shown in Equation 10.4, is another capture-recapture scheme that has been highly effective. It is based on the assumptions that defect types are equally probable and inspector skills differ. Experience indicates that the Chao estimator consistently under-estimates the actual number of defects. Using the same two groups as previously described, its use would predict that 30 errors still remain in the inspected artifact. In addition, the Chao measure has been shown to be appropriate for two-person inspection teams although capture-recapture models are strongly affected by the number of inspectors [25].

$$D_4 = \frac{(m_1 + 1) \times (m_2 + 1)}{(m_{12} + 1)} - 1 - (m_1 + m_2 - m_{12}) \tag{10.4}$$

The Jackknife estimator, which is shown in Equation 10.5, is a capture-recapture method based on the assumptions that defect types have different probabilities of being detected and that inspector skills are the same. In practice, it tends to overestimate the number of defects [23, 27]. Using the two groups previously identified, this estimator predicts 33 defects, which is the same number as the basic technique and more than the Chao estimator predicted. Consequently, it has been recommended that organizations use the Chao and Jackknife estimators to predict lower and upper bounds of the remaining defects in software, respectively. Furthermore, it has been claimed that the Jackknife estimator is significantly better than detection profile methods (although advocates of detection profile methods contradict this assertion) or subjective estimation [28]. Unfortunately, one drawback of all capture-recapture techniques is that they do not work when inspectors are focusing on finding different types of defects [25].

$$D_5 = \frac{m_1 + m_2}{2} + m_{12} \tag{10.5}$$

10.4 Summary

This chapter has presented three important topics. The first topic discusses ways to write useful user documentation. It emphasizes the presentation of information in terms of real tasks. Such information should be clearly presented to readers in an action-oriented manner that emphasizes the user's knowledge and prior experience in a practical manner. This information should be organized in such a way that the user always knows the relevance of the information already presented to him and how it will influence the material that will be presented to him. That is, no extraneous information should be presented to the user, and the information presented to him should always support some larger goal, of which he is aware. In addition, all information that must be presented to the reader should be presented, and it must be accurate.

The second topic of this chapter concerns the reuse of software artifacts. It discusses the cost of developing for reuse and the cost of reusing software. To be cost effective, artifacts must be reused at least three times for small products and thirteen times for large products. Thus, a simple and reasonably accurate heuristic for large systems is that an organization should not consider reuse unless it plans to develop customized versions of a product at least ten times. The chapter also indicates that the effectiveness of a reuse strategy is largely based on the level of abstraction of an artifact. Finally, it distinguishes between deep- and surface-structure approaches to software reuse. The deep-structure approach is based on capturing low-level artifacts and reusing them later in conventional ways. The surface-structure approach, however, attempts to abstract away the low-level details and focus on higher-level aggregated concepts, often expressed in a domain-specific language. The surface-structure approach should be the preferred approach because its requires less knowledge of the internal structure of the reused artifact.

The third, and final, topic of this chapter concerns the quantification of the number of defects that remain in software. Four primary techniques were discussed. One of these techniques hypothesizes that the number of defects introduced into software will be similar to those of past products. Another technique hypothesizes that the number of defects is related to the number of tokens that comprise the source code of a product. The remaining two techniques hypothesize that the number of defects is related to the number of people who find the same defects. It is unclear which technique is the best to use.

References

1. Smart, K.L., Madrigal, J.L., and Seawright, K.K., The Effect of Documentation on Customer Perception of Product Quality, *IEEE Trans. on Professional Communication*, 39, 157, 1996.
2. Carroll, J.M. and van der Meij, H., Ten Misconceptions about Minimalism, in *Minimalism beyond the Nurnberg Funnel*, Carroll, J.M. (Ed.), MIT Press, 1998, 55.
3. Dean, M. et al., Producing Quality Technical Information, *ACM J. of Computer Documentation*, 26, 66, 2002.

4. Hackos, J.T., Choosing a Minimalist Approach for Expert Users, in *Minimalism beyond the Nurnberg Funnel*, Carroll, J.M. (Ed.), MIT Press, 1998, 149.

5. Mirel, B. Minimalism for Complex Tasks, in *Minimalism beyond the Nurnberg Funnel*, Carroll, J.M. (Ed.), MIT Press, 1998, 179.

6. Redish, J., Minimalism in Technical Communication: Some Issues to Consider, in *Minimalism beyond the Nurnberg Funnel*, Carroll, J.M. (Ed.), MIT Press, 1998, 219.

7. van der Meij, H. and Carroll, J.M., Principles and Heuristics for Designing Minimalist Instruction, in *Minimalism beyond the Nurnberg Funnel*, Carroll, J.M. (Ed.), MIT Press, 1998, 19.

8. Klare, G.R., The Measurement of Readability: Useful Information for Communicators, *ACM J. of Computer Documentation*, 24, 107, 2000.

9. Frakes, W. and Terry, C., Software Reuse: Metrics and Models, *ACM Computing Surveys*, 28, 415, 1996.

10. Neighbors, J., Draco: A Method for Engineering Reusable Software Systems, in *Software Reusability*, Biggerstaff, T.J. and Perlis, A.J. (Eds.), 1, Addison-Wesley, 1989, 295.

11. Prieto-Diaz, R., A Software Classification Scheme, Ph.D. dissertation, Information and Computer Science Department, University of California, Irvine, 1985.

12. Kandt, R.K., Reuse of Design Information, Master's thesis, Information and Computer Science Department, University of California, Irvine, 1984.

13. Selby, R.W., Quantitative studies of software reuse, in *Software Reusability*, II, Biggerstaff, T.J. and Perlis, A.J. (Eds.), Addison-Wesley, 1989.

14. Krueger, C.W., Software Reuse, *ACM Computing Surveys*, 24, 131, 1992.

15. Yourdon, E., *The Decline and Fall of the American Programmer*, Yourdon Press/Prentice Hall, 1993.

16. Abbott, R.J., Knowledge Abstraction, *Commun. of the ACM*, 30, 664, 1987.

17. Gabriel, R.P., *Patterns of Software: Tales from the Software Community*, Oxford University Press, 1996.

18. Jones, C., *Applied Software Measurement: Assuring Productivity and Quality*, McGraw-Hill, 1991.

19. Paulk, M.C. et al., *The Capability Maturity Model: Guidelines for Improving the Software Process*, Addison-Wesley, 1994.

20. Halstead, M.H., *Elements of Software Science*, Elsevier North-Holland, 1977.

21. Beizer, B., *Software Testing Techniques*, Van Nostrand Reinhold, 1990.

22. Wohlin, C. and Runeson, P., Defect Content Estimations from Review Data, in *Proc. of the Int. Conf. on Software Engineering*, 1998, 400.

23. Stringfellow, C. et al., Estimating the Number of Components with Defects Post-Release that Showed No Defects in Testing, *Software Testing, Verification and Reliability*, 12, 93, 2002.

24. Thelin, T. and Runeson, P., Robustness Estimations of Fault Content with Capture-Recapture and Detection Profile Estimators, *J. of Systems and Software*, 52, 139, 2000.

25. Briand, L.C. et al., A Comprehensive Evaluation of Capture-Recapture Models for Estimating Software Defect Content, *IEEE Trans. on Software Engineering*, 26, 518, 2000.
26. El Emam, K. and Laitenberger, O., Evaluating Capture-Recapture Models with Two Inspectors, *IEEE Trans. on Software Engineering*, 27, 851, 2001.
27. Miller, J., Estimating the Number of Remaining Defects after Inspection, *Software Testing, Verification and Reliability*, 9, 167, 1999.
28. Biffl, S., Freimut, B., and Laitenberger, O., Investigating the Impact of Reading Techniques on the Accuracy of Different Defect Content Estimation Techniques, in *Proc. of the Int. Symp. on Software Metrics*, 2001, 51.

Chapter 11

Competing Approaches

This chapter contrasts and compares the proposed software development approach to those of other prominent approaches. This analysis is largely based on the core topics presented in this book: personnel management, project management, configuration management, requirements engineering, design, programming, and verification.

The Quality-Oriented Software Engineering approach proposed in this book is just one of many software development approaches. Others include Extreme Programming [1], the Rational Unified Process [2, 3], and Cleanroom Software Engineering [4]. In addition, there are several software development process models. An example of one of these is the Capability Maturity Model–Integrated® (Carnegie Mellon University, Pittsburgh, Pennsylvania) [5]. This chapter summarizes and compares these three approaches and model to the approach proposed in this book. This summarization is based on the primary topics of this book that are represented by each chapter: personnel management, project management, configuration management, requirements engineering, design, programming, and verification. In addition, this chapter discusses documentation as well as other important issues. Furthermore, because organizational change management is not addressed by any of these approaches this subject is ignored. A limitation of this analysis is that some key process areas of the Capability Maturity Model–Integrated (e.g., Supplier Agreement Management) are ignored.

11.1 Extreme Programming

Extreme Programming emphasizes the importance of a small number of key practices that have been empirically proven to yield a high return on investment [1, 6]. Because these practices are critical to rapidly delivering quality software, Extreme Programming advocates their repetitive and frequent application. The remainder of this section discusses Extreme Programming and periodically contrasts and compares it to the proposed Quality-Oriented Software Engineering approach.

Personnel Management. Extreme Programming advocates two critical management practices. First, it recommends the rapid removal of people from teams that are not meeting expectations. Second, it encourages teams to design or tailor their office space to suit themselves. This office space must be separate from the office space of other teams and should be a large room where all team members can work. Such a room is configured with computer monitors placed on top of desks or tables that permit two people to conveniently sit. These tables are placed in the center of the room without the use of wall partitions. Private office space resides on the outer edges of the room, which is used for making phone calls or conducting other business that is not suitable for the communal environment. For example, meetings may take place in these areas. This office space, however, is not composed of private offices; at most, low partitions may separate them from the communal programming area. Also residing on the outer edge of the room is a decompression area for people to relax when they need a break from their work. It is claimed that this configuration encourages collaboration among team members. A common rule is that people speak quietly among those who they work with; people who need to talk go to the far edges of the room.

My personal experience confirms much of this advice. First, I support the notion of removing problem employees (see Practices 3.15 and 3.16) and the provision of separate meeting areas (see Practice 3.13) and quiet work environments (see Practice 3.14). Second, I have worked in an environment very similar to what is described here and it worked very well. My main disagreement is that private *and* group office space really is needed to permit discussions that can become loud and distracting to others or to provide silence for times when intense concentration is needed. Furthermore, the success of such an environment is largely based on the professionalism of a workforce. The more professional it is, the more workable is such an environment. With an unprofessional workforce, the communal workspace will become too disruptive to perform work.

Although collocating teams is a highly desirable practice (see Practice 4.9), an organization must use common sense when doing it. For example,

I once worked for an organization that used a matrix organizational structure. Consequently, every time a new project was initiated, the organization would move people from disparate technical groups into an existing, common office space. This act displaced the workers who occupied the office space, which disrupted their work for about two weeks. In addition, the office space that was provided to the new project was always altered, meaning that the people in adjacent office spaces were disrupted for months while the office space allocated to the new project was being renovated to support its needs. I expect that the net loss in productivity of the workforces that were displaced and adjacent to the collocated workforce during the time of reconstruction outweighed the net gain of moving the new group to a common work area.

Furthermore, when a team is collocated, an organization must give the team what it promised to provide. I once belonged to a business unit that was moved to a new building. Because we were all involved in software development and dependent on a distributed computing infrastructure, we were vitally concerned about our networking needs in our new office space. We were assured that all our needs would be satisfied. When we got to the new office building, we were dismayed to learn that all the computers of our group did not share the same subnet. Instead, the network server machine was on its own subnet, separated by a gateway from all the client machines that were on another subnet. At the time, the networking software provided by the vendor of our workstations did not support such a configuration. With the aid of the manufacturer of the computers and our own staff, it took about two months to get this environment to work. Once working, distributed operations were about half the speed of our old environment. Obviously, a lot of ill-will was created by this fiasco.

Project Management. Extreme Programming is based on a small number of fundamental ideas [1]. Maybe the most important is the notion of iterative development using very short cycles — one- to three-month delivery cycles, one to four weeks for customer-requested features, and one to three days for internally planned tasks. Similarly, development activities are performed nearly continuously. For example, system builds and testing may be performed several times a day. The two primary benefits of these short cycles is the ability to rapidly respond to evolving business needs and to rapidly provide concrete feedback to system users based on executable software. Extreme Programming acknowledges that development teams of large systems may not be able to effectively use cycles of such short duration. I also feel that performing multiple daily builds yields little, if any, benefit.

When using Extreme Programming, development plans are developed incrementally. Managers of Extreme Programming teams only plan to the next foreseeable horizon, which is either the next release or the next iteration of a release that focuses on doing the most important things next [6]. Beyond the next horizon, planning is not detailed. The rationale for this approach is that it is better to defer making decisions until one has the greatest chance of being right, which generally occurs as one gains more knowledge and has a better understanding of the problem domain and user needs. In addition, the scope of work is based on business priorities and technical estimates, made by the people who will actually do the work. I generally agree with this just-in-time planning approach, although a consequence of it is that cost estimates cannot possibly be accurate given that detailed planning is not performed past the forseeable horizon.

Extreme Programming teams define a software development process and software development practices that suit their team members, and are not derived from an institutional procedure or recommended practices. The process, however, is changed when needed to work within the operational environment. That is, when the team recognizes that an improvement opportunity exists, then it actively seeks to resolve it by conducting experiments to find the best way to satisfy the objectives of the identified need. This approach is similar to that of the NASA Software Engineering Laboratory at Goddard Space Flight Center. That is, the team attempts to improve its processes in a bottom-up fashion that is driven by a need that has a high return on investment for a specific project. Thus, software process improvement functions within Extreme Programming in a very localized manner where its improvements are not necessarily passed on to other projects, nor is the improvement activity noted or rewarded by management. The result of this approach is that knowledge is acquired by an individual or group of individuals, but not by the organization — at least not formally. One assumption of this approach is that the team is knowledgeable and dedicated, which results in it doing the right thing. However, this may not always be true.

Change opportunities normally result from analyzing a small number of collected metrics. The primary metric that Extreme Programming teams track is actual development time versus estimated development time. This is similar to the earned value metric discussed in Practice 4.5. Beck says [1]: "You can make all the estimates you want, but if you don't measure what really happens against what you predicted would happen, you won't ever learn." Thus, it seems that the primary difference between the agile and defined process communities on this point concerns the number of metrics to collect. Unfortunately, Beck further states [1]: "The XP manager's most sensitive barometer of the need for change is awareness of his or her own feelings, physical, and emotional. If your stomach knots when you get in the car in the morning, something is wrong with your project and it's your job to effect the change." I claim that once you have such a gut feeling, the problem is well beyond being trivial. On the other hand, by collecting the right metrics, it is possible to identify problems earlier and in a more disciplined manner.

Extreme Programming defines the role of a coach, which is largely equivalent to conventional notions of a project manager of a small project or a technical lead of a subsystem or unit of a large project. The primary responsibility of the coach "is to get everybody else making good decisions," although no advice is given about how to do this. My belief is that you surround yourself with good people who are capable of making good decisions. Chapter 3 provides specific advice for hiring and retaining such people. People are the most critical resource, and employing the best people is the best way to deliver quality software that satisfies desired process qualities.

Configuration Management. Extreme Programming does not comment on configuration management, although practitioners of Extreme Programming most likely use and control it.

Requirements Engineering. Extreme Programming advocates the creation of stories, which essentially are rapidly created scenarios (see Practice 6.8), to describe what things a system needs to do. These stories are created to develop a shared understanding of the system by the development team and with the planned users of the system. In fact, they are generated with the aid of an on-site customer representative (see Practice 6.1). It is the premise of Extreme Programming that such a user representative is vital to the successful deployment of a system, and that the lack of access to such an individual indicates that the system lacks business value. Each of these stories is assigned a priority, which is used to assign tasks to development cycles (see Practice 6.15). The highest-priority items are implemented first. Developers, on the other hand, prioritize the stories assigned to a cycle according to their estimated risk. It is not clearly identified how risk is used, but I assume that those stories with the greatest risk are developed first.

Design. Extreme Programming focuses on building the simplest system having the minimal set of features that satisfy the defined stories (see Practice 7.10). The goal is to never include extra design elements. As new stories are implemented, developers continuously refactor the evolving design and refine the system architecture (see Practice 7.11). A clear belief is that it is better to fix an evolving design as you build it than to let it decay into a horrible mess, which is then fixed by reengineering it. That is, continuous, incremental change is preferred to infrequent but disruptive change. The goal of refactoring is always to reduce system complexity to achieve simple designs. No explicit rules are provided for reducing complexity, although some generic advice is given that essentially translates into reduced coupling, increased cohesion, and improved locality of reference.

Programming. Extreme Programming is an evolutionary style of programming — do a little now, do a little more later, and continue doing more until a project is completed. The primary motivation for this approach is that the earlier that an operational system is available to its users, the earlier the development team can get feedback about it. The premise is that only code — actually an executable specification — can give one the feedback that one needs to develop a system that satisfies the needs of the users. In other words, Extreme Programming advocates the continuous validation of the evolving system by its anticipated users to ensure that the right thing is being built and matches the users' desired workflow.

Extreme Programming advocates the use of pair programming, which is when two programmers work at one machine to develop the same code. When one person writes code, the other is supposed to be thinking more strategically. For example, the second person should consider the following questions. How will the proposed approach affect other parts of the system? What test cases should be written? Is there a way to simplify the system? That is, the second person is reviewing the software as it is written, writing test cases for it, and thinking about how to refactor the system to maintain design integrity. From this perspective, the second person is performing the verification activities necessary of a mature organization, but doing it in parallel with the development of the system instead of following the development effort, as is typical of most defined software development processes. The benefit of this approach is that peer reviews and testing get done early in the software development life cycle instead of being postponed to the end, where they are often not performed because of schedule pressure. In addition, the second person spends about the right amount of time verifying an artifact based on empirical data, although the effectiveness of the second person is unclear.

Because anyone can refactor code, advocates of Extreme Programming claim that the development team obtains a greater shared understanding of an entire system than with conventional development practices. Ownership, on the other hand, encourages stability at the expense of its evolution. My personal experience is that everyone should have the courage to change any code, but wisdom dictates that one should consult with the author of the code one intends to modify before making nontrivial changes.

Finally, the Extreme Programming approach recommends the adoption of coding standards, although it provides no guidance on what they should be (see Practice 8.3).

Verification. As mentioned, all work is continuously reviewed by one person of a pair programming team. In addition, an Extreme Programming project continuously — at least once a day — performs unit, integration, and functional testing to monitor progress and find defects. These tests are organized as a regression test suite that is executed after each change. The long-term benefit of regression test suites is that delivered systems remain in use longer because they are easier to maintain and evolve. Beck claims the following short-term benefit [1].

> *"Programming and testing together is also faster than just pro-gramming. ... The gain in productivity comes from a reduction in the time spent debugging — you no longer spend an hour looking for a bug, you find it in minutes."*

I have also observed this same phenomenon. By removing defects early in development and knowing that they have been removed, one is able to concentrate debugging efforts to a much smaller piece of code — that which one has most recently developed. However, executing a regression test suite for an entire system more than once a day yields marginal, if any, benefit.

Beck advocates the use of the following heuristic to determine whether or not a test should be generated [1]: "You are responsible for writing every test that you can imagine won't run immediately. After a while you will get good at reasoning about tests...." I, however, disagree with this statement. There is no evidence regarding the accuracy of people's intuition about what will work and what will not. A responsible philosophy is that every method can break — if not now, then in the future — unless it has been demonstrated to work. Thus, people should use a technique that generates effective test suites efficiently. This can be done using a code coverage tool and the procedure provided in Chapter 9.

Beck implies that the purpose of a test is to find a defect when he stated the following [1]:

> *"If I told you to test absolutely everything, pretty soon you would realize that most of the tests you were writing were valueless, and, if you were at all like me, you would stop writing them."*

However, the purpose of writing a test is not to find defects. Instead, it is to show their absence, which instills greater confidence in people that the software works. If I write a test suite that only tests half a program, I am confident in only the half that I tested. I may feel that the other half works but I would have little faith in it, at least not as much as in the half that was tested. In addition, if one does not write a test for a module because "it can't possibly fail," what prevents a future change from making it fail? With an existing test, the defect would be easily found and localized; without it, the defect may go undetected and cause failures to occur.

Documentation. A fundamental belief underlying Extreme Programming is to impose as little overhead on work as possible. Hence, meetings are short and held only as necessary to convey information when needed. In addition, few reports are generated, and when generated they are short. Hence, Extreme Programming emphasizes oral communication and close collaboration among programmers and the involvement of system users to communicate system structures and intent. The premise is that the need for written design documentation implies that successful verbal communication did not occur among the team. I, however, believe that the creators of ideas do not truly understand them until they write them down. While writing, authors generally find several errors in their thoughts or realize that the thoughts have not been sufficiently elaborated. What this means is that if people do not write down their ideas first so that they can inspect them before communicating them to others, the communicated ideas will not be fully developed and will contain omissions and inaccuracies.

Miscellaneous. Extreme Programming advocates never work overtime two weeks in a row because the need to do so indicates a serious problem that cannot be solved by simply working more hours (see Practice 3.20). Finally, Extreme Programming acknowledges that [1]: "Lines of code is a useless measurement in the face of code that shrinks when we learn better ways of programming" (see Practice 4.4).

11.2 The Rational Unified Process

The Rational Unified Process [2, 3] is a component-based software development process framework that emphasizes iterative development to develop software architectures. The process framework permits tailoring of software development processes to meet the needs of an organization and its projects. The Rational Unified Process defines the responsibilities of people who perform tasks, how they perform the tasks, and when they perform them. It also clearly identifies milestones and various decision points (see Practice 4.6). The Rational Unified Process uses the Unified Modeling Language® (Object Management Group) to prepare blueprints of software systems. The Unified Modeling Language, in fact, is integral to the process and is used to describe behaviors and workflows using state charts and sequence and activity diagrams.

Personnel Management. The Rational Unified Process neither discusses the hiring and retention of quality employees, nor does it provide any significant advice about how to create good software teams. However, its advocates do acknowledge that people are the most important asset. For example, Kroll and Kruchten [3] state that matrix organizational structures lower communication effectiveness of personnel because of the grouping of people by the functions they perform and that this structure views the most important asset — people — as being interchangeable, although nothing could be further from the truth.

Project Management. Before development begins, the Rational Unified Process first demands the creation of a vision statement (see Practices 4.1 and 6.3); the establishment of a business case for the effort (see Practice 4.1), including the identification of the return on investment (see Practice 2.8); and evaluation criteria for determining success. Throughout the whole process, planning what to do is always done before performing tasks. Because the Rational Unified Process advocates iterative and incremental development, these plans identify the number of development cycles, the number of iterations per phase, the major milestones, and the allocation of time (see Practices 4.2 and 4.6). The planning process also identifies significant risks (see Practice 4.3), which are managed as activities, and the tools that will be used by the project. Finally, this information is used to estimate the cost of a software development effort (see Practice 4.4).

Thus, this approach acknowledges that requirements cannot always be fully defined at the beginning of system development — sometimes they can only be developed gradually as people gain a better understanding of the problem and the problem domain. The Rational Unified Process defines each cycle of development as a collection of phases, each terminated by a major milestone. Each milestone is defined by the completion of a set of artifacts, which generally are expressed as documents that represent a variety of models. The purpose of each milestone is to act as a gate where a decision is made whether a development effort is ready to progress to the next phase of a cycle or, in the case that a cycle has been completed, to the next cycle. At the end of each cycle, software is integrated and executable images are built. Cycles are typically defined to be three to six months long. Hence, integration does not occur frequently enough to avoid difficult, and potentially time-consuming, integrations. Instead, integration should occur when a unit of work is completed, which implies that it has successfully passed defined criteria allowing it to be published (see Practice 5.5). This generally means that the unit has passed a series of regression tests and possibly a quality assurance assessment.

Configuration Management. The Rational Unified Process advocates using a configuration management tool to manage software artifacts (see Practice 5.16). It also advocates the use of a change management procedure that is controlled by a change control board (see Practice 5.8). Beyond this, it makes no other recommendations.

Requirements Engineering. The Rational Unified Process expects stakeholders to participate in the definition of requirements (see Practice 6.1) and advocates the following process for defining requirements:

> **Step 1.** Define the actors, which are people or external systems that interact with the system (see Practices 6.5 and 6.7).
>
> **Step 2.** Identify the desired features of the system to be developed.
>
> **Step 3.** Construct a domain model to understand the system context (see Practice 6.13). The domain model should identify the responsibilities (i.e., services) of each concept class.
>
> **Step 4.** Construct use cases, such that each use case corresponds to a functional requirement important to an actor (see Practice 6.8). Use cases should be described in the language of the user.
>
> **Step 5.** Capture nonfunctional requirements and associate them with individual uses cases (see Practice 6.9). Important nonfunctional requirements to define are those that define desired product quality (see Practice 6.10).
>
> **Step 6.** Prioritize the collection of use cases, select the ones to implement, and assign them to development cycles (see Practice 6.15). This helps to develop a development schedule, as well as resolve system scope. That is, the functional requirements that

underlie the use cases yield the highest level of tasks contained in a work breakdown structure.

Step 7. Prototype the user interface (see Practice 7.12).

As one can see, most of these requirements are described by the several practices contained herein. In addition, the desired features of a system are explicitly stated within the development of a concept of operations or the highest level of functional requirements.

Design. Create a design model that is derived from the domain model and forms a blueprint for the resulting implementation. The primary difference between the domain and design models is the introduction of supporting infrastructure and additional refinements of the concepts of the domain model. The basic design process follows, but it should not begin until about 80 percent of the use cases are specified.

Step 1. Define infrastructural classes and the ancestral relationships among all classes using class diagrams (see Practice 6.13).

Step 2. Define the interactions among the classes using sequence diagrams (see Practice 6.13).

Step 3. Define how system modules are deployed in the physical environment using deployment diagrams.

Step 4. Partition the system into subsystems and define their interdependencies using package diagrams (see Practice 6.13).

Step 5. Define the interfaces of each subsystem (see Practice 6.13).

Step 6. Identify the classes that are active (i.e., can run asynchronously as a thread or process) (see Section 7.5).

Step 7. Identify concurrency issues among the active classes (see Practice 8.5).

Step 8. Identify architectural mechanisms (see Section 7.5).

Step 9. Identify the attributes of each class and the operations that can be performed on each class (see Practice 6.13).

Step 10. Identify the associations and aggregations among classes (see Practice 6.13).

Step 11. Identify the classes that have state and design the states and transitions among them (see Practice 7.3).

Step 12. Identify the classes whose instances are persistent and design a database schema for them.

The approach proposed in this book is largely consistent with these design requirements. However, I believe that the identification of the deployment of system modules within a physical environment is of little value. Few, if any, bugs arise from this issue; even if they did, they would be trivial to resolve. Similarly, although it is important to development data persistence, it is a system function of no more importance than other system functions so it does not make much sense to give this topic any special significance, and I have not. On the other hand, concurrency is an extremely important issue but a detailed treatment of it is beyond the scope of this book.

Programming. The Rational Unified Process provides no real programming guidance other than to define how the system will be built.

Verification. The Rational Unified Process specifies the execution of functional, integration, system, and unit tests. All test cases are captured in a regression test suite that is executed during each build. Functional tests are created from defined use cases (see Practice 9.6). Integration tests are created, but it is not specified how they are created. Thus, the creation of integration tests may not be efficient nor effective. Unit tests are created using the equivalence class testing technique (see the similar Practices 9.8 and 9.9). Furthermore, it is recommended that most interesting paths be tested — those that are most common, most critical, the least followed, and the highest risk (see Section 9.2.2). Configuration, installation, and stress testing comprise the system testing strategy. Test coverage metrics are collected (see Practice 9.7), which are indicative of the effectiveness of a test strategy; and it is recommended that 100 percent of the statements be tested. In addition, the Rational Unified Process recommends monitoring discovered defects to estimate the reliability of a system and when to stop development (see Section 10.3). Finally, the Rational Unified Process recommends reviewing the artifacts (see Section 9.1.1) although no guidance is given on how to do it. Again, the material described in this book is largely consistent with the Rational Unified Process. The primary difference is that this book identifies a specific review process that is based on a formal inspection technique.

Documentation. The Rational Unified Process advocates using use cases to write user manuals, which implies that user documentation will focus on tasks that users will perform (see Practice 10.1).

Miscellaneous. The Rational Unified Process advocates:

1. The use of software tools
2. The development of adaptable software (see Section 7.1)
3. The development and reuse of software components, although no guidance is provided for creating reusable software
4. The development of an executable architecture early in the software development life cycle

I agree with all these points. The use of software tools, however, is beyond the scope of this book. I believe that most bookkeeping and many analysis activities can be automated by software tools, especially when they are designed as an integrated suite of tools. Software reuse is very likely the most important thing an organization can do to increase product quality and the productivity of software personnel, once it has taken the necessary steps to hire the best people. Unfortunately, the development of a successful reuse strategy is also beyond the scope of this book. However, by following a disciplined development process that uses the practices described herein, an organization can overcome many, if not most, of the difficult issues underlying the development of reuse libraries. Finally, the process identified in Section 7.6 advocates the continuous development of an executable architecture from the first day of design to the last day of coding.

11.3 Cleanroom Software Engineering

Cleanroom Software Engineering is a response to the following observation [4]:

> *"The vast majority of software today is handcrafted by artisans using craft-based techniques that cannot produce consistent results. These techniques have little in common with the rigorous,*

theory-based processes characteristic of other engineering disciplines."

As a result, Cleanroom Software Engineering emphasizes the design of correct software using rigorous specification, design, and verification practices that precisely and predictably define, verify, and measure software quality and reliability.

Personnel Management. Cleanroom Software Engineering focuses completely on the software development process, and does not comment on personnel issues whatsoever.

Project Management. Project managers who follow Cleanroom Software Engineering create software development plans to control incremental development and process improvement activities. Projects adopting Cleanroom Software Engineering are generally small — three to eight people — to minimize communication and coordination. Tasks are assigned to people based on individual responsibilities and schedule priorities. Reliability requirements influence these schedule priorities because they have the greatest impact on system reliability [7]. For larger projects, an initial group of the most experienced people are composed, who define the system architecture, develop the initial increment or two, and write specifications for individual subsystems. Later, these same team members lead the various subsystem development teams. (This approach is a characteristic feature of the Chief Architect Team discussed in Section 7.6.)

Configuration Management. The software development plan defines configuration management and change control policies, practices, and procedures. However, Cleanroom Software Engineering does not specify specific practices or procedures to follow.

Requirements Engineering. Cleanroom Software Engineering defines scenarios based on events that correspond to canonical sequences of behavioral specifications. This follows an algorithmic process of all sequences of length 1, 2, 3, etc. For each new sequence, one determines if it is illegal, equivalent to an existing sequence, or represents a new sequence. For each new sequence, traces to existing requirements are made, although there is no mention of how these requirements were created. If no trace is possible for a sequence, a requirement has been omitted. In this case, the person creating the behavioral specifications will derive a new requirement. Similarly, if a requirement is not traced to any canonical sequence, then the requirement is either unnecessary or one or more events have been omitted.

The produced artifacts of this process comprise four tables. One table describes every event and the associated responses to them. Another one identifies the behavioral sequences, their associated responses, their equivalence to other behavioral sequences, and the traces to defined requirements. A third table identifies the behavioral sequences, the state variables required by each one, and the values before and after the occurrence of the last event of the sequence (i.e., the stimulus). The final table identifies each state variable and associates an initial value and range of legitimate values for each one. For a more thorough description of the process underlying the creation of these tables, see [8] and Practice 6.30.

Design. Design follows a strict refinement process. First, functional black boxes are specified by identifying input (including input history) and output pairs. Then, these black boxes are refined into state boxes, which identify the elements of the input history that must be captured as internal states to achieve the external behavior. Next, transitions are identified that transform a current state and new input to a different state and corresponding response. Finally, a clear box representation is produced that identifies the procedures for performing the transitions and may introduce new black boxes to represent important decompositions. Hence, this approach advocates transformational implementation [9], which means that any expression of the evolving solution can be replaced by any other equivalent expression. A benefit of this approach is that given an initially correct specification, one only has to verify the transformational rules to verify a system, instead of verifying the entire resulting system. Although I also advocate this approach, it was barely discussed in Section 10.2.

Programming. No specific guidance is given for developing code.

Verification. Verification of software is based on peer review and testing procedures. Every work product is reviewed at each cycle of development. There are two types of reviews. A *verification review* focuses on the correctness and completeness of software artifacts through a formal verification process that requires designers to make function-based correctness assertions, for which the reviewers must unanimously agree. In essence, verification reviews involve mental and verbal correctness proofs. *Development reviews*, on the other hand, examine technical strategies and alternative ideas, and help educate the development team. Simplification of a work product is an explicit object of every review. Hence, refactoring is encouraged because it is easier to verify a simpler product than a more complex one, and its quality is generally higher.

Testing, on the other hand, is achieved by creating a usage model, formalized as a state machine, that represents all possible system uses. The usage model is then used to produce functional test cases. The number of functional test cases is determined by randomly selecting different stimuli, with associated probabilities, until a desired level of statistically based reliability is achieved. This verification approach is similar to the Quality-Oriented Software Engineering approach, although its inspection procedure is more rigorous and its testing procedure is less so.

Documentation. Cleanroom Software Engineering provides no guidance concerning documentation.

Miscellaneous. The basic practices underlying Cleanroom Software Engineering include:

1. Define quality objectives (see Practice 6.10).
2. Use quantitative measures to measure the process and product, and take corrective action (see Practice 4.5).
3. Create traces between artifacts (see Practice 6.20).
4. Do peer reviews (see Section 9.1).
5. Define the host environment and tools (see Practice 4.12).
6. Define mission, goals, and objectives (see Practices 6.2 and 6.3).
7. Define the organizational structure (see Section 4.2).
8. Define deliverables, schedule, and available resources (see Section 4.1).
9. Analyze opportunities for reuse.
10. Analyze and manage risks (see Practice 4.3).
11. Identify applicable standards (see Section 4.3, Step 9).
12. Identify training requirements (see Practice 3.7).
13. Identify configuration management procedures (see Section 5.6).
14. Control changes and analyze their impact (see Practice 5.8).
15. Manage interactions with customers and others outside the team (see Practice 6.32).
16. Evaluate new technologies and processes as part of process improvement.
17. Define all software boundaries (see Practice 6.7) and stimulus-response pairs.
18. Specify, analyze, and validate the software architecture (see Sections 7.2, 7.4, and 7.6).

11.4 Capability Maturity Model–Integrated

The Capability Maturity Model–Integrated was developed to integrate the best practices of process development, product development, software engineering, supplier sourcing, and systems engineering into a single model. Similar models are in widespread use in other parts of the world, but this model has become the most common model for assessing the process maturity of a product development organization in the United States. The Capability Maturity Model–Integrated is described according to the categories previously used, not in terms of its defined key process areas.

Personnel Management. The Capability Maturity Model–Integrated does not discuss the management of personnel. It strictly discusses development processes.

Project Management. The Capability Maturity Model–Integrated discusses project management, both broadly and specifically. Following are some of the practices used to better manage projects:

- Establish a shared vision (see Practice 4.1), align it with business needs (see Practice 4.1), and establish a contract between the team and its sponsor (see Practice 6.32).
- Identify the necessary team tasks (see Practice 4.2) and the knowledge, skills, and expertise required to perform them.
- Establish a work breakdown structure and schedule that explicitly identifies major milestones, assumptions, constraints, and task dependencies (see Practice 4.2).
- Identify and analyze development and deployment risks (see Practice 4.3).
- Estimate the effort and cost based on models of documented experience (see Practice 4.4).
- Make develop, buy, and reuse decisions.
- Review the plan with high-level management (see Practice 4.1).
- Establish and maintain formal agreements with suppliers (see Practice 6.32).
- Assign appropriate people to teams and define their roles and responsibilities (see Practices 2.5, 3.1, 3.9, 3.10, and 4.10).
- Monitor and control the process and quality objectives (see Practices 4.5 and 4.6).

The project management practices identified in this book are similar to those identified by the Capability Maturity Model–Integrated but are stated differently. For example, although the identification of knowledge, skills, and expertise is not specifically discussed in any of the practices described in this book, it is indirectly identified by the specified human resource categories associated with each software development task. Similarly, constraints are documented as nonfunctional requirements, and assumptions are explicitly documented during requirements definition and design. Finally, decisions involving whether a requirement should be satisfied by developing, buying, or reusing software is an explicit responsibility of the design process and should be documented as part of the design rationale. Contrarily, formal supplier agreements are not discussed herein because the topic lies outside the scope of the book. However, I believe that formal supplier agreements should state that the supplier must fulfill the same practices fulfilled by the customer. That is, a customer should not contract out services to suppliers that do not meet the quality standards of the customer.

Configuration Management. The Capability Maturity Model–Integrated requires the establishment of a configuration management system that fulfills several requirements. These requirements include:

- Configuration items must be identified following specified criteria (see Practices 5.1 and 5.2).
- Configuration items must be assigned unique identifiers (see Practice 5.12).
- The person responsible for each configuration item must be identified.
- Configuration items must be stored and accessible (see Practice 5.16).
- Versions of configuration items must be archived and recoverable from archives (see Practices 5.18 and 5.19).
- Transaction records must be stored and accessible (see Practice 5.16).
- Multiple levels of management control (for different phases or cycles of a project, for different types of systems, and for different roles) must be provided.
- Baselines must be established (see Practice 5.12).
- The configuration items comprising a baseline must be documented (see Practice 5.13).
- Configuration control boards should authorize baselines (see Practice 5.8).
- Track change requests (see Practice 5.8).
- Analyze the impact of change requests (see Section 5.6).
- Authorize changes to configuration items before changing them.
- Validate that changes do not have unintended side effects.
- Record the rationale for a change.

I disagree with some of the configuration management practices identified by the Capability Maturity Model–Integrated. First, it is unclear what it means to hold a person responsible for each configuration item. Obviously, one person should be the primary author of an artifact when it is first created; but after creation, any person should be allowed to change an artifact if such a change is an outcome of satisfying an authorized task. Second, it is not always possible to authorize changes to every configuration item before one needs to change them. That is, it is impossible to always predict every artifact that needs to be changed as a result of a change request; in actuality, this rarely can be done. Instead, when artifacts are changed as a result of a change request, someone should validate that it was necessary to modify the changed artifacts in response to a change request. Third, it is not feasible to validate that changes do not have unintended side effects. Instead, the goal should be simply to satisfy the defined verification criteria for the artifact that have been identified by the applicable software development process.

On the other hand, I agree with the remaining configuration management practices of the Capability Maturity Model–Integrated, some of which are not documented herein. For example, I believe that the rationale and estimated impact of a proposed change should be identified so that a change control board can analyze the merit of the proposed change and the cost to make the change. Similarly, I believe that a configuration management system should provide multiple levels of management control.

Requirements Engineering. The Capability Maturity Model–Integrated asks that the management and definition of requirements satisfy the following practices, which are consistent with those proposed in this book:

- Establish operational concepts and associated scenarios (see Practice 6.8).
- Describe operating modes and states (see Practice 6.4).
- Collect stakeholder needs and transform them into requirements (see Practice 6.1).
- Define interface requirements (see Practice 6.9).
- Define functional requirements.
- Define requirements for desired qualities of a work product (see Practice 6.10).
- Allocate requirements to product components and life-cycle phases and cycles (see Practice 6.18).
- Maintain relationships among requirements (see Practice 6.25).
- Validate requirements for necessity and sufficiency (see Practice 6.29).

Design. The Capability Maturity Model–Integrated requires that design interfaces be established and that alternatives be evaluated when making decisions. To improve the decision-making process, the Capability Maturity Model–Integrated recommends that practitioners perform the following activities:

- Establish and maintain criteria for evaluating alternatives and ranking the criteria (see Practice 7.14).
- Document the rationale for selecting and rejecting criteria (see Practice 7.15).
- Identify the process for measuring criteria.
- Select evaluation methods (e.g., simulation, prototyping) (see Practice 7.12 and Section 7.6).
- Identify and evaluate assumptions.
- Perform a sensitivity analysis of the alternatives.

These requirements are consistent with those practices described herein, with the exception that I believe the profession is not mature enough to perform sensitivity analysis and it is unclear how meaningful such results would be. On the other hand, several metrics have been identified for collection throughout the book and should be collected in an automated manner using an integrated tool suite.

Programming. The Capability Maturity Model–Integrated provides no guidance regarding the writing of code.

Verification. The Capability Maturity Model–Integrated recommends the following practices, although it provides little specific guidance on how to perform them.

- Select the products to be verified and validated.
- Select the evaluation methods for verification and validation (see Chapter 9).
- Identify criteria for successful verification and validation (see Chapter 9).
- Establish and maintain a verification and validation environment (see Practice 9.13).
- Analyze the verification and validation results.

I agree with all these requirements except that I believe that all artifacts should be verified through the execution of regression test suites. However, when a test fails, someone must correct the defect, identify its source, and determine its cause so that other defects of the same kind can be reduced or eliminated. This behavior is not specifically identified within this book during the development activities, although it is discussed within Chapter 2 for larger-grained change efforts.

Documentation. The Capability Maturity Model–Integrated requires that virtually everything be documented and recorded. It, however, provides no guidance on how to construct good documentation. This book, on the other hand, rarely specifies the actions that should be documented and recorded, although it does provide guidance on how to write good documentation. The reason this book provides no guidance on what should be documented and recorded is because I feel that all information should be captured within a repository, which can be later used for reporting purposes. Thus, I have chosen to emphasize doing work instead of documenting what work is to be done or has been done.

Miscellaneous. The Capability Maturity Model–Integrated identifies four other very important goals:

1. Establish an integrated work environment.
2. Establish incentives as part of a reward and recognition program that is consistent with the organization's vision, goals, and objective, and that recognizes teams as well as individuals (see Practice 2.5).
3. Establish and maintain life-cycle models and tailoring guidelines.
4. Identify risk sources and categories.

I interpret an integrated work environment as an integrated software tool suite that supports software development personnel during all phases of the life cycle and for all tasks they need to perform. Unfortunately, no such environment exists today. I propose an iterative development life-cycle model and feel that other models are unnecessary. I expect that all these practices will be followed; when they are not, a rationale must be provided explaining why they are not followed. Each rationale must be reviewed by an authoritative person capable of judging its adequacy. Finally, I view that each practice not performed or not performed as stated is a risk; hence, most of the key risks are already identified and classified.

11.5 Summary

This chapter briefly described four schemes for developing software. Extreme Programming was developed by real programmers and has been successfully used for building many systems. I know of no documented successful use of this approach beyond 50,000 lines of source code, and it is unknown whether this approach breaks down at some point or what such a point would be. Extreme Programming focuses all activity on the development of code; other artifacts are developed only to support the generation of code and are developed no further than necessary to support such activity. Hence, Extreme Programming emphasizes the skill of the developer and discourages the creation of documents that large organizations typically mandate. This approach has led many to erroneously claim that Extreme Programming lacks maturity or discipline. Instead, it is a disciplined approach that emphasizes the frequent repetition of a small number of proven practices that focus on the development of quality products.

The Rational Unified Process, on the other hand, was largely developed by methodologists whose actual development experience is unclear. The Rational Unified Process has been successfully used in a variety of domains and for numerous projects of varying size — from the very small to the very large. Thus, one could argue that it has been demonstrated to work in the real world. The Rational Unified Process does not focus on one specific activity; instead, it treats software as an end-to-end process. It emphasizes processes that are supported by software tools, while acknowledging that people are the critical ingredient for successfully developing software. It is a very mature and disciplined process that is tailorable to meet the objectives of a software development effort.

Similar to the Rational Unified Process, Cleanroom Software Engineering was developed by methodologists and has been validated to achieve its goals by practitioners. It has been successfully used on several applications, but one might argue that its approach is not suitable for the typical programmer because of its formal basis. Cleanroom Software Engineering focuses on the specification, design, and validation of software. Hence, it is a very mature and disciplined process, like the Rational Unified Process, but one that involves much more rigor.

Finally, the Capability Maturity Model–Integrated was developed by representatives of numerous organizations. Some of these representatives were process methodologists and many were managers; it is unclear what practical experience these people had. Such experience may or may not be significant. Regardless, their effort has resulted in the definition of numerous high-level strategies useful to organizations that have significant expertise in the area. However, by not specifying useful tactics for successfully achieving these strategies, many organizations may have difficulty achieving effective change efficiently. As a result, the satisfaction of the goals and practices defined in the Capability Maturity Model–Integrated will not necessarily lead to improved product quality. For example, empirical data for the Capability Maturity Model for Software indicate that higher levels of organizational maturity typically result in better product quality and increased human productivity. However, the data also shows that the best performing organizations of the lowest level of maturity outperform the lowest performing organizations of the highest maturity level. Hence, this fact demonstrates the importance of validating the benefit of each proposed change in an operational environment.

References

1. Beck, K., *Extreme Programming Explained: Embrace Change*, Addison-Wesley, 2000.
2. Jacobson, I., Booch, G., and Rumbaugh, J., *The Unified Software Development Process*, Addison-Wesley, 1999.
3. Kroll, P. and Kruchten, P., *The Rational Unified Process Made Easy: A Practitioner's Guide to the RUP*, Addison-Wesley, 2003.
4. Prowell, S.J. et al., *Cleanroom Software Engineering: Technology and Process*, Addison-Wesley, 1999.
5. Chrissis, M.B., Konrad, M., and Shrum, S., *CMMI: Guidelines for Process Integration and Product Improvement*, Addison-Wesley, 2003.
6. Beck, K. and Fowler, M., *Planning Extreme Programming*, Addison-Wesley, 2001.
7. Poore, J.H., Mills, H.D., and Mutchler, D., Planning and Certifying Software System Reliability, *IEEE Software*, 10, 88, January 1993.
8. Prowell, S.J. and Poore, J.H., Sequence-Based Specification of Deterministic Systems, *Software — Practice and Experience*, 28, 329, 1998.
9. Balzer, R., Cheatham, T.E., Jr., and Green, C.C., Software Technology in the 1990's: Using a New Paradigm, *IEEE Computer*, 16(11), 39, 1983.

Chapter 12
Summary

This chapter summarizes the material presented in this book. It recounts that the software industry is rarely successful in developing quality software, partly because industry does not know how to orchestrate organizational change. Then, it briefly reviews the key practices identified within the book and compares these practices to those advocated by other schemes. Finally, it mentions that these practices are largely the result of failures that I have been a part of — some I have helped to create and others I have observed.

The difficulties of developing quality software have been known since at least 1968 [1]. Today, most organizations still have not come to grips with these difficulties and still have problems developing quality software. Without positive change, this situation will continue to worsen because the growth in software is increasing about four times faster than productivity growth.

12.1 Software Development

Several factors affect the development of software. Critical factors affecting software cost and quality are product complexity and human capabilities. Product complexity factors include product size, product reliability needs, and various timing and space constraints. Vital human capabilities include knowledge of the problem domain, modern programming practices, and software tools. In addition, the stability of software development artifacts, the adopted technologies for developing them, and the personnel used to develop them also are significant factors affecting software. Hence, a successful way to produce quality software is to embrace these critical success factors through core software development practices. The Quality-Oriented Software Engineering approach proposes the following critical concepts.

- Hire and retain a highly skilled, learning workforce and properly match its members with development tasks.
- Manage software so that reliable deliveries can be created and recreated at any time.
- Identify and verify requirements with the involvement of all stakeholders.
- Define availability, efficiency, extensibility, portability, reliability, reusability, robustness, testability, and usability requirements in addition to functional requirements.
- Design software to minimize coupling among modules that fulfill single responsibilities and aggregate them to maximize cohesion.
- Manage software development by planning for change, managing the approved changes, monitoring risks, and measuring software quality.
- Use an integrated tool suite to develop and manage software.
- Use a small number of defined reference architectures and solution frameworks.
- Adopt software development standards.

These critical concepts are realized by the definition of several critical practices emphasizing people, tools, and techniques that are embodied in several procedures. However, before one can apply these ideas within the workplace, one must ask how one can change human behavior so that members of an organization will accept these new ideas.

Organizational Change Management. The software industry has defined several software process standards, requirements, and guidelines to help it develop quality software. Even with these aids, developing quality software has proven an extremely challenging undertaking because organizations largely ignore or incorrectly handle the human issues surrounding organizational change. Consequently, most software quality initiatives fail.

Several practices, however, can significantly ease the introduction and continuity of a software process improvement program. These practices are based on four imperatives that involve the understanding, commitment, and involvement by the members of an organization. First, an organizational vision must be clearly defined and communicated to the entire workforce so that each individual will understand the goals of the organization and how he or she helps to achieve those goals. Second, nearly every member of the entire organization must be committed to achieving the goals defined in the organizational vision. Third, practitioners must assist in defining the policies, procedures, and processes to achieve the organizational goals. Fourth, the defined policies, procedures, and processes must be clearly communicated to the affected workforce.

Management plays a critical role in organizational change management. It must inculcate an organizational vision, commit to a software process improvement program, create a software engineering steering group and a software engineering process group, and align the human resources organization with the organizational vision. A software engineering steering group should be composed of executives and senior line management and led by the head of the organization. The software engineering process group, on the other hand, should be composed of highly respected people having expertise in and a demonstrated commitment to software engineering, process definition, organizational change, and information technology. In addition, group members should be highly motivated individuals who have spent many years developing software. Although the software engineering process group is responsible for improving software processes, the human resources organization could have the most significant impact on a software process improvement program because people are the most important resource that an organization has. As a result, the human resources organization must hire a resilient workforce compatible with the characteristics of the desired organizational culture, establish a defined career path for software professionals, establish quantitative and objective promotion criteria, provide a problem-solving-based training program, and align the reward system with the objectives of a software process improvement program.

Because a software engineering process group is responsible for making successful software change happen, it must perform three essential functions. First, it must periodically assess how the organization develops software and determine if and when change is needed. Second, it must demonstrate that proposed changes are beneficial. Third, it must obtain the commitment of practitioners to adopt the proposed changes.

Personnel Management. The most important asset of a software organization is its talented people. These people are often 15 to 30 times better than the less talented people in terms of both productivity and quality factors. Hence, an organization must follow very selective hiring practices to hire these high performers. As a result, it should define minimal standards of knowledge for software personnel based on a broad base of computer science, software engineering, and application domain knowledge. It should verify that prospective employees have this knowledge by performing the following actions.

1. Interview candidates using a checklist of questions that tests their knowledge, identifies their problem-solving skills, illuminates their interpersonal characteristics, and evaluates their enthusiasm for the tasks that they will perform on the job.
2. Examine a portfolio of work provided by a candidate and evaluate its quality.
3. Require candidates to give a short presentation on a technical subject of their choice, which allows them to demonstrate their technical knowledge, communication skills, and personality traits.

If possible, an organization should hire potential employees on a short-term basis so that it can evaluate their performance before hiring them. In addition, an organization should attempt to hire personnel who have actually delivered software systems because delivering software systems requires a unique combination of skills and experience. Once hired, new employees should attend an orientation program that identifies an organization's expectations of its employees and communicates to them the organization's business values and practices. In addition, recent hires should be provided with on-the-job training that describes the institutional software engineering policies, practices, and procedures.

To keep its best people, an organization should provide its employees witth a stimulating and friendly environment that permits them to work efficiently and effectively. Such an environment is one whereby software engineers are given private, noise-free office space (at least ten feet by ten feet) that contains a whiteboard and a workstation. In addition, the organization should encourage interaction among people through various events. They do not have to be elaborate affairs — getting together for bagels and cream cheese once a week has a tremendously positive effect on group dynamics.

Finally, an organization must fairly compensate its people for their work. If not, few of the best people will stay with the organization. Thus, an organization must develop quantitative and objective guidelines for recognizing and rewarding outstanding performance. Such a compensation scheme should also plan for the removal of poor performers because the best performers often quit because of their frustration with having to work with these less-talented individuals. In sum, an organization must hire the best people it can by following a defined process and retain them by providing a conducive work environment and a fair reward system.

Project Management. To overcome the difficulties of cost-effectively delivering quality software, an organization should conduct feasibility studies to estimate the cost of developing quality software while assuming a manageable level of risk. The primary goal of a feasibility study is to determine early in the software development life cycle whether a project should be cancelled or continued. A feasibility study should include a risk assessment and an estimate of the work to be done and its cost. One can estimate the cost by creating a detailed work breakdown structure, identifying the dependencies among the project's tasks, and noting the most critical path. Personnel should derive cost estimates based on experience with similar projects. When doing this, they should explicitly identify all source code modules to be reused and estimate the effort to integrate each reused module. In addition, the minimum estimated development time should use a maximum personnel growth rate of 30 percent per year.

The management of a software organization can be optimized in several ways. For example, it should be structured hierarchically and project offices should be created for large projects. Similarly, before real work begins, an operational infrastructure should be added to the work environment. The operational infrastructure, in part, should be determined by key technology experts, who are assigned to a project during the earliest stages of development. Once the key personnel and the necessary infrastructure are in place, full-scale project staffing can begin. Once a project is fully staffed, management should use several metrics to track projects. These metrics should measure schedules, budgets, productivity, defects, quality, and risk.

Configuration Management. Software artifacts and their configuration must be managed. Essential to this management is the maintenance of the integrity of each artifact, its derivation history, and the configuration of software releases over time. Hence, it is vital that all source artifacts and those artifacts used to produce a delivery be under configuration control. Control should govern how artifacts are created, edited, changed, and deleted. Practically speaking, this means that an organization or project must define policies for branches, codelines, and workspaces.

An organization must control how its software is changed because it is the primary way to stabilize software development efforts. Two key ideas of a formal change management process are to use a change control board to control system change and to use change packages to define units of work. When a defect is discovered and the change control board has authorized its correction through a defined change package, it should be recorded for future process improvement. Furthermore, once the correction has been made, the type of correction should be recorded and applied to each release that may share the same defect. Finally, the building of software releases for internal and external use should use common tools and processes that ensure the integrity of each release and the artifacts that comprise them.

Requirements Engineering. Requirements define necessary, quantifiable, and verifiable capabilities, characteristics, and constraints of systems, and are generally imposed by multiple stakeholders. Functional requirements define the capabilities that systems provide, whereas nonfunctional requirements identify the constraints imposed on systems or their development. Nonfunctional requirements should identify operational, performance, user interface, and site adaptation needs because these are extremely vital to the successful operation of a system. Such requirements are especially important when dealing with subcontractors. For example, a contractual specification should specify guarantees covering availability, mean time between failures, mean time to repair, throughput, etc. In addition, nonfunctional requirements may constrain the construction process and should constrain product quality.

Requirements engineering can be described in terms of the following activities: elicitation, analysis, specification, validation, and management. Requirements elicitation is the process of identifying and consolidating various stakeholder needs. The involvement of stakeholders in the definition of requirements is important because productivity is significantly higher when stakeholders participate in specifying requirements and their involvement ensures that their needs are better satisfied. When involving stakeholders, a clear, crisp project vision should be defined that explains what a system will be and the reasons for building it, which should satisfy one or more business needs. Such a vision statement helps all stakeholders come to a shared understanding of the system. One way to elaborate this understanding is to define a concept of operations that describes how a system is used and what it does in a typical day. These descriptions should include how a system is developed, verified, deployed, installed, operated, maintained, upgraded, and disposed. The viewpoints of all stakeholders — developers, inspectors, testers, end users, customers, trainers, and maintainers — should be considered when writing these descriptions. In addition, these descriptions should identify all external and enabling systems required by the system being built.

Requirements analysis is the process of analyzing a problem to derive a complete and appropriate set of requirements. This analysis typically involves the development of a conceptual model, which is an abstraction of the real world. A good model of a system represents the aspects of a problem critical to its solution. That is, it should describe the important concepts of the real world, including their attributes and behaviors, and the relationships among them. The conceptual model is usually derived from the concept of operations, as are several requirements. The rationale for each requirement should be explicitly stated so that others can understand why it exists or question its existence. Finally, the analysis activity should include an evaluation of the relative merit or importance of the defined requirements, based on cost, dependency, and importance, which is used to select the functionality of each software release or build.

A requirements specification identifies what a system is suppose to do and provides a basis for developing schedules, estimating costs, and verifying requirements. A requirements specification should uniquely, completely, and consistently define a consistent set of requirement statements that clearly convey intent. Furthermore, a verification method should be associated with each statement. If one cannot be identified, then it is not possible to demonstrate that a requirement has been satisfied. On the other hand, if a verification method can be documented, it can be used to write test cases to verify its satisfaction.

Throughout the entire requirements engineering process, managers must perform two critical activities. First, they must ensure that all interested parties have a common understanding of the system requirements. Second, they must control how requirements are introduced, changed, and removed because requirement volatility is a leading cause of software project failures. In sum, paying attention to all these issues should result in quality requirements that are easily verified, especially when an organization invests 10 to 15 percent of total project development funds in the engineering of requirements.

Design. The design process results in the creation of solutions that satisfy specific goals or needs. Software design is different than other forms of design because it is not constrained by physical laws or structures. Consequently, software design is more complex than most forms of design because it is conceptually unbounded. However, software design can be efficiently and effectively performed once one understands important software principles, practices, and procedures. Fundamental design principles include separating design concerns, modeling real-world objects, and minimizing the interactions among cohesive design components.

When applying these design principles, one should plan for change, plan for failure, and adopt a core set of ideas for each system design to improve its conceptual integrity.

There are two ways to separate design concerns: (1) by viewing only the important aspects of a software system (i.e., abstraction) and (2) by delegating individual responsibilities to modules (i.e., modularity). Modularity is a measure of the decomposition of a system into well-defined modules. Abstraction, on the other hand, is the act of focusing on the important aspects of a phenomenon and ignoring what is unimportant. The purpose of abstraction is to create a new semantic level where one can be absolutely precise and work with concepts appropriate for solving a particular problem. One type of abstraction views a specific aspect, or perspective, of a problem and another views a problem at different levels of granularity. Although the use of abstraction is a highly effectively form of managing complexity, knowledge cannot be strictly categorized within a single hierarchy or multiple disjoint hierarchies; instead, these hierarchies are tangled and the tangles tend to create problems.

An important goal of design is to achieve high cohesion and low coupling. Remember that cohesion is a measure of the relative function strength of a module and coupling is a measure of the relative independence between modules. The maximization of cohesion and minimization of coupling make software systems easier to understand, modify, and reuse because it improves a system's locality of reference.

A conceptual model is a simplified representation of reality and can be used to express concepts at different levels of precision. A useful technique for developing software is to develop a conceptual model of the application domain and then derive an implementation from it. By matching the structure of the design to the problem, the developer reduces the translation effort between conceptualizations, which improves design quality and shortens the design process.

To develop quality architectural designs, software engineers should follow several important practices that emphasize the principles just discussed. For example, large systems should be decomposed into small modules that separate the control logic of functions from the services they provide. In addition, models of critical system-level concepts — measurements, clocks, data queues, events, and threads — should be provided. The use of measurements ensures that interface requirements are not violated. Clocks are useful for scheduling the start and end of asynchronous activities. Data queues commonly buffer sensor and user input. Events represent real-time, dynamic situations that occur within the real world. Finally, threads permit asynchronous processing to occur within the application.

To produce quality detailed designs, software engineers should apply several important practices. They should encapsulate detailed descriptions of behaviors within functions and use program structuring techniques that optimize locality of reference. In addition, they should minimize their use of goto statements and avoid using redundant data. Finally, throughout the entire design process, software engineers should use an unambiguous notation for modeling designs, formally analyze design decisions, compute quality metrics, and improve software designs when the quality metrics indicate that quality goals are not being achieved.

Programming. The primary artifact of the programming process is the development of one or more executable applications. To produce quality applications, it is essential that an organization follow a few critical practices. First, it should program in the highest-level programming language subject to defined constraints and other practical considerations because this approach results in more reliable software and greater programmer productivity. This occurs because the higher-level programming languages operate at higher levels of abstraction. Second, it should further increase programmer productivity using an integrated development environment. Finally, it should adopt coding standards based on fundamental principles and practices known to positively affect quality, as well as other conventions that ease readability.

Verification. Because it is impossible to deliver defect-free software for nontrivial programs, an organization should use an efficient and effective defect detection approach based on software inspection and testing that finds defects at the earliest possible stage in the software development life cycle. Software inspections are recommended because they have proven to be a cost-effective technique for removing defects, although their effectiveness can vary widely. Chief architects should inspect requirements documents and code because they understand the interactions of the system components and are responsible for maintaining the conceptual integrity of entire systems. Similarly, chief programmers should inspect architectural designs for simplicity, low coupling, high cohesion, and adherence to applicable standards. When performing inspections, inspectors should use standard checklists, which are tailored to achieve the goals of each inspection.

Testing, like an inspection, cannot show that an artifact is free of defects but it can identify their existence. Structural testing verifies the structural aspects of code. Effective and efficient structural testing is based on basis path and boundary value testing. Basis path testing independently tests the outcome of each condition that affects control flow, whereas boundary value testing verifies the correctness of each condition. Functional testing, on the other hand, verifies that the functionality of the system behaves as intended. Hence, functional tests are derived from the functional requirements defined in earlier stages of development. Finally, system testing verifies that one or more nonfunctional characteristcs are satsfied. System testing exists in a variety of forms. Performance testing verifies that the speed of a system satisfies specified performance requirements. Likewise, capacity and stress testing ensure that software properly handles excessive volumes of data for both short and long periods of time while operating under varying workloads. In conclusion, an organization should use a code coverage tool that provides quantitative evidence on how thorough a test effort is.

Documentation. Good user documentation is critical for achieving customer satisfaction. One way of gaining such satisfaction is by orienting the documentation around descriptions of real tasks performed by system users that reflect the way they actually do their work. This documentation should be written in a brief, action-oriented manner that emphasizes the key ideas and uses the preferred terminology of the user community.

12.2 Comparison to Competing Approaches

Chapter 11 summarized three different approaches to software engineering: (1) Extreme Programming, (2) the Rational Unified Process, and (3) Cleanroom Software Engineering. Extreme Programming is representative of the lightweight methods that characterize the agile software development movement. The Rational Unified Process is probably the most popular process-oriented approach to software development. Cleanroom Software Engineering is arguably the most rigorous approach to software creation. On the other hand, Chapter 11 also discussed the Capability Maturity Model–Integrated, which is a process model that identifies high-level goals and strategies that represent best software development practices. Table 12.1 provides a comparative analysis of these four approaches, as well as the one proposed herein, based on the practical advice given by each approach. The comparative analysis is provided in terms of simple rankings, such that a ranking of "1" is the best and "5" is the worst.

One way to characterize these different schemes is as follows. The Capability Maturity Model–Integrated is very good at providing specific

TABLE 12.1   Comparison of Competing Approaches to Software Engineering

	Capability Maturity Model– Integrated	Cleanroom Software Engineering	Extreme Programming	Quality- Oriented Software Engineering	Rational Unified Process
Organizational Change Management	2	2	2	1	2
Personnel Management	4	4	2	1	3
Project Management	1	4	5	3	2
Configuration Management	2	4	4	1	3
Requirements Engineering	4	2	5	1	3
Design	4	2	5	1	3
Programming	3	2	2	1	3
Verification	4	1	5	2	3
Documentation	3	3	3	1	2

guidance for managing a project and the artifacts produced for it and for the technical activities of analysis and design. Extreme Programming, on the other hand, emphasizes the importance of people and the process of developing programs. The Rational Unified Process is different from both of these approaches because it focuses on the technical aspects of analysis, design, and verification, and monitors those activities very closely. Contrarily, the Cleanroom Software Engineering approach applies a very formal and rigorous approach to specifying the behavior, decomposition, and verification of a software system. However, the Quality-Oriented Software Engineering approach is an amalgamation of all these approaches and therefore provides significant guidance on all technical aspects of software development, in addition to acknowledging the importance of people in the software development process. To this end, it provides guidance on how to recruit and nurture extremely talented people so that they can improve their development processes. The weakness of this approach is that it provides minimal guidance for, or insight into, managing software projects.

12.3 Early Thoughts of the Software Pioneers

The pioneers of the computing profession realized that the methods that programmers of their day were using to develop software were inadequate. Consider that Naur and Randell [1] defined the phrase "software engineering" to imply "the need for software manufacture to be based on the types of theoretical foundations and practical disciplines, that are traditional in the established branches of engineering." McIlroy's thoughts were even harsher when he said [1], "We undoubtedly produce software by backward techniques. ... Software production today appears in the scale of industrialization somewhere below the more backward construction industries." Unfortunately, these comments are largely applicable to the people who develop software today, although almost 40 years have passed since these comments were made.

These pioneers understood the importance of team composition, which most organizations largely ignore today. Buxton said [1], "if I'm setting up a software group ... I'm extremely careful that all the people working on it are close personal friends, because then they will talk together frequently, and there will be strong lines of communication ..." He went on to say that "the good systems that are presently working were written by small groups. More than twenty programmers working on a project is usually disastrous."

These pioneers shared several thoughts on incremental development, which even today are not as commonly accepted as most people would like to believe. Ross commented on the foolhardiness of the waterfall model of development, still in predominate use today for large systems development, when he said [1], "The most deadly thing in software is the concept ... that you are going to specify what you are going to do, and then do it." Similarly, Fraser said [1], "program construction is not always a simple progression in which each act of assembly represents a distinct forward step and that the final product can be described by the sum of many sub-assemblies." He went on to say that the "escalation [of system complexity originates] in the conceptual inadequacy of the basic design. By replacing the appropriate [module] we simultaneously removed an apparent need for a growing number of specialized additions to the superstructure and considerably enhanced the quality of the final product." In other words, he is saying that rework is inevitable and that initial designs often must be changed (e.g., refactored) to accommodate unanticipated design complexity or other inadequacies.

Several others also commented on the necessity of iterative and concurrent specification of design, verification, and documentation. For example, Perlis said [1], "A software system can best be designed if the testing is interlaced with the design instead of being used after the design. ...

Through successive repetitions ... of interlaced testing and design the model ultimately becomes the software system itself." Graham further supports the importance of concurrent top-down design and verification when he says [1], "Simulation is a way to do trial and error experiments. If the system is simulated at each level of design, errors can be found and the performance checked at an early stage." Similarly, Dijkstra recalled an experience he had with a graduate student who was writing a program. Dijkstra concluded that documenting an artifact immediately before it is built (he called this predocumentation) was vital to efficiently constructing it. He said [1], "making the predocumentation at the proper moment, and using it, will improve efficiency with which you construct your whole thing incredibly."

Naur probably best makes the case for concurrent design, verification, and documentation when he said the following [1].

> *"Both the need for documentation of software systems, and the difficulties in filling these needs, are well-known items in software work. It is my experience that the most constructive way to solve this problem is to insist that the production of essential parts of the documentation is a natural part of the production of the software program, and that the two proceed in parallel.*

> *In discussing documentation one should keep in mind that this is aimed at the human reader, and should be developed along the principles of report writing set forth in several different texts on the subject. Of particular significance is the insistence, among competent report writers, that reports be structured hierarchically and written from the top of the hierarchy, i.e., starting with a brief synopsis. I feel strongly that in software production this principle should be followed carefully, at all levels of the work. If this is done, the first thing to be done by the software producer about to start writing a piece of software, is the writing of a synopsis of what his piece of program is supposed to be doing. The next level may consist of a description of a few pages describing the essential structures and the major processes to which they will be subjected. This description should include carefully selected examples, to illustrate the functions and their most important variations (these will be useful as test cases). The lowest level of the hierarchy is the program text itself.*

> *This way of work not only has the advantage that important parts of the documentation are actually produced. It also leads to better programs. In fact, when working out the higher level*

descriptions in written form, the software producer inevitably will be forced to think out his data and program structures more carefully than otherwise. This regularly leads to programs with clearer structure, higher efficiency, and fewer bugs.

This way of developing the software and its documentation also allows for mutual review, check, and criticism within small groups of software programmers. This should take place frequently while the work is in progress and can very well be done within groups of two people who look into another's work. In my experience this is a highly effective way of organizing the software work."

Why were all these things known decades ago, but only beginning to be accepted now? There are two primary reasons. First, we often are unreasonably constrained, as Dijkstra pointed out in 1969 when he said [2], "software engineering techniques should be improved considerably, because there is a crisis. But there are a few boundary conditions which apparently have to be satisfied. ...

1. We may not change our thinking habits.
2. We may not change our programming tasks.
3. We may not change our hardware.
4. We may not change our tasks.
5. We may not change the organizational setup in which the work has to be done.

Now under these five immutable boundary conditions, we have to try to improve matters. This is utterly ridiculous." These boundary conditions often result because organizations unnecessarily constrain change efforts. In addition, they generally do not know how to introduce change into an organization, which was the topic of Chapter 2.

12.4 My Final Thoughts

In conclusion, the guidance given in this book is the result of my experience with software development, accumulated over 30 years. I have participated in the development of software systems for academic institutions while pursuing research problems in artificial intelligence and software engineering. I have also helped develop large software systems for the financial and telecommunication industries. Most of the guidance contained within this book is the result of software development failures, both large and small. In other words, I have learned more from my failures than from my successes. A short parable summarizes this experience quite eloquently. A young boy and an old man were sitting down one day. The young boy asked the old man, "How did you become so wise?" The old man responded by saying, "Through experience." The young boy then asked the old man, "How did you gain experience?" The old man said, "By making lots of mistakes." This book has described ways to avoid past mistakes that I have made or witnessed. I hope this advice helps you create better software by avoiding these same mistakes.

References

1. Naur, P. and Randell, B., *Proc. of the NATO Software Engineering Conference*, 1968.
2. Buxton, J.N. and Randell, B., *Proc. of the NATO Software Engineering Conference*, 1969.

Index